PENGUIN BOOKS

INDEPENDENTS DAY

Lou Dobbs is the anchor and managing editor of CNN's *Lou Dobbs Tonight*. He has received the Peabody Award, the Luminary Award from the *Business Journalism Review*, and the Horatio Alger Association Award for Distinguished Americans, as well as an Emmy Lifetime Achievement Award.

Independents Day

Awakening the American Spirit

LOU DOBBS

PENGUIN BOOKS

PENGUIN BOOKS

Published by the Penguin Group

Penguin Group (USA) Inc., 375 Hudson Street, New York, New York 10014, U.S.A.

Penguin Group (Canada), 90 Eglinton Avenue East, Suite 700, Toronto,
Ontario, Canada M4P 2Y3 (a division of Pearson Penguin Canada Inc.)

Penguin Books Ltd, 80 Strand, London WC2R 0RL, England

Penguin Ireland, 25 St Stephen's Green, Dublin 2, Ireland (a division of Penguin Books Ltd)

Penguin Group (Australia), 250 Camberwell Road, Camberwell,
Victoria 3124, Australia (a division of Pearson Australia Group Pty Ltd)

Penguin Books India Pvt Ltd, 11 Community Centre,
Panchsheel Park, New Delhi – 110 017, India

Penguin Group (NZ), 67 Apollo Drive, Rosedale, North Shore 0632,
New Zealand (a division of Pearson New Zealand Ltd)

Penguin Books (South Africa) (Pty) Ltd, 24 Sturdee Avenue,
Rosebank, Johannesburg 2196, South Africa

Penguin Books Ltd, Registered Offices:
80 Strand, London WC2R 0RL, England

First published in the United States of America by Viking Penguin,
a member of Penguin Group (USA) Inc. 2007
Published in Penguin Books 2008

10   9   8   7   6   5   4   3   2   1

THE LIBRARY OF CONGRESS HAS CATALOGED THE HARDCOVER EDITION AS FOLLOWS:
Dobbs, Lou.
Independents day : awakening the American spirit / Lou Dobbs.
p.   cm.
Includes bibliographical references and index.
ISBN 978-0-670-01836-9 (hc.)
ISBN 978-0-14-311419-2 (pb.)
1. United States—Politics and government—2001–   2. Political culture—United States.
3. Political parties—United States.   I. Title.
JK275.D63   2007
323.6'50973—dc22   2007031354

Printed in the United States of America
Designed by Carla Bolte • Set in Dante

To my wife, Debi, and the kids:
Chance, Buffie, Jason, Michelle, Heather, Hillary,
and new granddaughters Malaya and Devon

Acknowledgments

First and always, thanks to my wonderful family for their love and support, and, yes, for still putting up with me. And thanks to the great team of journalists who produce *Lou Dobbs Tonight* and report with diligence and distinction every day on the events and issues that confront the American people.

It's my privilege and honor to work with the diligent, professional journalists who work so hard to bring the truth as best we can discern it to our audience each evening. We've been reporting for five years now on issues that influence and shape the lives of all Americans: failing public education, disastrous free-trade policies, outsourcing of American jobs, the assault on working Americans and their families, our aging and crumbling national infrastructure, e-voting and voter fraud, runaway costs of health care and energy dependency, illegal immigration and lack of border and port security, political and corporate corruption, dysfunctional government, massive federal and trade debts, the global war on terror and our wars in Iraq and Afghanistan. Our broadcast deals with all these issues and more, and our work is heavy lifting for journalists in any medium. I'm proud of and grateful to the whole team at *LDT* who get it done every day: Jim McGinnis, Chris Billante, Leslie Bella-Henry, Kevin Burke, Jill Billante, Kitty Pilgrim, Bill Tucker, Casey Wian, Christine Romans, Lisa Sylvester, Philippa Holland, Tom Evans, Warren, Lewis, Carmen Martin, Claudine Hutton, Adrienne Klein, Rene Brinkley, Jessica Rosegaard, Lisa DiLallo, Chris Murphy, Megan Clifford, Paul Vitale, Marci Starzek, Kimberly Cardinal, Nicole Duignan, Stacy Curtin, Vandana Agrawal, Angela Ramos, Richard Dool, April Harris, Kate Goldrick, Britton Schey, Jaison Manns, Klair Odumody, John Herrick, and Kelly Carty.

My thanks as well to CNN News Group president Jim Walton for his strong encouragement and support of me and my work over many years, and to Time Warner CEO Dick Parsons and president Jeffrey Bewkes, who are steadfast in their commitment to world-class journalism.

I believe the 2008 election will be pivotal for the American people, who must make a choice between self-determination or acquiescence to the rule of establishment elites who now control our destiny as a nation, a choice between independence and partisanship, and populism and elitism. This book is my view of the reality that faces all of us as American citizens, the issues that we must understand and resolve, the tasks we must undertake if we are to succeed as a people and a nation in this new century.

I want to thank Rick Kot, Viking Penguin executive editor, as always for his encouragement, patience, and skillful editing. Thanks to my friend and counselor Wayne Kabak of William Morris Agency, who keeps me out of the ditches and who came up with the idea for this book; to my friend and compadre Harvey Newquist, whose humor and talent makes this fourth book in seven years possible; and to my colleague Slade Sohmer, for his journalistic instincts, research, and humor. And for their assistance each and every day, my thanks to Arlene Forman and Mario Spagnola.

Contents

Independents Day

Introduction

The 2008 presidential campaign is upon us, and there should be no doubt that we are at a critical historic juncture, and the very survival of our nation may well depend on the electoral choices we make. When one scans the number of candidates seeking their party's nomination for the highest office in the U.S. government, what has seemed an interminably long campaign seems too brief and inadequate a period in which to choose a leader of great quality and character to successfully lead us in the twenty-first century.

America is a great nation whose leaders have become intoxicated with the idea that the accomplishments and achievements of preceding generations assure them not only of success, but of only limited consequences for their failures of judgment and infidelity to traditional American values. Nearly all of our political leaders seem to believe that America's wealth is so great that it cannot be exhausted; the elites of politics and business seem to believe that their power flows from a superior DNA structure that confers upon them an omniscience in economic and geopolitical affairs that three hundred million citizens cannot hope to comprehend. Their arrogance now threatens the future of our nation, and their elitist sense of entitlement has reached such heights that our leaders are now openly dismissive of the will of the people. They no longer honor our fundamental national values but instead attach themselves to the interests of multinational corporations and political parties, and recognize no duty to the nation in which they prosper. Many of our political leaders rationalize their careless exercise of power and their disregard for the consequences of their decisions with their religiosity; that is, God's providence has guided and favored America throughout its history and therefore favors the faithful, if incompetent, leaders in all walks of American life. Let us pray.

Many of our corporate leaders are even more disdainful of our national values and interests than our politicians. Business leaders, if anything, seem more committed to their personal belief systems, which have been elevated to religiosity, the foundation of which is a blind faith in what they perceive to be the higher perfect power of economics and markets. "Mr. Market" knows all and knows best for these corporate masters of the universe.

These lofty elites wield their awesome social, economic, and political powers without apparent regard for the common good, the national interest, or the traditional values that have historically informed and guided America's leaders. These elitists have abandoned American ideals for self-interest, and are ignoring ordinary citizens as unworthy of their concern, obligation, and duty.

For too long the American people have deluded themselves that failures of leadership will in the fullness of time resolve themselves in our great republic, because our history has given us the assurance that partisanship is an acceptable substitute for citizenship. We've accepted our own apathy and tolerated what has become a frontal assault by the establishment elites on our national sovereignty, the welfare of our people, and our future as a nation. But there are now promising signs that the American people will soon be ready to reclaim this nation.

As I write these words, the U.S. Senate has just rejected a cloture vote on so-called comprehensive immigration reform legislation by a vote of 53 to 46. The defeat of President Bush and the Democratic Senate leadership all but ends the efforts in this session of Congress to grant amnesty to twelve million to twenty million illegal aliens and to keep our borders wide open.

For four years I have fought almost daily the advocates of open borders and amnesty, and despite this Senate victory, I know that the fight will go on. That fight will likely intensify, because the political, social, and economic interests driving open borders and amnesty are powerful, the stakes could hardly be larger, and American citizens are only slowly awakening to the threat to our nation that emanates from both the left and the right, the establishment and the radical. But the American spirit is no longer slumbering. On my broadcast we have reported the facts that should form the parameters and foundation of what has at long last become a national dialogue, even if now only incipient, on our illegal immigration and border-security crisis. I have put representatives of all sides of the debate and discussion on the broadcast in an effort to examine the facts, to put the facts as we know them in perspective from the points of view of the advocates, to debate the merits and failings of those views, and to expose the varied agendas and interests of the elites who have tried to ram their positions through Congress and down the throats of American citizens who were just a few years ago unaware of the nature and extent of the threat to the American way of life.

The political contest that has resulted from our immigration and border crisis produces great passions and every bit as much heat as light. Unfortunately, the facts and the independent, nonpartisan reality that my colleagues and I try to report to our audience each night are inconvenient obstacles for the ideological orthodoxies and conflicting partisan, establishment, ethnocentric, and even radical agendas that motivate most of our national dialogue and debate on so many critical issues, and nowhere more powerfully than on the illegal immigration and border-security crisis. Too much of our national mainstream media is content to devote more airtime, ink, and kilobytes to Paris Hilton and Anna Nicole Smith than to the events, ideas, and issues that will determine our quality of life and our future as a nation. Ours is a national entertainment media that is incentivized to appeal to the lowest common denominator in our society, a national news media that reports the ideological postures and rhetoric of both Republicans and Democrats and regards such journalistic efforts as fair and balanced. As I've said frequently, the truth is seldom fair or balanced, and it is certainly seldom represented by the partisanship and ideology of our two principal political parties.

Even before the final Senate vote on "comprehensive immigration reform legislation" was tallied, e-mails and telephone calls of congratulations started pouring into my office. But I was surprised by my reaction to that vote and to all the congratulatory messages. I felt great satisfaction, to be sure, that many of our elected officials had actually listened to their constituents, but I felt more a sense of relief at the prospect of a pause, for a while at least, in the political and media battles that might well give us all the opportunity to reflect and consider carefully our future course. And I was grateful that for the first time in a long time that senators, both Democrats and Republicans, stood up and acted like they really cared about our nation and found the courage and good judgment to demand better of themselves and the leadership of the upper house of our Congress. Senators Jeff Sessions, John Cornyn, Jim DeMint, Claire McCaskill, Jim Webb, Bernie Sanders, and and Byron Dorgan stood out in the fray on the Senate floor as people of character, quality, and commitment to our fundamental national values, the common good, and our national interest.

Fifteen Democratic senators and thirty-seven Republican senators voted to kill the legislation, and each of them played an important part in asserting the public good against what has become the almost always overwhelming political influence and power of corporate America and special interests, particularly the business associations and ethnocentric activist organizations that have played a disproportionately dominant role both in the national media and on Capitol Hill.

As Senator Lindsey Graham, Republican of South Carolina, said to his colleagues before the vote, "Remember this day if you vote no." Senator Graham was issuing a warning to his colleagues, seeking their support in favor of amnesty in the upcoming vote. But not only our senators but all of us should remember that day because it may well and truly have been the dawning of reasonable hope that we the people can still influence and shape our future as a nation; it was the beginning of a reason to believe, with some confidence, that we can still save the once great democratic republic inherited.

We have much to overcome in the months and years ahead, but it's been a long time since I felt as confident as I do now that we can succeed in restoring a broad commitment to our great national values: equal rights of individual liberty and opportunity, both economic and educational. I can actually imagine the American people demanding that excellence be restored to our public education system, that a better quality of life for our working men and women and their families be the goal of domestic public policy, and that the restoration of our national sovereignty and security can become an attainable governmental goal. My growing confidence is predicated on the belief that most of us are learning that America can no longer tolerate inadequate and incompetent leadership in either the White House or the Congress. Nor can we any longer tolerate our own indifference, apathy, and cynicism, which have given rise to a succession of weak and short-sighted leaders who have spoken and have acted as if our citizens were strangers to them in what they now regard as their land, not ours.

I actually believe that populism is gaining the power to defeat elitism and that our government can one day soon again legitimately claim to be "of the people, by the people, and for the people."

We Americans are surely strangers to any person who could say, "America must not fear diversity. We ought to welcome diversity." Who would utter such condescending words about our land and our people, the most diverse nation on earth? None other than President George W. Bush. Can we be such strangers to this president that he does not comprehend that this great nation's citizens are from every country, practice every religion, and are of every race and ethnicity on the planet, and that Americans will never submit to any fear of any kind? We as a people welcome millions of legal immigrants to our country each and every year, more than all other countries combined. Americans speak over 120 different languages in the New York City public school system alone. Afraid of diversity, Mr. President? What in the world are you thinking?

Let me acquaint you with the America I know. We are a nation of immigrants. But foremost we are a nation of laws. We are a nation of unprecedented diversity, and we are a people of laws. Even foreigners who visit and who are guests of this nation enjoy the same legal protection guaranteed our citizens under the Constitution. That Constitution begins with the words "we the people," and so far we have persevered, in good times and bad, in war and peace, in poverty and prosperity, because we honor our Constitution and the laws that flow from it. To paraphrase our president, our leaders must not fear the people, and our leaders must welcome democracy. America is first a nation and Americans are first citizens, despite those corporate and special interests and political partisans who insist that America is only an economy and a market and Americans are just consumers and laborers. America is a great nation, Americans are a great people, and we are desperate for great leaders who know us, understand us, and respect us. We will no longer tolerate elitists who would have Americans be strangers in our own land.

The ever-enlarging size, scope, and scale of government, business, and media are often celebrated by establishment elites who are indifferent to the rights and lives of ordinary citizens whose interests are poorly served by many of the powerful institutions that once stood for all that is best of what has been America and American. While our elites have perverted our great national purpose of providing for the life, liberty, and pursuit of happiness of all our citizens, they exalt ideology, partisanship, greed, and privilege. Our elites no longer talk straightforwardly and plainly. They speak instead in the jargon of Wall Street and the lexicon of globalization. Elites in business and government promote efficiency, productivity, and competitiveness rather than their responsibilities to our citizens, to the quality of life of our working men and women and their families, to the education of our young, and to our American way of life.

Straightforwardly, we have allowed our elites to mortgage our future, literally and figuratively, and to constrain our individual liberty and freedom, and it is time that we examine with clear eyes who we've become, who we are as a nation, and how American citizens will shape our own future. Both Republicans and Democrats, the president, and the congressional leadership would have us focus on fears and limitations rather than on our aspirations and hopes, and accept elitist direction toward the fate they favor. The elite establishment fears nothing more than the awakening of the American spirit and the empowerment of American citizens to determine our national destiny. Until now, the elites have had their way. It's time for the American way.

Irrespective of your politics or partisanship, your ideology or socioeconomic status, our elites would much prefer we avoid important questions. Questions such as: Why, if we are the world's only super-power, why are we also the world's leading debtor nation? Why, if we have the world's most advanced military, can we not defeat an insur-gency and sectarian conflict in a third-world nation of only twenty-five million people? Why, engaged in a global fight to the death with radical Islamist terrorists, does our government refuse to secure our borders and ports? Why, six years after September 11, do we have fewer allies and not more in that global battle against radical Islamist terror? And why, if ours is the world's strongest economy, have we run thirty-one consecutive years of trade deficits, lost the ability to clothe and feed ourselves, and now find ourselves dangerously dependent on other nations for our oil, computers, consumer electronics, and, increasingly, even our basic daily sustenance in almost every respect?

Those are a few of the questions we must answer, honestly and directly, if we are to shape our future and assure security and prosper-ity for generations of Americans to come. And we can no longer rely upon our elites to ask the right questions, and we certainly can no longer trust them to provide truthful, relevant answers.

The issues and forces, global and domestic, that challenge us and our future are all the more daunting if we lose sight of our history as a people and nation, if we forget who we are as individuals, as citizens, and if we permit ourselves to be defined by those whose ideologies and interests compel them to deny our uniqueness as a people and a nation. Should we really subordinate the interests of our fellow Americans and our nation to those of the United Nations, NAFTA, and the World Trade Organization, to multinational corporations and even the gov-ernments of other nations? I don't think so. But the orthodoxy that has built up among most of our elites in politics, business, academia, and media certainly does. Many of those elites have declared me a "nation-alist" because I care about our country and our fellow citizens, and on every single issue, whether domestic or international, strongly believe that our government should put the common good and the national interest of America ahead of all else. The "internationalists" seek the demise of national sovereignty around the world, the end of borders, and an integration of commerce and economies that observes no dis-tinction among people in France, Indonesia, Venezuela, and America, and they cheer the "flat earth" corporatist society that recognizes people only as consumers or producers. Our elites increasingly look upon themselves as the owners and managers of this land we call America, our government as something simply to be bought and bro-kered, our borders as outdated obstacles to international commerce, and American citizenship as an annoying conceptual relic of the eigh-teenth, nineteenth, and twentieth centuries that interferes with effi-cient production and distribution and heretofore predictable consumer patterns. So who and what are we if we cannot declare America as our land and ourselves to be Americans? Our elites don't want you to even consider that question, and they sure as hell don't want any of us to make a declaration. So, I will.

First, I'm an American, and damned proud of it. I'm also deeply grateful to this nation because I was born poor and this country gave me and millions upon millions of others the chance to live the Amer-ican Dream. I'm also a devout believer in our fundamental national values of equality of liberty and opportunity and in the irrepressible American spirit. And I believe that each of us must be as vigilant and protective of the rights of equality and opportunity of our fellow Americans as we are of our own, and honor our obligations to our nation and future generations of Americans.

Nearly all of us have an ideal of what America ought to be. My ideal was shaped by elementary school teachers who taught us that George Washington didn't lie and took responsibility for his actions. An ideal framed in the classroom by portraits of presidents on the wall, looking down on us from their lofty perches in history. Biographies of Jefferson, Lincoln, and Teddy Roosevelt. And Benjamin Franklin. Stories about Tom Sawyer and Huckleberry Finn. Frank and Joe Hardy. An ideal shaped by Fourth of July parades in my small hometown of Rupert, Idaho. An ideal passed on by a high school teacher, Elizabeth Toolson, who made me believe, as did she, that a poor boy born in Texas and raised in Idaho could go to Harvard. At Harvard, Professors Oscar

Handlin and Frank Freidel taught me how powerful ideas and working people built the country, and saved it more than a few times.

My ideal of America was also shaped by the Vietnam War, and by the protests against it. The struggle for civil rights and the death of Martin Luther King, Jr. The Apollo project and Neil Armstrong's first steps on the moon. The OPEC oil crises and the Persian Gulf War. The stock market crash of 1987 and the greatest bull market in Wall Street history. Presidential impeachment and the collapse of the Soviet Union. More than thirty years in journalism have revealed the best and the worst of us, the base and the uplifting, the ordinary and the spectacular, the cruel and the truly good, including all that this country can accomplish and all that it is capable of becoming.

After the tragedy of September 11, the corporate corruption scandals, and now the war in Iraq, I cannot imagine most Americans are content to allow our elites to continue to further debase the ideals of our nation and determine our course into the future. Both of our major political parties have become little more than well-funded marketing organizations, advertising brands that the corporate and special-interest elites manage for their own benefits, with almost no regard for the common good and the national interest. We have much to overcome, and much to do. That's why I'm an independent and a populist. I no longer believe the Republican and Democratic parties are capable of serving the people: Their priorities and focus are the special interests and corporatists who fund them, and now direct them and the rest of us. The consent of the governed is the foundation of our government and its endurance over the past two hundred years. If the American people are to prevail against the challenges of the next two hundred years, we must end our apathetic and uninformed acquiescence to elitist unrepresentative governance and demand that our political leaders respectfully seek our consent rather than take for granted our submission.

I believe that only the energized, active engagement and participation of our citizens at every level of politics and government will change our national direction. We will succeed if the vast majority of us can reject partisanship and end what are nothing more than brand loyalties to the Democratic and Republican parties, and replace those partisan brands with a passionate commitment to our ideals of independence and equality, to the common good and the national interest. Populism requires no political apparatus, no party machine. Populism as a philosophy and movement requires only that we put our people and our national interest first, that we honor our Constitution and nation, and that we respect one another's rights of individual liberty and equality of opportunity. Populism requires that we Americans be neither timid nor retiring in asserting our rights and the equal rights of our fellow Americans, and that we prize our American heritage of self-reliance and compassion and our independence as a people and a nation. I truly believe all of us should live every day as Independence Day.

We must make this our day, the day of the independent American.

1

A Superpower Struggles

If destruction be our lot, we must ourselves be its author and finisher. As a nation of freemen, we must live through all time, or die by suicide.

—Abraham Lincoln

I don't know a single person who believes that this country is headed in the right direction, let alone on an intelligent, positive path to the future—not my family, my friends, neighbors, audience, colleagues, not even a single elected official, in his or her honest moments. There is a palpable anxiety in this country about where we're headed, whether as workers, parents, providers, citizens, or as a nation. Until fairly recently we Americans were confident to the edge of cockiness, and beyond. Where once I saw most Americans from all walks of life imbued with a strong independence and individual pride, I now sense the onset of doubt and hesitation. That's not just the result of economic insecurity and partisan divisiveness, though they're surely a part of it. There's also been a dimming of the American Dream, a widening gulf between the governed and our government, a disconnect between the rhetoric of our leaders and the needs and hopes of our people. Americans don't wear insecurity and uncertainty well—nor for long. The American spirit doesn't require genuflection from others, or dominance, but we Americans do require respect for our rights, and for our liberties. It's just who we are, and ought to be.

Not so long ago, the idea of being the world's only superpower was, well, empowering to Americans. When the Berlin Wall fell, when the Soviet Union and Marxist-Leninism collapsed more than a decade and

11

a half ago, we were shocked by the suddenness of it all, by how abruptly the Cold War came to an end. We breathed a national sigh of relief, our leaders started talking about the peace dividend, and no matter how young or how old, how much or how little we earned, how lofty or lowly our job (or position, if really lofty), we were united in our pride that the American way had prevailed against the evil empire. Today that World's Only Superpower title isn't quite what it used to be, is it? The peace dividend turned out to be just another bad promissory note on the part of our leaders, and the federal budget deficits just keep mounting. The notion of being a "superpower" no longer puts an extra bounce in the step of any American I know. I believe that our leaders need to be reminded that our nation's superpower status doesn't automatically assure our survival or guarantee our success as a nation. Wise and responsible policies are part of our leaders' contract with the people, and our national character demands that we, too, be both confident and humble, whether as leaders ourselves or in granting our consent to those we elect, but also impatient with folly and excess. And yes, we as a people benefit from hearing that reminder from time to time.

Of course we all know that the United States is still the world's only superpower. We have the world's best military, we have more intercontinental missiles, more warheads, and more nukes than any other nation. We could destroy not only the world but the solar system, if our weapons could only reach those other eight planets. (I'm sticking with Pluto as a planet.) We also have more jet fighters, bombers, ships, and subs. We have the world's back. I'm not sure why, but we do, and we have had it for more than a half century. Even before the global war on terror was declared, our troops were stationed all over the world, not just in Iraq and Afghanistan, but in nations on every continent. Our troops are still posted in Germany and Japan, as if some government functionary expected them someday soon to grow nostalgic for World War II. Perhaps some of the geniuses in Foggy Bottom or the Pentagon aren't aware that Germany and Japan are now democracies themselves and have two of the strongest economies in the world. The economy of the European Union is, in fact, now larger than that of the United States. Surely, they can afford a world-class military of their own, if they really want one.

We also know that we can't afford to allow our leaders and our government to continue acting as if superpower status grants America some kind of magical, supernatural dispensation that relieves us of the political and economic consequences of ill-considered and harmful public and foreign policy decisions and actions. We may be the world's only superpower, but we're also the world's biggest debtor nation, and we have the world's biggest trade deficits. We are also the third-largest oil producer in the world, but we're also the world's biggest oil importer. The truth is, there will be wrenching consequences if we don't acknowledge our folly, failings, and yes, limits as a superpower, and correct our policies, our attitudes, and our course as a nation.

Course corrections in this country have historically resulted from landmark events, such as wars, economic recession and depression, and our national elections. A confluence of those factors may occur in our elections next year. With the dollar falling in foreign exchange markets—being overtaken by the euro, near parity with the Canadian dollar, and at more than a twenty-five-year low against the British pound sterling—there is sufficient reason to expect that the economy may be a central issue in the 2008 election, along with the war on terror and the wars in Iraq and Afghanistan. I hope not, but it is certainly a proximate possibility.

I wish that I had more faith that next year's election would produce the leaders we require to overcome our mistakes, to meet our challenges, and to chart a bright way forward for our country. But I don't, in part because we've allowed our elections to become a bazaar for special interests and corporatists to broker their support for favor and influence, if not to dominate the electoral process entirely.

There's no question that we have a government for sale. The only real outstanding questions are how high its price will go and, come election time, which of the two political parties will be the successful bidder for the majority of offices around the country. The Democratic and Republican presidential candidates are pushing the price of the presidency to new heights and will spend an aggregate of at least a billion dollars trying to get elected in 2008. Senators Barack Obama and Hillary Clinton have already set quarterly fund-raising records, and the top-tier candidates of both parties appear to be having little trouble raising lots of money, although the Republican candidates are running behind their Democratic rivals in the early stages of Campaign 2008.

And then there's Congress, with 435 seats up for election, and the Senate, with 34 seats at stake. With the average cost of winning a House seat estimated to be $1.2 million, and the cost for a seat in the Senate pegged at almost $10 million, that's at least another $800 million. In total an estimated $2 billion will be spent on Campaign 2008. And what will all of that money buy? My guess is more of the same, unless all of us decide that it's time for a change—not just a change in which party will be sending the majority of its candidates to Congress or the Senate, or who will be sitting behind the desk in the Oval Office, but a change in the role of the voter in our upcoming elections, and a change in the attitude of Americans about our role in our society, our economy, and our politics and government. All are necessary for us to take control of the direction of this country.

I believe that we have begun, barely, to do just that—to create change. Voter turnout in 2006 was the highest for a midterm election in twenty-four years. While it wasn't a tectonic shift in our body politic, the election did produce a change of control in both the House and the Senate. Voters, argued the pundits, were driven to the polls because of their disillusionment with President Bush and his mismanagement of the war in Iraq. While that was certainly true, the pundits, strategists, and political mavens of the mainstream media overlooked other issues that also weighed heavily on the minds and the hearts of many voters. Exit and opinion polls revealed their concern about the economy and the impact of free trade, about the war on terror, and about border and port security and illegal immigration. The intense disappointment with our leadership and worries of our middle class were clearly on display last November, but most of the national media is as hidebound in its herd mentality and orthodoxy as the two political parties and the corporate interests they favor. In particular, the liberal establishment press couldn't bear to break with the Eastern elites' orthodoxy of free trade and international-ism, which would have required it to report a careful, honest examination of the loss of middle-class jobs caused by the multinational practices of outsourcing American jobs and offshoring of what was once Ameri-can production.

While the mainstream pundits at the *Washington Post*, the *New York Times*, and *Newsweek* reported without pause about the war in Iraq, and the intelligence failures and manipulations at the outset of the war, they barely mentioned illegal immigration and its impact on our society and on the budgets of our local and state governments. Not only have they demonstrated no concern for the well-being of our own middle class, but none of those mainstream media mavens saw fit to indulge their one-world cant and detail the failure of the last two administrations to organize and carry out an intelligent foreign policy with Mexico, or the truly devastating consequences of NAFTA on the Mexican people. Nor has the establishment Eastern press covered the astounding levels of investment by corporate America in China, which if it had been deployed instead to Mexico and other Latin American nations might well have changed history for the better. But opening their editorial vision to include the well-being of American workers and their families, and to the construction of a productive American foreign policy in the Western Hemisphere, must be considered rather parochial to most of the national media, who obviously prefers to pander to the corporatists and spew their flat-earth apologias for the multinationals. These pun-dits obviously believe themselves to be possessed of a superior global perspective, and think little of our outmoded sense of sovereignty, citizenship, and allegiance to our mere nation.

The media is not alone in ignoring obligations to our fellow Amer-icans, and to this country. I think too many of us have lost sight of our country's traditions and values, our responsibilities as citizens of this great nation. Some of us have lost sight of who we are, and take too little note of who we may become if we continue on the course that has been set for us.

So who *are* we? We can look to demographics and economics for part of the answer, but certainly only part. We're now a nation of more than 300 million individuals, and growing rapidly: The Census Bureau estimates that there are 302,568,533 people living in the United States. Our diversity is unrivaled. Other countries in the world, especially the largest, are relatively homogeneous by comparison, whether to China, India, Indonesia, Mexico, or the rest of Latin America, or to African, Middle Eastern, or European nations. Whites make up approximately 69 percent of the American population, followed by Latinos and Hispanics, with just over 14 percent, and blacks, with 12 percent. Asians make up about 4 percent, while other groups, such as American Indians, native Alaskans, and Hawaiians, make up approximately 1 percent. More than half of our population is female: Women are in the majority by a relatively slim margin of approximately 5 million. Most Americans now live in cities, and in 48 of our 100 largest cities whites are in the minority. Fifty-eight percent of us choose to live in cities, while 21 percent choose the suburbs. Nearly 21 percent still live in rural communities or on farms. Our population also remains younger than that of most industrialized nations.

By 2050, we're expected to be a country of nearly 420 million people, and nearly half of our population will be over the age of 45. By some estimates the United States will be the only developed and industrialized nation that also ranks in the world's twenty most populous countries. Much of that growth will come from the millions of legal immigrants we welcome here each year, and certainly the millions more who come to live here illegally.

Our superpower economy's gross domestic product, the goods and services we produce each year, is definitely impressive but is being vigorously challenged by the European Union and, ultimately, by China. Our GDP has risen to more than $12 trillion and is projected to grow at a rate of more than 2 percent this year. That's better than that of, say, Germany, where GDP has grown by less than 1.5 percent annually this decade, but far below that of China, which has experienced annual GDP growth of more than 10 percent.

Our working men and women earn comparatively high wages and salaries. Arguably American workers are the most productive in the world, and inarguably they should share in the wealth our supereconomy has generated. The average American's income is $32,660 per year, while the median household income is $46,326. But Americans are hardly alone in earning good pay, and are not the world's highest paid: The average worker in Britain makes $36,851, and in Japan, $35,593. The prospects for significant improvements in the pay of our middle-class workers are problematic, at best. Because of so-called free-trade policies, American middle-class workers are now competing directly with third-world labor forces. Workers in Mexico make only $7,180 a year, while a worker in China earns only $1,533.

Americans are defined by the rights we enjoy as citizens, and our Constitution guarantees a degree of individual liberty and freedom that exists in no other nation on earth. We are also defined by our attitudes and our behavior, and there's no question that we've developed an American sense of entitlement. American adults spend more than three thousand hours a year watching television, surfing the Internet, reading daily newspapers, going to the movies, and listening to radio and personal music devices like the iPod. Those of us who help out at our schools, churches, and charitable organizations give an average of only fifty hours a year of our time to work as volunteers. Americans have the world's greatest democracy, but we vote erratically and carelessly. Voter turnout in the 2006 midterm elections was relatively high by historical standards, but still included only 40 percent of registered voters. The average voter turnout in presidential elections during the past fifty years has been just over 50 percent, and it has dropped substantially since the 1960s, when over 60 percent of voters went to the polls for each presidential election.

It can be readily argued that Americans don't vote in great numbers because of their dismay at our choices of leaders, or their lack of confidence in the talents of the those we do elect to represent us. I believe that until recently we took for granted that our elites shared our values and views, that they would preserve the interests of the nation without reservation. But even our self-identity as Americans is attacked by many of them.

There are those one-world advocates who would in all sincerity and sanctimonious political correctness demand that we not call ourselves Americans, because that might offend citizens of other countries in this hemisphere. Interestingly, they and their acolytes seem to care little for any offense they might give to Americans or America. The fact that Americans remain the world's most individualistic and independent people may explain in large part the elites' aversion to us.

Most Americans believe strongly in the essential value of individualism, and in the personal freedoms our Constitution guarantees. But we are witnessing the erosion of those rights, as global economic integration creates a global interdependence that threatens to overwhelm our national identity. Our elected leaders once spoke to us with a clear and strong voice of America's can-do spirit, of our values of independence and self-reliance, of our capacity to sacrifice for the needs of one another and the nation, of our ability to overcome any hardship and meet any challenge. No longer. Now our leaders darkly bemoan the competitive burdens of this nation's health care, environmental protection, and workplace rules and regulations; worker retirement and pension costs; the lack of education; and the high wages of our workers. Make no mistake, elites in business, politics, and academia mean to roll back a hundred years of progress in the quality of life for working Americans and their families.

Americans must awaken to the challenges posed by the new postmodern geopolitical and economic reality, understand that America's destiny is not guaranteed and unconditional, and come to terms with the fact that our own elite orthodoxies now pose one of the most dangerous threats to the American way of life. It is time to actively engage in politics at every level, to fully participate in our democracy. It is time to raise up the American spirit.

2

Inflection Points

The preservation of the sacred fire of liberty, and the destiny of the republican model of government, are justly considered perhaps, as deeply, as *finally*, staked on the experiment entrusted to the hands of the American people.

—George Washington

We Americans have inherited a great nation, one that has been blessed with equally great leaders during times of the most critical challenges throughout our history. We have also been an imperfect people and a society with many flaws. Yet even our shortcomings have led not to our failure as a nation but rather to success in historic struggles in war, depression, and social division. That success has been guided by a fidelity to our founding values and principles: energy, resilience, strength, and the American spirit, which demands that we confront rather than shrink from problems.

My deep concern for the well-being of all our citizens and the national interest, and my criticism of those who lead our society, economy, and political system, are in no way nostalgic or retrospective, but rather aspirational. I do, however, believe our capacity to shape the nation's future depends greatly on our understanding of our history. The struggles of the generations that preceded ours and their success in overcoming their own weaknesses and the obstacles of their day should imbue all Americans with the confidence and commitment to recognize our own failings honestly, and to openly embrace the admittedly difficult task of confronting the issues that now face America within our nation and throughout the world.

I have no doubt that we will prevail against each and every challenge so long as our nation is guided by a faithful allegiance to our founding values, principles, and philosophy. We can resolve any conflict or fix any problem so long as we are united in a common fidelity to one another's equal rights of individual liberty and opportunity, and dedicate ourselves to ensuring this great nation's future.

The history of America is one of glorious accomplishment and individual achievement. America is a free and vigorous nation in which every citizen has the right and opportunity to live as he will, respecting the rights of his fellow citizens, while fulfilling his obligations to the nation. Liberty and equality are the essential, fundamental values and principles of the American nation. Each generation is called upon to renew our people's pledge to those ideals and ensure that they and the nation endure.

Individuals as diverse as Martin Luther King, Jr., Abraham Lincoln, and Helen Keller succeeded because of the opportunities afforded them by our nation. Their flourishing as individuals has always inspired us, and has shone as a reminder of what America can offer.

This country has always been at its best when it provides opportunity to, and supports the endeavors of, the individual citizen. Unfortunately we are at a point in our history where institutions and special interests have come to take priority over individuals. Institutions are operating for the sake of their own self-perpetuation, rather than for any benefit they might bestow on society, and now exist at the expense of individuals. It's true of government, big business, the media, our educational system, and those special-interest groups that purport to be working for the common good.

You can see their values clearly in their disregard for the will of the people. More disturbing, those values are evident in the behavior of our elites, from elected officials to the overpaid and underperforming CEOs of corporate America. It takes only a quick look around to recognize that something nefarious has happened to our country. We're immersed in a nonstop barrage of business scandals, Capitol Hill ethics violations, White House spin, and corporate layoffs measured in the tens of thousands.

Such events used to be the deviation from the norm. Now they are the status quo. We have to ask ourselves: How did we let it get this far?

This was not the kind of behavior that exemplified our nation for the first two hundred years of its existence. Scandals and corruption of the scale we now see all too frequently were isolated events in the early days of the twentieth century, notable for how anomalous they were in contrast to the expected and accepted standards for individuals and institutions. In fact, before the 1940s, we worked hard to build this country into a model that would demonstrate our values of freedom and liberty, economic potential, and individual accomplishment to the rest of the world.

There was a time when the United States had checks and balances in the government, regulations for corporate behavior coupled with the threat of punishment, little tolerance for ethically challenged public figures, discipline for children, and rewards for jobs well done. Each of these notions has seemingly disappeared, a development that has been given scant thought and less notice.

Many would deny that the level of scandal we see today is any different than it was in the past. If the media was as pervasive then as it is now, the argument goes, we'd have been aware of just as much corruption as we witness today. While I have no illusions that shameful behavior has always been present in society, a review of our history shows that such conduct, coupled with the deterioration of our institutions, has never before come close to the near-epidemic levels that it currently enjoys.

In fact, the dramatic changes in our country over the last hundred years can be charted by pinpointing those events in which government and corporate America consciously extended and exercised their power over citizens and the national interest. There are certain inflection points, especially after World War II and during the 1960s, when America tilted away from being a nation dedicated to the good of everyone to being a nation that sought to benefit a select few. Their effects have multiplied to the extent that, in the last decade, it seems that they've snowballed out of control.

Reviewing the high and low points of the last century reveals how quickly and thoroughly the infractions against American citizens have accumulated. It's instructive as a guide of how to fail an entire nation and its people in a few tumultuous decades.

Outside of military skirmishes, the United Stated entered the twentieth century intent on realizing its potential, building its industrial base, and providing for its citizens. The first dent in the fender was delivered rather painfully by Standard Oil. In the early days of the century Standard Oil was accused by Theodore Roosevelt's administration of monopolization. The company then controlled an estimated 90 percent of America's oil production and exported its refined products all over the world, which arguably represented our nation's first encounter with the power and scope of a multinational corporation. The Supreme Court discerned enough anticompetitive activity in Standard Oil's business practices to break the company up in 1911. The resulting entities formed the basis of today's Seven Sisters of the oil business.

A half decade later—a period that equates to an eternity in modern news cycles—America entered World War I. We only committed to the conflict in 1917 after a number of U.S. ships had been sunk by Germany, and there was real concern that our allies in Europe were in danger of being overrun. Taking part in the war was not a decision arrived at hastily. There was extensive political debate on Capitol Hill, and continued provocation from Germany—no imaginary plots or illusory weapons of mass destruction were necessary to demand a response. When U.S. troops were sent to Europe in 1917 and 1918, it signaled our first military engagement on a truly international scale. We acted decisively and admirably in support of our allies and literally turned the tide of that war. When the conflict was over, the United States focused its attention back on domestic matters.

Four years later, in 1922, Secretary of the Interior Albert Fall took control of several of the nation's public oil reserves, including the Teapot Dome oil field in Wyoming, and leased them out to interested oil companies. As head of the Interior Department, Fall was allowed to grant such leases. However, as a member of President Warren G. Harding's cabinet, he was not allowed to accept cash and favors in return for the leases. But he did so nonetheless, and made himself wealthy in the process.

The *Wall Street Journal* reported that Fall had assigned leases without competitive bidding, which ultimately led to a Senate investigation of what became the Teapot Dome Scandal. By the time it was over in 1929, Fall was sentenced to a year in prison after being found guilty of bribery. The case had occupied an entire seven years of the country's attention, far more time than the several weeks given to recent scandals involving Tom DeLay, Mark Foley, Duke Cunningham, and Bob Ney. Far from being protracted and isolated scandals, these four all involved individuals who were forced to give up their elected positions in the course of a single twelve-month period over 2005 and 2006.

Little outside World War I and the Teapot Dome convictions could be considered inflection points in the early part of the century. Prohibition was certainly a major development, but I think you'd have to agree that Prohibition laws were created with the intent that they would stop people from acting scandalously.

At the end of 1929 the stock market crashed, and its effect on the national economy was compounded when the Great Depression followed in its wake. Consumer debt, bank failures, and Federal Reserve restrictions on the money supply all contributed to the worst economic crisis this country has ever faced.

While Americans focused on trying to pull ourselves out of the economic morass of the 1930s, war had already begun again in Europe. We kept our distance from the fighting until Japan attacked Pearl Harbor in December 1941. Again, we joined an international war to defend ourselves and to support our allies in Europe, who were being mowed down by the Axis. Again, it was not a step taken lightly. Our leaders estimated the costs, in terms of both human lives and financial commitment, and made a decision based on those factors. They made plans, they set goals, and they set out with a determination to accomplish those goals given the data at hand.

America changed dramatically in the aftermath of World War II, and I think it was then that we saw the first breakdown in the underpinnings of our nation. First of all, we were the only country to come out of the war virtually unscathed, as no enemy forces had attacked our homeland. (Hawaii was then still a territory.) Our losses had been military losses, and unlike the people across much of Europe, U.S. civilians at home suffered no carnage.

Second, we had emerged as the greatest military power in the world. We had the bomb. We had tremendous fighting forces and military technology. We oversaw the carving up of Europe into a group of new nations, with half of it given away to Russia and the other half rebuilt under the auspices of the Marshall Plan. We later did the same thing with the Korean peninsula.

In many respects we believed ourselves to be invincible. That thinking, to my mind, led to the period of America's greatest arrogance in our history. From the final days of World War II in 1945 and up until 1951, our government chose to flex its muscles both at home and abroad in ways that would have been unthinkable just twenty years earlier.

To begin with, President Harry Truman had decided to use the atomic bomb on Japan. Regardless of his rationale, the bomb was a dramatic demonstration of American strength and technology. And Truman used it despite there being no clear understanding of its true power.

Two years later, the Truman Doctrine stated that America would fight to contain the spread of communism, whether that spread had any direct bearing on America's interests or not. The first two countries granted aid under the doctrine were Greece and Turkey, areas in which we hardly had a vested national interest. But they were very close to Russia.

The following year, 1948, the United States was instrumental in gaining independent statehood for Israel. Not only had America overseen the redrawing of European boundaries, we had now helped create a brand-new nation. Given the increasing turmoil in the Middle East and Eastern Europe, we also promised to come to the aid of any country worried about incursion from the Soviet Union.

The first opportunity to exercise this military guarantee came in Korea in 1951. Eager to show the American people and Senator Joseph McCarthy that he was tough on communism, and without consulting Congress, Truman sent troops to fight in what was essentially a Korean civil war. Part of the rationale for the "police action," as it was called, was America's interest in South Korea after Korea had been divided into post–World War II American and Soviet occupation zones.

The Korean War was the first time that America had "opted in" to a conflict that posed no immediate threat to any of our national interests or to American soil. As soon as our troops showed up in Korea, the genie was officially out of the bottle. The United States initially helped repel North Korea when it attacked South Korea, but then our forces moved onward into North Korea. From that point forward, we were no longer providing defense against communist aggressors; we were actively going after them.

The military advance into North Korea was led by General Douglas MacArthur at the behest of the Truman administration. A popular, almost iconic figure in the aftermath of World War II, MacArthur was the Supreme Commander of the Allied Forces in Asia. His military instincts were widely praised, and his direction of the rebuilding of Japan helped that country on the road to becoming a significant economic power in the years ahead.

But MacArthur didn't agree with Truman's assessment of how to deal with the conflict in Korea. He wanted to press on into China, but Truman disagreed. When MacArthur took his arguments to the press, and thus the American people in 1951, Truman removed him from command. MacArthur wanted to win the war that the country had entered, but for all its posturing, the administration was not ready to see its commitment through to a definitive conclusion. Truman's emasculation of the general was the ultimate assertion of presidential authority over the military. MacArthur returned to the United States, where he had become so popular that many people expected he'd run for president against Truman.

Now America was entrenched in a war in which it had no viable interest other than the tenets of the Truman Doctrine. Dwight Eisenhower, a military man, was elected to succeed Truman as president and in 1953 oversaw the cease-fire in Korea. Back at home, Joseph McCarthy, one of the most unscrupulous people to ever hold public office, was censured for a crusade that recklessly victimized innocent Americans.

The Korean War and McCarthyism were the blights on an otherwise idyllic-seeming decade. We do tend to forget that Eisenhower sent troops to Lebanon in 1958, getting us involved in another conflict in which we had no stake. But Lebanon was viewed as a useful site in the Middle East, one where America could keep friendly governments in power. We were there for barely half a year, and most Americans didn't think much about Lebanon again until Ronald Reagan returned in the 1980s.

The 1950s provided a setting for our ideals that we look back on with nostalgic fondness. We focused our attention on matters at home and concentrated on what we could do as a nation. The revised G.I. Bill of 1952 offered loans and educational benefits to American soldiers. Some 7.8 million of 16 million World War II veterans used those benefits to enroll in college or get vocational training. An estimated 1.5 million Korean War veterans used the bill to obtain home loans.

The Federal Highway Act of 1956 created the interstate highway system, which ultimately linked our country from end to end and provided a means for people to move out beyond the cluster of cities. Its effect on creating our mobile society cannot be overstated, and the open road and cars became a hallmark of intrepid Americans.

TV became the preferred mode of home entertainment, and Elvis Presley and Chuck Berry sowed the seeds of rock and roll. America was living its Golden Age, with very little in the way of scandal to taint the air.

Then came the 1960s. That period stands as a watershed decade for our nation, not simply because of Vietnam, the assassinations of the Kennedys and King, the civil rights movement, and the cultural and social upheaval. It was also a decade when citizens seriously considered what the nation's priorities were, and didn't like what they saw. For the first time our government adopted an "us vs. them" mentality toward the populace, a sentiment that has reverberated far too strongly in recent administrations. The initial cracks in our government, resulting from its condescending belief that it knew what was best for the nation regardless of the will of the people, began to show.

The relative tranquillity of the Eisenhower years started to unravel on May 5, 1960, when Russian premier Nikita Khrushchev announced that the Soviet Union had shot down an American U2 spy plane. At the same time, he claimed that the United States had undertaken an act that constituted "aggressive provocation." President Eisenhower, who was under the belief that the plane had been destroyed and that its pilot, Gary Powers, was dead, felt no reason to acknowledge the flight was actually a spy mission. Instead, he approved the release of a fictitious NASA statement that claimed the plane was most likely a weather research craft flying over Turkey that had strayed off course when its pilot has suffered oxygen loss.

Two days later, Khrushchev produced the pilot—alive—along with the wreckage of the plane. Eisenhower had been caught in lie, a lie he had told because he was confident he wouldn't get caught. Ike had to acknowledge the deception and thus scorched his reputation as an honest man. He had, in effect, breached the public trust, and from that point forward, a palpable level of distrust of government leaders—men who would lie because they thought they could get away with it—would pervade the media and the public.

In his farewell speech on January 17, 1961, little more than a year after the U2 incident, Eisenhower introduced the famous term "military-industrial complex." Specifically, he said that "this conjunction of an immense military establishment and a large arms industry is new in the American experience. The total influence—economic, political, even spiritual—is felt in every city, every State house, every office of the Federal government. We recognize the imperative need for this development. Yet we must not fail to comprehend its grave implications. Our toil, resources and livelihood are all involved; so is the very structure of our society.

"In the councils of government, we must guard against the acquisition of unwarranted influence, whether sought or unsought, by the military industrial complex. The potential for the disastrous rise of misplaced power exists and will persist."

Eisenhower's allusions to the perils of business and the military working together proved to be perfect fodder for conspiracy theorists and a media ready to catch the president in another bit of contrived wordplay. In retrospect, it was a bizarre comment for Eisenhower—the top general in World War II, commander of the armed forces in Europe, a national hero, and now president—to make on his last day. In effect, he was warning the country against some of the leading institutions of the country itself: beware of your military, and beware of industry—and this from a president who was considered a friend of business. Ike's statement gave the media impetus to take an adversarial stance against the presidency, the military, and big business. More important, it was all too prescient: The "rise of misplaced power" and its involvement with our toil and our livelihoods are perfect descriptions of what's taking place in the United States today.

Eisenhower's comments served as the hallmark of a strange era—that of the Cold War. For many Americans, it was a time of trying to find out what the truth was and who the villains were. The Cold War had no Hitlers and Mussolinis; the enemy was faceless and remote, and information about it came primarily through the government. The fact that Eisenhower and his vice president, Richard Nixon, were Republicans helped craft the image of the GOP as being secretive and controlling, and thus in opposition to the media. Hidden agendas came to be associated with Republicans, a perception that Nixon did nothing to help in years to come.

When John F. Kennedy moved into the White House, there was a tangible shift in public opinion, as well as in the perception of the presidency. Kennedy, apart from being a Democrat, was also a truly media-savvy individual. He played on his looks and his charm to court the media, and in return it gave him significant leeway in all aspects of his administration, public and private. His dalliances went unreported, and it is unlikely that even Eisenhower in his prime would have gotten away with such flagrant behavior.

As a public and media figure, Kennedy was at the opposite end of the spectrum from Ike and certainly from Nixon. Dick Nixon looked like a bad guy—his five-o'clock shadow and nervous perspiration during the presidential debates are still a source of constant glee and discussion—talked like one, and had no inclination to be ingratiating. Kennedy was in every respect a breath of fresh air for the nascent broadcast media. The fact that Kennedy's win over Nixon in the popular election was razor-thin was generally overlooked in the media coverage of the Kennedy administration.

The Kennedy years also ushered in an era of government and media chumminess with liberal thinkers and their respective academic institutions. Products of Ivy League schools, whose students and faculty prided themselves on their liberal intellectualism, entered the government and the media in droves. The self-described "best and the brightest" grabbed the reins of the country and set about crafting it in the image of their own ideals.

Kennedy was enamored of conducting politics well beyond our borders and involved America in some of the most dangerous international conflicts since World War II. Just four months after being sworn in, he authorized the Bay of Pigs invasion in Cuba. The attempt to overthrow Fidel Castro and his Soviet-friendly regime ended in abject and public failure. It thoroughly embarrassed the new president, who believed that the operation could be conducted covertly and without the approval of Congress or the knowledge of the American people.

In 1961, Kennedy sent U.S. military "advisers" to South Vietnam to train soldiers to fight the North Vietnamese, ostensibly as a means to contain the spread of communism into Southeast Asia. Eisenhower had already deployed "advisers" to Vietnam to support French troops there, but Kennedy felt the situation required greater U.S. involvement. This was the beginning of our active interest in Vietnam, another country that posed no direct threat to our interests at home. However, Kennedy and administration adherents of the Domino Theory, which predicted the eventual fall of one country after another to communism, were determined to use Vietnam as a beachhead in the escalating climate of the Cold War.

Kennedy also promised to put a man on the moon within a decade. Having made it a priority, America achieved that goal with less computer power than you probably have in your home right now. While there is no doubt that this nation is ingenious enough to do something like this again—whether it be developing alternative energy sources or improving schools—no one is willing to commit to such ambitious goals.

The following year, Kennedy found himself in the thick of the

Cuban Missile Crisis. Here was an occasion, the first in nearly two decades, where an American president had legitimate concerns for the safety of our national borders. The Soviet Union was intent on installing missiles in Cuba, a mere ninety miles off the Florida coast, as a means to threaten the U.S. for putting missiles in Europe. In October 1962 Kennedy's standoff with Russian premier Nikita Khrushchev almost pushed the world into its first nuclear war. The crisis was ultimately defused in America's favor, but not until substantial bluffing, saber-rattling, and sweating had been brought to bear. Brinksmanship was now officially part of the U.S. government's diplomatic arsenal. As a people, we took our cue from the administration and became wary of the intentions of every country that was not an avowed ally.

While it was hardly all bright and cheery during the period of various run-ins with Cuba, we have assigned those days a glow in retrospect that they didn't possess in reality. The notion of Camelot, for example, was never applied to the Kennedy administration while he was in office; it came from a later reference that Jacqueline Kennedy made about the president's favorite line from the musical. "Camelot" is nothing more than a media construct after the fact, a hoped-for place that never existed.

Nevertheless, when Kennedy was killed, our national mood grew substantively darker. The country and the media had little time to get to know new president Lyndon Johnson before the elections of 1964. Barry Goldwater entered the fray with his hawkish and aggressive demeanor, and the press had a field day with him. The Democrats ran a commercial—once—that showed a little girl holding a flower. Halfway into the ad, the girl and the field in which she stands are annihilated by a fiery mushroom cloud. The implication was clear: Vote for Goldwater, and he'll use the bomb.

Johnson won the election and soon came to personify the authoritarian presidential style that had already begun creating distrust within the country. Not only did he take it upon himself to dig America deeper into Vietnam, but he also stonewalled the American people and the media about just how involved we really were in that war.

Johnson managed to push through many of the programs he inherited from the Kennedy administration, programs designed specifically to help individual Americans, from education to warning labels on cigarettes. He also pushed through the Civil Rights Act of 1964, granting equal rights to women and minorities. But racial tension in the United States had increased during the early 1960s, and the passage of that law could not contain it. Malcolm X was assassinated in February 1965, and the following month state troopers attacked and beat civil rights marchers in Selma, Alabama. The National Guard was called in to stop a race riot in the Watts section of Los Angeles that summer. Throughout the year Americans watched their fellow citizens being beaten by police and soldiers on national TV. Hearing about Vietnam or reading about race riots and police brutality was one thing, but witnessing it in our living rooms on the evening news was something else entirely. For millions of Americans, the televised images we saw during the mid-1960s were the first time we truly understood what was happening in our country.

College campuses, which had always fostered independent thought and cultural experimentation, now became hotbeds of analysis of the government's behavior at home and in Vietnam. Students increasingly viewed the government—actually, authority of any kind—as being responsible for the deaths of innocent peasants in Vietnam and innocent minorities in decaying U.S. ghettos. The students also wanted no part in personally fighting North Vietnamese soldiers.

Johnson's popularity dropped precipitously throughout the sixties, even though he managed to get Medicaid and Medicare off the ground. Rioting escalated around the country, notably in Newark and Detroit during July 1967. Dozens of people were killed in those riots, and Johnson had to call in the army to stop the violence in Detroit.

Then came 1968. January began with the Tet Offensive, a significant North Vietnamese military operation. The media covered the fighting on the ground as it was happening, and reported primarily on American losses. Although the Viet Cong were ultimately turned back, and the military viewed Tet as a U.S. battle victory, the media presented it as a disaster for America and its prospects in Vietnam. Popular opinion, given the media spin, turned strongly against continued involvement.

Martin Luther King, Jr., was assassinated in April. Robert Kennedy was assassinated in June. In August came the Democratic National Convention in Chicago, and it was there that any pretense of civility between the government and its citizens was dispensed with. Antiwar protesters, many of them college students, were beaten by Mayor Richard Daley's police and the National Guard. Battlements were set up—literally and figuratively—between the media as "the eyes and ears of the people" and the government. Journalists were hassled in and around the convention center, and our government looked as if it were running nothing so much as a police state.

With assassinations and rioting taking place on an apparently nonstop basis, Johnson realized that he had become ineffectual. Walter Cronkite had recently stated after the Tet Offensive that he personally didn't think the United States could emerge victorious from the Vietnam War, and that remark allegedly pushed Johnson to his own brink, feeling that if he'd lost the support of "Uncle Walter," then he'd lost the support of the common man. It was a critical juncture: The media had grown powerful enough to affect the decisions of the government. Johnson dropped out of the presidential race, beaten and bowed by a television news anchor's words ringing in his ears.

Hubert Humphrey, the Democratic candidate in the election of 1968, was viewed as more of the same by voters, so Richard Nixon won handily, but nothing improved. There were no assassinations in 1969, but media reports from Vietnam were bloodier and more disheartening than ever. Protests continued in increasing numbers. Students at Harvard seized the administration building in April. In May, California National Guard helicopters bombarded protesting students at UC Berkeley with skin irritants. Gays rioted in New York City in June. The first troops were withdrawn from Vietnam in July, and that same month Senator Edward Kennedy drove off a bridge in Chappaquiddick, killing his female passenger. Two days later Neil Armstrong walked on the moon. Charles Manson and his "family" began their murder spree in August. The next week was Woodstock. More than a hundred Vietnamese civilians were killed by U.S. soldiers at My Lai in September. The Days of Rage riots took place in Chicago in October.

A second successful moon landing occurred in November, a mere four months after the first one. December brought the reinstatement of the draft. And a murder at the Altamont rock concert took the wind out of the sails of the "peace and love" movement.

The events of the 1960s eclipsed almost everything that America had experienced in the twentieth century. Government and the media would never be the same, and business upheavals were soon to follow. As citizens we understood that our government wasn't interested in involving us in setting our nation's course. Echoing the government's position, we took more interest in ourselves than in one another, sowing the seeds for the "Me Decade" of the 1970s.

Nineteen seventy unfolded ominously. The U.S. Army charged fourteen officers for withholding information about the My Lai massacre. On May 4 the Ohio National Guard was sent to the Kent State campus after several days of student protest. By the end of the day four students were dead. Ten days later two students were killed by state troopers during a protest at Jackson State College in Mississippi.

In full view of all of us, our government had aimed, and fired, guns at our children.

There was outrage in response, but the sixties had taken a toll on the protest movement. Each presidency since Kennedy's had become more intransigent and less willing to brook dissent. Nixon, more than any president before him, was not going to let anyone or any organization interfere with the decisions he was determined to make for the country. He and his cabinet were secretive, combative, and dismissive of the press and the populace. His administration adopted a bunker mentality that polarized the nation.

Nixon can be credited with reaching out to China and for withdrawing troops from Vietnam in the early seventies, but his involvement in Watergate ensured that his presidential legacy would be one of scandal and embarrassment. Protest and racial violence had dropped off significantly after 1970, the government having created the fear of armed retaliation in its citizens. The *New York Times*, determined to reveal an administration out of control, published the Pentagon Papers in 1971 in defiance of Nixon. The publication of these Vietnam War documents proved that a committed journalistic ethic could expose flaws in the government, and the Pentagon Papers proved that the government had been lying to the nation for years. One of the reasons we look back reverently on the media's role in this period is that it has since failed to act so diligently and nobly in pursuit of the truth.

The Republican administration devolved into paranoia and suspicion, especially of the Democratic Party. Nixon was reelected in 1972 and began covering up the Watergate burglaries that would bring his presidency down, showing a disregard for the law and the responsibility of a president. The end of the Vietnam War, as established by the Paris Peace Accords, was relegated to secondary importance in the administration as Nixon tried to ward off the effects of the Watergate scandal. While that was happening, oil-producing Arab nations decided in October 1973 to embargo shipments of oil to the United States, and Vice President Spiro Agnew resigned amid accusations of tax evasion and taking bribes while he was governor of Maryland. Agnew pleaded no contest to the charges, paid a fine, and was given probation. A month later Nixon famously announced to the media, "I am not a crook."

By the middle of the following year, it was clear that Nixon *was* a crook. With the House and Senate ready to impeach him for Watergate, Nixon resigned. Before an angry nation could prosecute him, the new president, Gerald Ford, issued a pardon, setting the entire executive branch above and beyond criminal reproach.

Our presidents had gone from moral and ethical lapses (Eisenhower's and LBJ's lies) to outright criminal activity (Nixon's) to immunity from prosecution. By the mid-1970s it seemed there was almost nothing a president wouldn't do to further his own agenda.

It was this type of audacity that in 1975 prompted the creation of the Church Commission, a Senate committee that investigated abuses of power by intelligence agencies in the wake of Watergate and the Pentagon Papers. The Church Commission uncovered U.S. plans to assassinate political opponents in other countries as well as to create unrest and destabilize foreign governments. It also learned that the CIA and FBI had been opening and keeping records of American citizens' private mail since the 1950s.

In the aftermath of the Church Commission, attempts were made to completely overhaul the intelligence agencies, but they were halted by none other than Ford's secretary of defense, Donald Rumsfeld. Ultimately Ford could not distance himself from Nixon's ugly legacy, and Jimmy Carter became president.

Carter was elected in large part because he was not a Republican and he was not involved in Washington's climate of deceit. He had emerged from relative obscurity to lead the nation during a period of economic turmoil that included double-digit inflation, a second OPEC-driven energy crisis, high interest rates, and high unemployment. He deregulated the airline industry in 1978, took restrictions off the savings and loan business, and also created the Carter Doctrine, which stated that the United States would not allow any one country to control the Persian Gulf and threaten our interests in the region.

Whatever he may or may not have accomplished while in office, Carter realized that the mood of the country had changed. In July 1979 he delivered a speech that included the following comment:

> I want to talk to you right now about a fundamental threat to American democracy . . . I do not refer to the outward strength of America, a nation that is at peace tonight everywhere in the world, with unmatched economic power and military might.
>
> The threat is nearly invisible in ordinary ways. It is a crisis of confidence. It is a crisis that strikes at the very heart and soul and spirit of our national will. We can see this crisis in the growing doubt about the meaning of our own lives and in the loss of a unity of purpose for our nation.
>
> The erosion of our confidence in the future is threatening to destroy the social and the political fabric of America.

Carter's eloquent warning fell on deaf ears as America's troubles at home soon included troubles abroad. On November 4, 1979, fifty-three Americans were taken hostage at the U.S. embassy in Iran by radical Islamic fundamentalists, an episode that would consume Carter's administration for the remaining year of his presidency, even as he tried to address domestic problems and keep the Cold War at bay. He reinstated the draft, canceled the Russian wheat deal, and kept America out of the 1980 Summer Olympics, which were held in Moscow.

America, its economy, and its confidence had been undermined by Nixon, but now we were being undermined by other countries. Americans responded to Carter's international ineffectiveness by electing the tough-talking Ronald Reagan by a landslide in 1980. Reagan returned the country to international and domestic stability, an achievement for which he is not given enough credit. Beginning with the release of the hostages in Iran (an event the media has never investigated to the point of finding an explanation), Reagan methodically set about addressing the ills of the nation by cutting taxes and increasing military strength.

Reagan was shot and hospitalized in an assassination attempt two months into his term. Four months later he fired the nation's air traffic controllers when they went on strike in violation of federal law. Reagan's action was a blow to unions everywhere, which realized—and still have not come to terms with the fact—that they no longer had as much leverage in as many industries as they once had.

The nation was drawn back into the Middle East in October 1983 when 241 American soldiers were killed in a barracks bombing in Beirut. Reagan did not retaliate; instead, we sent troops to the little Caribbean island of Grenada just days later in order to put down a coup orchestrated by pro-communist rebels.

Throughout his presidency Reagan focused on the Cold War and restoring the confidence of American citizens. His hands-off approach to business allowed corporate America to start playing fast and loose with the law, not to mention any perceived code of ethics. Mergers and acquisitions, leveraged buyouts, junk bonds, corporate raiders, and greenmailers all came to prominence during the 1980s; there were nearly three thousand mergers in 1986 alone. Many of these deals were not designed to increase shareholder value, increase competitiveness, or spur innovation; they were not designed to do anything other than line the pockets of the dealmakers. Companies were broken up, shut down, and even held up for legal ransom at the hands of a new style of businessman who squeezed money out of the transactions rather than building up core businesses or investing in future growth.

Names like T. Boone Pickens, Michael Milken, Ivan Boesky, Martin Siegel, Dennis Levine, and James Goldsmith, along with companies such as Federated, Revco, Disney, Revlon, Beatrice, Union Carbide, Fruit of the Loom, and Owens Corning, all represented the new climate of doing business where the deals were more important than the production of anything of lasting value.

Insider trading took the decade's newly minted "greed is good" ethos to a new level. Not only were the dealmakers getting rich at the expense of strong companies and the average investor, but Wall Street traders were cashing in early on tips about impending deals. It seemed that everyone in the stock market was growing immensely rich, except for those individual investors who played by the rules.

Lined up at the money trough right behind the dealmakers were the savings and loans. Unfettered by deregulation and unsupervised because of a decrease in the number of examiners, S&Ls made incredibly risky investments that ended in the collapse of more than a thousand financial institutions, nearly half the total of all savings and loans in America. The bailout for these businesses came not from those who had profited from the investment deals, but from taxpayer money—$41 billion worth. The S&L crisis of the eighties ensnared a number of elected officials, including Senator John McCain, who was accused of taking improper campaign funds from embattled Charlie Keating, chairman of the failed Lincoln Savings and Loan. That scandal ended the careers of several senators, but McCain survived and adopted the mantle of reformer for, ironically, campaign finance reform.

After five years of strong growth, the U.S. economy was dealt a nasty blow with the October 1987 stock market crash. But the markets rebounded quickly, and the country avoided any long-term effects. Reagan abandoned détente with the Soviet Union and instead upped the Cold War ante, forcing the communists to try to keep pace with U.S. military spending. Playing catch-up took its toll on the Soviet populace, reducing the superpower to the economic ranks of a third-world country. Determined to eliminate threats to America on every front, Reagan misstepped badly when he allowed the sale of arms to Iran in order to fund the anticommunist Contra rebels in Nicaragua. It was a blatant violation of law, and one that would eventually tarnish Reagan's reputation and legacy.

Significantly, two of Reagan's top aides, former chief of staff Michael Deaver and adviser Lyn Nofziger, were convicted of violating lobbying rules soon after leaving the White House. Lobbying scandals, a result of the increasing coziness between politicians and big business, were soon to become a staple of modern business.

By 1988 our country had reached a stage where the public could almost count on an administration scandal, a president caught breaking the rules or lying, and a nefarious role for the country in an international conflict.

Reagan was followed by George H. W. Bush, who was fortunate enough to be president when Russia withdrew from Afghanistan and the Berlin Wall was torn down in 1989, effectively ending the Cold War. Bush spent his four years concentrating on international matters, not the least of which was protecting our oil interests in the Middle East. After invading Panama in December 1989, he then went to Kuwait in 1991 to oust Iraqi forces in the first Gulf War.

Bush largely avoided any scandals, although he was tainted by Iran-Contra. When he raised taxes after promising not to, however, the American public decided it would relegate Bush to the ignominious fate of a one-termer and put Bill Clinton in the White House. He was not elected by a majority of the American public—only 43 percent of it. In fact, it's worth noting that Clinton didn't win a majority in either of his two victories.

Despite economic stability the United States was subjected to significant terrorist attacks on its citizens. The World Trade Center was bombed in 1993 by radical Islamists. In April 1995, the Oklahoma City bombing occurred, killing 168 people. An apartment building housing U.S. military personnel in Khobar, Saudi Arabia, was blown up in June

1996. U.S. embassies in Africa were car-bombed in 1998. The USS *Cole* was attacked in Yemen in 2000, killing seventeen sailors. We got involved in Somalia, leading to the infamous murder of soldiers in the Black Hawk Down episode. The Cold War was over, and America was facing an entirely different kind of foe: the religious and political zealot determined to die attacking the United States.

Clinton could not shake the taint of scandal from the moment he took office. There was Whitewater, Travelgate, Troopergate, Filegate, Vince Foster's suicide, Paula Jones, Gennifer Flowers, Kathleen Willey, and Henry Cisneros, among others. Fighting scandal became a full-time preoccupation of the White House.

Due to deregulation and military buildup, the government began to become beholden to business in the 1980s under Reagan, a process that was accelerated under Clinton. Clinton was happy to be playing in the same league with big business, and his administration was actually friendlier to business than any Republican president's ever had been. It was Clinton's SEC that permitted ENRON to occur, and the Clinton administration permitted CBS to get scooped up by Viacom, GE to buy RCA, AOL to buy Time Warner, and Disney to buy Capital Cities/ABC. The tentacles of big business in its most insidious form were allowed to grow unrestrained during the 1990s. Clinton's administration was happy to let business run without oversight and intervention, and unlocked the handcuffs that the financial institutions claimed were hindering and hampering their growth.

Clinton ended his presidency with yet another scandal, that involving Monica Lewinsky, which led to impeachment. Then the millennium was upon us. The Internet bubble burst, sending investors for the exits and destroying paper dot.com fortunes. The election of 2000 was bitterly fought, even more bitterly contested, and wound up in the hands of the Supreme Court. George W. Bush emerged as the victor, although many in the country refused to see it that way.

After handling the September 11 attacks with dignity and true leadership, President Bush and his administration took America down a path that has led us to a forfeiture of nearly everything that our nation values. We are involved in a war that has no specific goals. We have been unable to respond appropriately or adequately to natural disasters. We are allowing illegal aliens to enter the country in defiance of the law—while the president is trying to find them jobs. The administration has seemingly not met a corporate favor that it won't grant. Lobbyists like Jack Abramoff have been shown to hold immense power over legislation that affects all of us. Elected officials have been resigning at record rates due to personal and professional scandals that occurred while they were supposed to be looking after our interests as a nation. There are so many low points across the spectrum of government, corporate America, and the media that describing and analyzing them all would entail an entire book. Even a list barely hints at what has gone wrong: Weapons of Mass Destruction. Colin Powell's fall from grace. Dick Cheney and Halliburton. Corporate miscreants Ken Lay, Jeff Skilling, Bernie Ebbers, Dennis Kozlowski, Richard Grasso, and Martha Stewart. The Dubai Ports World deal. Abu Ghraib. Dan Rather's phony Bush military letters. The response to Hurricane Katrina. Attorney General Gonzales's firing of attorney generals. The White House paying columnists for positive press coverage. Scooter Libby and Valerie Plame. The fall of Tom DeLay, Mark Foley, Duke Cunningham, Jack Abramoff, Bob Ney, Bernard Kerik, James Traficant, Robert Torricelli, and Jim McGreevey. All this and more, and the decade isn't even over.

Even worse than scandal, to my mind, is that our political discourse today relies on guesswork and public shouting in order to achieve an end. Hard evidence, data, and facts are given short shrift in every branch of the government. Logic is ignored in favor of faith and beliefs. Gut feelings and hoped-for results direct our public policy.

The federal government has exercised power in a broader range of issues, both domestic and international, than ever before. The empirical and the factual is defined by the corporate and the special interests that lobby our federal elected officials as never before. And when reality and the limitation of resources and our national values impede the elite's pursuit of their preferred public policy, our government rationalizes away the common good and our national interest. The American people must demand that our elected officials and our federal government rigorously research the facts of each issue, the impact of all public policy options and choices, and replace what are now decades of policy rationalization with reason and rational governance.

3

Two Parties, No Choice

Let us not seek the Republican answer or the Democratic
answer, but the right answer.

—John F. Kennedy

Purely partisan Republican and Democratic answers abound, and
America is well on its way to becoming the nightmare that James Madison feared two hundred years ago: a nation whose government is in the
sway of factions and special interests, which form an all-powerful cor-
poratocracy that dominates both our electoral and legislative systems.
Madison believed that our great republic would, through democratic
representation, create a government of wise and strong public servants
who would look beyond transitory and special interests, whether small
or large, and lead with thoughtful and prudent judgment, creating policies that would support the common good and the national interest.
Not even the great Madison could have imagined that the American
people would go to the polls like sheep and pull levers for partisan brands
rather than for candidates who faithfully reflected the values, character,
and interests of the voters of each congressional district and state. Nor
could Madison have envisioned the awesome power of corporate America and the insidious influence of special interests in our political system
and government in the twenty-first century.

This country's two-party political system, in my opinion, is no longer
working effectively to represent the will of the people, and it could reasonably be argued that the very legitimacy of our government is now in
question. If the Republican and Democratic parties no longer function
in our political process to demonstrate and manifest the consent of the

43

governed, why do they exist at all? If our public servants serve best those who work against the public interest, what is the purpose of popular support of one partisan brand over the other? Today, both major political parties are far more supportive of corporate and special interests than the will of the majority, upending the fundamental tenet of democracy itself.

Democrats campaigned in 2006 against the "culture of corruption" and the conduct of the war in Iraq. They pledged to change government after winning control of the House and Senate in the midterm elections. While it remains early in their control of Capitol Hill, they've failed to realize their plans to withdraw our troops from Iraq, and over a six-month period have accomplished scarcely more than the Republican "Do Nothing" 109th Congress. They did pass the important and much needed minimum wage law, but only by attaching it to a supplemental funding bill for the war in Iraq.

The Democrats took over control of the Senate and House promising they would roll back the corruption of lobbyists and set a new, higher standard of ethics in Congress. I hope you're not still holding your breath. Instead of working to fulfill their promises to the people, the Democratic congressional leadership has squandered committee and staff legislative time on investigations of pre–Iraq war intelligence and of the Justice Department's firing of eight U.S. attorneys. Ultimately the Democrats couldn't even pass a no-confidence resolution against Attorney General Alberto Gonzales, whose political deference to the White House and indifference to the Constitution qualify him as one of the country's worst attorney generals in history.

It's no wonder that a recent Gallup poll delivered Congress an approval rating of only 14 percent. That's even lower than President Bush's approval rating, and the lowest in the thirty-five-year period since polling on Congress began. Certainly, part of the reason for the nosedive in this Congress's ratings is simple disappointment that the Democrats have been unable to deliver even a meaningful articulation of a new strategy in Iraq and the Middle East, let alone a withdrawal of our troops. But I believe the reasons go well beyond that disillusionment, all the way to a general frustration with two political parties that can no longer deny they're just opposite wings of the same bird. And that particular bird may soon take its place alongside the dodo. The American people are a hell of a lot smarter than the two political parties and their candidates, strategists, and corporatist funders believe. We're certainly smart enough to no longer discount the proof before our own eyes, as we witness the political charade that has been played out by Republicans and Democrats over the past thirty years.

Neither party honors the legacy of its past, nor represents its partisan adherents in any meaningful way. That's not to say Democrats can't fire up their base and raise a lot of money by mentioning the term "abortion," or that Republicans can't do the same by just whispering the word "gays." Now I don't know about you, but fundamentally I don't see much of a difference between Republicans and Democrats. And for the life of me, I can't figure out what constitutes a liberal or a conservative these days. Democrats were once the party of working men and women, organized labor, and civil rights. Republicans were the party of business, large and small, fiscal prudence and restraint, and reserve in foreign policy. Not anymore. Thanks to the influence of the Democratic Leadership Council, President Bill Clinton was just as friendly to big business as President George W. Bush, although quieter about it. President Bush has expanded the federal government more than President Clinton, and they both support free trade at the expense of working Americans. President Clinton reformed welfare, and President Bush put through the largest increase in entitlement spending in decades. President Clinton balanced the federal budget, and President Bush has set new budget deficit records. They both went to Yale, both hired Goldman Sachs CEOs to run the Treasury Department, and both will have left the presidency with low public approval ratings.

If the distinction between Republicans and Democrats is blurred and increasingly unclear, it's in large part due to the fact that both parties are dependent upon the financial largesse of corporate America and the influence of special interests. President Bush has sent tens of thousands of our troops around the world to fight the war on terror, and hundreds of thousands to Iraq and Afghanistan, yet for six years he has insisted upon leaving our borders and ports open to the illegal traffic of millions of illegal aliens and billions of dollars in illegal drugs. Democrats have acquiesced, for the purpose of pandering to the socio-ethnocentric special-interest factions for votes. Both Democrats and Republicans are loath to displease their corporatist masters by impeding in any way international commerce.

President Bush and the Democratic leadership of Congress readily agreeing to grant amnesty to twelve million to twenty million illegal aliens would have meant amnesty for their illegal employers as well. Thankfully, enough Republicans and Democrats in the Senate showed the courage to represent their constituent citizens and the national interest to kill what would have been a socially and economically devastating piece of legislation. President Bush and proamnesty senators of both parties acknowledged as much with their common mantra of "a bad bill is better than no bill." How pathetic, and how alarming, that so-called bipartisanship can only come about as a result of the indifference of both Republicans and Democrats to the well-being of our citizens and the national interest. There is no doubt what James Madison and the Founders of our country would think of those we've elected to represent us in the early twenty-first century.

The key difference between our two parties is purely partisan: While Democrats describe themselves as liberal, progressive, and committed to civil liberties, and Republicans describe themselves as conservative and committed to tradition and social stability, the truth is, their only guiding principles are that Democrats are anti-Republican while Republicans are anti-Democrat.

Each night thousands of viewers send e-mails to *Lou Dobbs Tonight*, expressing their thoughts on the news and issues of the day. This one from Joe in Tennessee is especially pertinent:

> "When an old Reaganite like me finds himself in total agreement with an old socialist like Bernie Sanders and conservatives like Bush and McCain are pushing the same agenda as liberals like Kennedy and the Clintons, it's high time to redraw the lines in American politics." (June 22, 2007)

Political science and government scholars, and most pundits, cheered the demise of the smoke-filled rooms and cronyism of the classic political machines. Chicago's mayor Richard J. Daley, who ran the city from the 1950s to the 1970s, is the best known of the latter-day bosses. I can't help but believe there would be far less cheering for the end of kind had we known what would replace local grassroots politics in this country. Big money, big media, and national branding and marketing organizations posing as the two principal political parties have stepped in to fill the vacuum left by the dissolution of political power at the local and state levels.

While no one would welcome the return to corruption of much of the machine system, local politics in America today are anemic by comparison to the role they played in the past. Today every senator and congressman speaks to three constituencies: those in his or her district and state, the national media, and lobbyists and special interests. Only to the latter group do our elected officials listen more than they speak. Local media seldom has the budget to cover their elected officials in Washington, and the national media covers congressmen and senators only when they are relevant to an important or interesting national issue. It's no wonder that such a large disconnect exists between the voters of this country and their elected officials on a whole host of issues.

For most representatives campaigning and basking in the limelight of the national stage is the part of their job that seemingly trumps everything else, and it is far more important than getting involved in state business, or even than spending time in their state. Most Americans live their lives without ever seeing, let alone talking with, their congressman or senator, let alone the president. President Bill Clinton made 133 trips to foreign nations while he was in office, while President Bush has at this writing made just over a hundred trips to other countries. How many times did either of them visit your state? If you don't live in either New York or California, where the big-money contributors throw fund-raisers, then the number of presidential visits probably didn't exceed an average of more than one per year during the course of their terms in office. That figure does not represent even one visit every year, because several of those trips are typically campaign stops in one particular year.

It's equally doubtful that you'll see a U.S. senator, yours or anybody else's, in person during your lifetime. You may see a governor, possibly, but you'd better go to the state or county fair, because odds are that the governor isn't going to come to your neighborhood—unless you've had a major disaster that needs to be surveyed in front of the television cameras.

These politicians' behavior is nothing against you personally, because none of them is going to be talking to your first selectman or local mayor, either. All the state- and federal-level politicians are too busy "taking care of national interests," which happen to be removed far from the interests of your local community. Washington is where they all spend their time: All the TV cameras and national correspondents are there, in rooms down the street from the biggest lobbyists. You rarely see a national news correspondent covering events in Kentucky or New Mexico. Even the politicians from those states make it easy on the media and the lobbyists by going to Washington. That way, everybody saves time and effort, and they can focus on "the business of running the nation." Oh, yes, and they do have to attend sessions of Congress.

While the world has become smaller for our elected representatives, the distance between them and the people has increased. It is no wonder that lobbyists and special interests, and even other nations, enjoy an advantageous proximity to our government.

Thousands and thousands of viewers have written in to the show on this topic, outraged at the behavior of our elected officials, but even more troubling are e-mails like the following and the sense of resignation they convey:

John in Arizona: "They surrendered our jobs to China, our borders to Mexico, our ports to the Middle East and now they want to surrender in Iraq. There isn't a whole lot left for Congress to surrender." (April 23, 2007)

There would have been much less left to surrender had Congress passed the grand compromise immigration bill in the summer of 2007. The number of senators who acknowledged that they had not even read the four-hundred-page document was astonishing. The Democratic-controlled Senate, led by Harry Reid and Edward Kennedy, along with President Bush, knew full well that according to the Congressional Budget Office, the amnesty legislation would effectively curtail only 25 percent of illegal immigration, and that according to the Heritage Foundation, the retirement cost for illegal immigrants and the families who would join them would amount to $2 trillion. President Bush and Senator Kennedy talked about the legislation as "the right thing" to do for America, while countenancing a Senate debate of only five days to deal with the most critical legislation on illegal immigration in a generation. The arrogance and the ignorance of our leadership in Washington were breathtaking, and the furor they provoked among American citizens demonstrated that there is a limit to the insults that the American people will bear from their elected elites.

The Democratic leadership in both the House and Senate was convinced it could deliver, with the help of the president, a bill for him to sign. The legislation was defeated not only by a majority of Republicans, but by a minority of newly elected Democrats.

The senators who voted for the legislation should be embarrassed, but more important, they should be held accountable for what is nothing less than a betrayal of the common good and the national interest. There is simply no excuse for such devastatingly ill-conceived legislation to have ever made its way to the floor of the U.S. Senate. That a president of the United States could call for such legislation and support it so vigorously is outrageous, and heartbreaking evidence of just how far our political system, and the quality of our leaders, has declined.

The Republican 109th Congress was called the do-nothing Congress. This Democratic 110th Congress was elected in the national cry for change in 2006. But to this point it's been business as usual in Washington. Far more change and real reform must be achieved. Both political parties are dependent on the K Street lobbyists for their money, their guidance, and their largesse. The Democrats, with a handful of exceptions, have disappointed.

After sweeping back into power in 2006, the newly victorious Democratic Party proclaimed it would change the culture of corruption in the "first hundred hours" of its new Congress. And pass bills they did, but only one has become law: the increase in minimum wage. That is a significant achievement, but the sole achievement of this Congress to this point. It has backed down on substantive reform of the all-powerful role of those K Street lobbyists, and has been unable to generate an intelligent and focused debate on the conduct of the war in Iraq. The distance between voters and their elected officials, whether Republican or Democrat, remains vast.

> *Vincent in Illinois:* "As a Democrat, I'm very upset that my party uses the polls and the will of the people to justify their position against the Iraq war direction, while on the immigration direction they totally ignore those polls and the will of the people." (May 22, 2007)

Those of us who were hopeful that this newly elected Congress would mean a departure from the previous gaggle of partisan marionettes have listened to the same partisan blather and cheap political theatrics that we heard from the previous one, whether on the conduct of the war, trade, committee investigations of prewar intelligence, or a call for censure of President Bush.

This is the same Democratic leadership that promised it would not waste the opportunity to accomplish meaningful work by conducting needless and purely politically motivated hearings. It is no surprise that the American people hold Congress in even greater disdain than the president. As Frank Newport of the Gallup Organization said on the show, "It's the lowest level of confidence that we have ever measured in Congress for the decades that we have been doing this particular measure here at Gallup."

Our representatives have become little more than the middlemen and -women between the self-interests of corporate America and the lawmaking process. The duties we entrust to them are apparently not worth their time and trouble, despite the fact that we vote for them and that our taxes pay for their salaries, their health insurance, and their pensions. They are secure in their devotion to a two-party system that is no longer based on ideology and the good of the country, but rather is committed to helping the largest campaign contributors and corporate supporters.

We've had much to overcome in our national political life, but there has never been a time when both political parties offered voters so little choice. The Republican and Democratic parties rally to issues like flag-burning, gay marriage, faith-based initiatives, the Ten Commandments, evolution, and gun control. At a time when our nation is at war in Iraq and in Afghanistan and in a global war against terror, when the value of the dollar is plummeting on world exchange markets, when the housing market is in recession, and our public schools are all but collapsing, it is inconceivable that our elected officials do less than contend with those policy challenges. Is it unreasonable for us to ask whether there remains any decency, any sense of proportion and higher purpose in our nation's capital? Is it unreasonable to ask that both political parties, their leadership, our elected officials, and the candidates for president in 2008 commit themselves to the national interest and the common good?

As we approach the 2008 presidential election, it is clear that Republicans and Democrats would have us choose among their candidates based on superficial and often supercilious presidential debates. With the amount of money they have raised, our political parties have replaced smoke-filled rooms and brokered deals with massive fundraising organizations, big media buys, and political strategists poring over their computer screens triangulating acceptable political positions, and slicing and dicing demographic and attitudinal surveys of voters. The candidates' biggest challenges in this process seem to be determining what position will attract the most voters who are most supportive of their fund-raising efforts and financial supporters.

I have to believe that these candidates are entering the 2008 presidential election quite confident that the electorate will again acquiesce to the establishment and the sophisticated media machines that have arisen as boosters of cynical brands posing as political parties. On the great issues of the day, the leaders of both political parties are not significantly different. While there are populist-inclined "Lou Dobbs Democrats," the party itself remains committed to the same free-trade-at-any-cost principles espoused by many Republicans. All of the Democratic presidential candidates supported the comprehensive immigration reform legislation that would have left our borders and ports wide open and given amnesty to as many as twenty million illegal aliens, and as many as half that number who would follow them in short order. No Child Left Behind is bipartisan and has failed to live up to its promise. And not a single candidate of either party has proposed an urgent and dramatically needed bold national initiative to repair our public schools.

Both political parties and their candidates are driving for an ever larger federal government and ever larger entitlements that are both unwise and unsustainable. Nearly all the presidential candidates of both parties are avoiding any meaningful discussion of the importance of the new role that America must assume in our increasingly complex and dangerous world. Our resources are more limited and our military is strained and exhausted from the poorly led and poorly managed war in Iraq. What are the visions of the political parties and their candidates for America's involvement and engagement in the Middle East? What is to be the strategic relationship between the United States and Europe, China, India, Russia, and the nations of this hemisphere? Should we not have a national discussion and debate of America's geopolitical economic and military role in the twenty-first century?

Should a superpower not be able to provide all of its people a superior health care system, and should we not have specific road maps from each candidate for that achievement? The 2005 Energy Policy Act was a dismal failure on the part of the Bush administration and the 109th Congress. How can we achieve energy independence in short order, safely and efficiently?

And what are the competing visions of our principal political parties and their candidates? Will this nation's commitment be to the economic and social needs of our citizens, or do any of these candidates, or either party, envision international interests as more pressing?

As voters we require answers to these questions from our candidates, and as a nation we require these answers for our survival and prosperity.

As citizens, we view our ability to engage in the political process as one of the most important benefits of our democratic society. As of today, 142 million Americans are registered to vote—about 72 percent of the eligible voting population of 197 million Americans. Because the media and our politicians operate as if there were only two parties in this country, we typically just choose to align ourselves to one or the other. Thus, 51 percent are registered as Democrats, and 40 percent as Republicans, though not very many of us are completely committed to the ideals of one party or the other.

Outside of those actually running for office, there are very few 100 percent Republicans or Democrats anymore. Not every Republican is in favor of the death penalty, and not every Democrat wants to follow the ACLU in taking down Christmas decorations at town hall. Most rational people are probably somewhere in the moderate realm of the political spectrum. Because the parties have veered to their furthest extremes, though, there is no centrist position that serves as a platform for measured and thoughtful discussion between the two. Democrats and Republicans are like awkward kids at a dance, committed to standing on opposite ends of the room until someone makes the first step to meet the other side halfway.

I'm not surprised that no one has taken the first step, a gesture that requires breaking ranks with the party orthodoxy. Typically those politicians who have moved toward the middle ground or have adopted an independent stance have done so after they've been rejected by their own party, or when they can find no comfortable place within the party. Look at Joe Lieberman. In the space of six years he went from being the Democrats' candidate for vice president of the United States to being tossed out by party leaders in favor of a better financed newcomer. Lieberman, undaunted, ran as an independent and handily won his Senate seat back. The voters obviously didn't feel the same way about the candidate pool as the Democratic Party leaders did. Lieberman proved that we don't have to stand for the unacceptable candidates that the two-party system imposes upon us.

The issues facing us in 2008 are too important to allow the two major parties to define their scope and too pressing for candidates to avoid taking clear, definitive positions on them. The number of Americans who identify themselves as independent voters is on the rise. Those who claim to be unaffiliated with either of our two primary parties is now almost 32 percent—an increase of roughly 8 points since the 2004 election. And based on an average of CNN/Opinion Research Corporation polls in 2007, my show reported that 42 percent of Americans now consider themselves to be independent. Thirty-three percent identify themselves as Democrats, while 25 percent now say they are Republicans.

This is a telling trend. The majority of people no longer identify with either of the two parties' perceived or stated stances on issues of real import. From the people I talk to, Republicans are fed up with being dictated to by the small but influential group that forms the extreme religious right, while Democrats are tired of being associated with a party that appears unable to commit to a single principle and stick with it.

By November 2008 it could well be that a majority of Americans will consider themselves independent. I believe that only an independent voter rebellion against the two established political parties can roll back the influence of lobbyists and special interests in Washington and establish a government of committed populists dedicated to our traditional values, our constitutional government, the common good, and the national interest. Whether an independent populist candidate emerges in 2008, and whether a populist movement can emerge, is an open question. For all our sakes, I hope so.

I truly believe that many voters want a way to take that step toward a middle ground where the issues are discussed and debated without the stench of partisanship. There is precedent for bringing the debate back to a point where it involves the people of this country and their concerns. It entails breaking the hegemony of the two-party system and allowing more rational voices to be heard.

The creation of a third, independent choice, one that has the concerns of American working people as its basis, is the way we must proceed.

4

Power to the People

The issue today is the same as it has been throughout all history, whether man shall be allowed to govern himself or be ruled by a small elite.

—Thomas Jefferson

Populism puts the interests of our people first, and it is the only political philosophy and movement whose every principle is embodied in the Constitution of the United States. Populism recognizes as its first precept the founding value of our nation: equality of all.

Populism, without question, strikes fear into the hearts of this country's political, academic, and business elites. Populism as both a philosophy and a movement is the opposite of elitism, and our twenty-first-century elite establishment is mightily inconvenienced and perturbed by engaged and active citizens who demand the representation of all citizens, the common good, and the national interest.

The establishment media has often labeled me a populist—an angry populist, a pin-striped populist, and even what I call myself, an independent populist. When attacking me for my populist philosophy, critics have tried to establish a direct connection to figures like William Jennings Bryan, Father Charles Coughlin, and Huey Long.

William Jennings Bryan was an early crusader against the unrestrained growth of large corporations and a believer in the rights of the individual. His platforms were immensely popular with many Americans and led him to run for president three times. But his inability to separate religion from his political message, along with chaos in his political party, doomed Bryan's efforts. His final appearance on the

American stage was as the defender of creationism during the infamous Scopes Trial in 1925.

Huey Long, who served as both governor of, and senator from, Louisiana in the 1920s and 1930s, rose to power on a populist platform of first and foremost tending to the needs of the people. His promises of social reform, coupled with his distrust of big business, rallied the electorate around him. He instituted a number of populist programs that included taxing corporations to help fund social programs and proposals for free college education. Long, however, soon became a national symbol of overreaching power and cronyism, and his legacy is one of political battles rather than progress.

One of Long's contemporaries, Charles Coughlin, was a Catholic priest who used his radio show to promote interest in the common good. He pushed for economic reform, seeking to limit Wall Street and its influence on government. At his peak, it was estimated that Father Coughlin had tens of millions of listeners. But his advocacy devolved into fascist and even anti-Semitic rants, and such views rightly cost him his show and his popularity.

Opponents of populism attempt to define and categorize the concept by pointing to the downfall of these individuals—as if their behavior were representative of populism. That makes no more sense than trying to define the Republican Party by the behaviors of presidents Bush and Nixon, or the Democratic Party by presidents Clinton and Carter.

Critics are also fond of dismissing the grassroots campaigns and the populist movements of the late nineteenth century and twentieth century, and point to the failure of the Populist Party in an effort to dismiss populism as an irrelevant political philosophy for the early twenty-first century. Many of these same critics delight in pointing out that the populism of the late nineteenth century was primarily an agrarian campaign that sought representation in the interests of farmers and laborers—as if to imply that modern populists were all merely hicks, hayseeds, rednecks, and retrograde irrelevancies in a postmodern world.

New York Daily News columnist Erroll Louis told me he believes that the populist uprising of the nineteenth century "showed the genius of democracy at work: at a time when corporations and the major political parties were unable to imagine or devise solutions to the great issues of the day—notably, a cramped, broken monetary system that left farmers starved for credit—the people created solutions of their own, such as the sub-treasury system that formed the outline of what later became the Federal Reserve System."

These propagandists neglect to mention that the populist movement was the origin of the direct election of U.S. senators and our modern progressive income tax system, which replaced the regressive excise fees and tariffs as a principal source of revenue for the federal government. Populism asserted a passionate egalitarianism against the dominant political influence of the robber barons and the Wall Street bankers and financiers of the 1890s and early 1900s. The populist movement also strongly influenced President Theodore Roosevelt, who used the power of his office and his bully pulpit to jealously and tirelessly work for the public good, the common good, and the national interest. Roosevelt toiled so vigorously for these issues that many of his friends and peers labeled him a "traitor to his class."

I am an independent populist and I have never felt more certain of my political philosophy. I grew up believing that class structure had no place in America, and I fervently believe so today. Populism is fundamentally egalitarian, and equality is the core, bedrock value of our nation. I enjoy referring to our Constitution as the world's most famous and important radical populist document, the preamble to which begins with these three treasured words: "We, the people." Our democratic republic was created to represent the will of the people and to restrain special interests, factionalism, and the political dominance of any one segment of our economy or society.

In this age of group and identity politics, as ethnocentrism, corporatism, and globalism dominate our political systems and processes, I believe populism may offer our best hope of creating a sufficiently powerful countervailing force to the elites and orthodoxies that are now unfettered in their direction of our economy and our government. Whether populism as a political philosophy and movement ever finds sufficiently robust support in either or both of our two major parties is an open question.

Louis told me he agrees with the potential power of the emerging populist sentiment, and that "all the polls today suggest that the modern populist uprising represents a similar level of major-party dysfunction and popular innovation: at a time when unions, corporations, and the major parties have failed to deal with pressing matters of war and peace, income inequality and the meaning of citizenship itself, it has fallen to the American people to set things right—and they are making their voices heard."

I also believe that if the Republicans, and certainly the Democrats, fail to accept populist ideas and policies, an independent political movement will embrace populism and give egalitarianism and our working men and women full-throated expression in the 2008 elections.

As Democratic national committeeman Robert Zimmerman said to me recently: "Regardless of an individual's Republican or Democratic registration, a growing and significant majority of them think and vote independently. The two major political parties have to wake up to the reality that the independent-minded voter will be the difference in 2008. The political leaders' rallying cry for party unity is being replaced by the voters' thunderous demand for ideas and competence."

I'm also convinced that both parties face the prospect of demise or diminishment to the point of irrelevance, because liberalism and conservatism have lost ideological meaning and significance in our new political reality. All that seems to remain of the Republican and Democratic parties is their partisanship, their labels, and their records of intransigence and ineffectiveness over the past forty years. Once we looked to our two-party system to produce leaders who worked in our nation's capital as public servants to resolve conflicts and to attend to real problems. Now most Americans see Washington, D.C., as the place where our problems and conflicts go to be perpetuated, and almost never fixed. The Republican and Democratic parties have little to point to in the way of achievement. They sustain themselves primarily with partisan rancor and by titillating their ideological bases with wedge issues, being beholden to corporate and special interests, trying to cloak their contempt for the popular will and the public good, and—bereft of a vision for our nation's future—looking only to their next elections.

The divide between the establishment and the American people has widened to the point of social and economic rupture, and all but certain political reaction.

Washington Times columnist Diana West disagrees with my assessment of the likely path of populism in the 2008 presidential election. West says, "The Democratic candidates all supported amnesty—indeed, Senators Hillary Clinton and Barack Obama voted for it—and the Democrats, of course, are still favored to win. While we saw the candidacy of John McCain, a leading amnesty bill supporter, sink in the bill's wake, we saw nothing new emerge—for example, no soaring support for, or even interest in, presidential candidate Tom Tancredo, a bona fide outsider when it comes to the GOP establishment, particularly on key issues of border security and illegal immigration. Maybe it's the case that populist movements put their foot down, but little else."

While West believes that the Republican Party will adapt to populist calls for national security and beef up their border security platforms, she believes that Democrats will resist populist and independent temptations and demands. I disagree and believe that both parties will fail to put our people first. And I believe that neither party has demonstrated either willingness or ability to represent the will of the majority. I'm an independent.

For me, being an independent means more than simply being unaffiliated with either of the two major political parties. I'm an independent in every sense of that word. For me, being an independent means not being taken for granted by either the Republicans or the Democrats. It means that, as a citizen, I believe that our first allegiance must be to this nation's values and founding principle of equality and to one another. It means that I will not associate with any political party or political movement that does not recognize and represent the common good and the national interest as its primary purpose in our political lives.

As an independent populist, I believe I'm in the very best of company. As an independent populist, I'm encouraged that the midterm elections of 2006 offered opportunities to populist voices that are now beginning to be heard, at least faintly, in the Senate and the House.

CNN senior political analyst Bill Schneider believes independents played an even bigger role in the midterm election. He said that "[i]n 2006, Independents came roaring back. They voted Democratic— meaning anti-Bush—in huge numbers. Now Independents are empowered, but they're still angry—at President Bush, at the Democratic Congress, at Washington. They're looking for change, big change, and they don't believe they can get if from conventional parties and politicians. They want new alternatives."

Freshmen senators Jon Tester (D-Montana), Jim Webb (D-Virginia), Sherrod Brown (D-Ohio), and Claire McCaskill (D-Missouri) won office in large measure on the strength of their economic populism. And in the House, Nancy Boyda (D-Kansas), Betty Sutton (D-Ohio), and Heath Schuler (D-North Carolina) embraced these values. Obviously, most of these newly elected senators and congressmen are Democrats, and their populist success in 2006 is not likely to be lost on candidates of both political parties in 2008. Both grassroots campaigns and the populist movement made inroads in making the voice of American citizens heard at the local and national levels.

Vanderbilt University professor Carol M. Swain tells me the growing numbers of disaffected independent voters are moving into position to determine the outcome of the 2008 elections. Professor Swain believes that "the American public is finally realizing its power, which is evident in the growing numbers of voters who have cast off their shackles and joined the ranks of independent voters positioned to demand and expect responsiveness from their government."

Democratic strategist Hank Sheinkopf told me he believes "Americans are moving away from positive party identification because today's Republicans and Democrats are non-ideological vessels used simply for campaign purposes. An unhappy electorate, worried about its economic safety and security, will thrash to populism seeking truth and justice, not empty slogans based upon polling data."

But populism is not a concept simply to be resurrected during election years or to be embraced by politicians triangulating positions to attract voters. Populism is a philosophy, behavior, and conduct, and a commitment to the interests and welfare of the majority of people over those of a select few. It is neither Democrat nor Republican, neither liberal nor conservative.

As Pulitzer Prize–winning *Daily News* columnist Michael Goodwin says of the 2008 elections, "The trick for those of us who want more independent voters is to push the issues that, because of their appeal, will force candidates to adopt them as their own. In that way, candidates and eventually the parties will expand beyond the narrow bases controlling them now. As always, however, what's essential is higher participation levels. Without more people voting, the narrow interests, money as well as unions and blocs, will keep their stranglehold on the process and the results." Independent populism can break that stranglehold and produce election results that serve American citizens.

Populism seeks what I believe is the attainable ideal of putting our country and our government back in the hands of the working men and women of America. Ours can again be a government of the people, by the people, and for the people. And in today's society, populism must become a powerful force for the interests and values of the people over those of corporations, lobbyists, and special interests that have for too long held pride of place in America's political economy.

5

The Imperious Presidency

> The President is merely the most important among a large
> number of public servants. He should be supported or opposed
> exactly to the degree which is warranted by his good conduct
> or bad conduct, his efficiency or inefficiency in rendering loyal,
> able, and disinterested service to the Nation as a whole.
>
> —Theodore Roosevelt

We'll have a new president on January 20, 2009, and I can't recall a
more eagerly anticipated inaugural for a leader who hasn't yet been
nominated, let alone elected. Our body politic may be divided and frac-
tious, but every public opinion poll shows that the people have simply
had a bellyful of George W. Bush, his administration, his policies and
proposals, and his failure to succeed in the war in Iraq. Americans are
overwhelmingly desirous of change, but we all need to be mindful that
a change of president isn't necessarily an assurance of betterment.

The United States hasn't had a lame-duck president in wartime since
Lyndon B. Johnson decided not to run for reelection in 1968, which led
to the victory of Richard M. Nixon. A desperate cry for change led to
the election of a president who presided over a disastrous economy
and was later forced to resign in disgrace. And while American casualties in Vietnam did decline dramatically after Nixon was sworn in, the
war that he was elected to end dragged on for another six years.

I believe we are at a critical point in our history, in which we have
a responsibility to make not only a clearheaded choice as to who will
be our next president, but also to take a tough-minded consideration
of the nature and power of the presidency itself.

The power of the presidency has grown substantially over the past forty years, to the point that, in my opinion, our constitutional system of checks and balances is as threatened today as it was in the 1930s under FDR. Certainly, there aren't many who would assert that the executive, legislative, and judicial branches are any longer coequal parts of our federal government. Limits to presidential power remain in place, but those limits seem to exist only at the outer reaches of constitutional and legal proscription, and the Bush presidency has pressed, and I believe in some cases exceeded, even those.

The Bush White House has so politicized every department of our federal government that our national media hardly takes notice that the chairman of the Joint Chiefs of Staff is dispatched by the political office of the White House to testify on immigration, and the CentCom commanding general to publicly support the private business sale of American port assets to Dubai. The Bush White House hasn't hesitated to reduce cabinet secretaries to political functionaries, sending them out before the cameras and microphones to attack, in Greek chorus unison, political and media opponents of free trade or outsourcing. It has enlisted the secretary of Homeland Security, who is responsible for our nation's border and port security, to lobby Congress for a guest-worker program to secure our borders. The attorney general supports warrantless wiretaps and torture, and tolerates White House intrusion into a Justice Department that has traditionally been independent of political influence. Secretaries in the Bush cabinet may nominally report to the president, but they seemed to be working almost full time for Karl Rove, the president's political guru and policy point man.

Expectations for George W. Bush were at worst relatively low and at best decidedly mixed when he took office in 2001, after winning the first legally contested presidential election in 130 years. But he almost immediately defied those expectations and demonstrated political adroitness. Five months into office, faced with the collapse of the stock market and the onset of a recession, he won passage of the Economic Growth and Tax Relief Reconciliation Act of 2007, the sweeping tax cuts he had promised during his campaign. Then, just nine days short of eight months in office, President Bush and the nation were confronted with the terrorist attacks of September 11. With shocked and angered Americans rallying behind him, his approval rating hit 90 percent in the weeks after September 11, one of the highest numbers ever recorded for a modern president.

But within six years President Bush's approval ratings hit historic lows, and the political capital that he believed to be immense after his reelection in 2004 was squandered.

Certainly, President Bush's decision to go to war against Saddam Hussein was the principal inflection point in his reversal of fortune. In August 2002, as the White House was considering whether or not to bring down Saddam Hussein, neither the United Nations, nor our traditional European allies, nor members of the previous Democratic administration disputed, at least publicly, the view that Saddam possessed weapons of mass destruction. But President Bush was calling for the use of military force not to remove those putative weapons of mass destruction but to bring about a "regime change" in Iraq.

However, much of the public and the press, as well as many members of Congress, were hesitant. Bolstered by its startlingly quick success in dismantling the Taliban in Afghanistan, the Bush administration obviously believed that the American people and Congress, still lusting for the blood of the radical Islamists who had supported the September 11 attacks, would support the use of American troops in Iraq, unilaterally if necessary. But criticism mounted rather than lessened. The Bush White House was confronted by three longtime advisers to the president's father, who publicly criticized his call for military force in Iraq. Former secretaries of state James A. Baker III and Lawrence Eagleburger, and former National Security adviser Brent Scowcroft publicly suggested caution, and urged that diplomacy and international economic pressure be used against Iraq rather than military action.

They were not shy about airing their opinions. Scowcroft wrote an op-ed piece for the *Wall Street Journal* entitled "Don't Attack Saddam" on August 15, 2002. In it, he stated, "The United States could certainly defeat the Iraqi military and destroy Saddam's regime. But it would not be a cakewalk. On the contrary, it undoubtedly would be very expensive— with serious consequences for the U.S. and global economy—and could as well be bloody. . . . The central point is that any campaign against Iraq, whatever the strategy, cost and risks, is certain to divert us for some indefinite period from our war on terrorism."

The following week Eagleburger told CNN: "I am not at all convinced now that this is something we have to do this very moment. . . . We need to understand that if and when we do take Saddam on, we will have to do it with massive force as we did the last time around, simply to be sure that we can do it successfully, and then we need to understand, that if we get him out of office, we'll probably have to stay there in Iraq for some period of time. All of those things need to be made clear to the American people."

A few days after Eagleburger's interview, Baker wrote an editorial for the *New York Times* entitled "The Right Way to Change a Regime." He argued that if America decided to invade Iraq, there was a right way and a wrong way: "Although the United States could certainly succeed, we should try our best not to have to go it alone, and the president should reject the advice of those who counsel doing so. The costs in all areas will be much greater, as will the political risks, both domestic and international, if we end up going it alone or with only one or two other countries. The president should do his best to stop his advisers and their surrogates from playing out their differences publicly and try to get everybody on the same page."

President Bush finally relented—but only in the use of regime change as the pretext for war and his transparent unilateralism, not in his determination to invade Iraq and topple Saddam Hussein. By the fall of 2002 the Bush administration was focusing on "weapons of mass destruction" and seeking the support of the United Nation for its campaign. That effort succeeded on February 5, 2003, when secretary of state Colin Powell, then considered to be the most respected person in American politics, went to the United Nations to offer irrefutable evidence of the presence of weapons of mass destruction in Iraq, and of the threat posed to the world by Saddam Hussein. Secretary Powell's performance won the support of the American people, the national media, and the enactment of UN Resolution 1441, authorizing the use of military force against Iraq.

Future historians will look upon Secretary Powell's acquiescence in the Bush administration's manipulation to misrepresent the facts at the United Nations as tragic. There's as much tragedy as irony in the fact that his UN speech also led to the administration's overthrow of his own "Powell doctrine," which called for the use of overwhelming military force as a last resort to achieve a defined strategic objective in the national interest with a clear exit strategy. When our troops defeated Saddam's woefully undermanned and underequipped army in a stunning twenty-five days, defense secretary Donald Rumsfeld appeared to have been proved correct in his insistence on the use of a small rapid strike force to carry out the invasion, and the Powell doctrine seemed discredited.

The invasion was so swift and apparently so successful that on May 1, President Bush could stand on the deck of the aircraft carrier USS *Abraham Lincoln* and declare the end of major combat operations, while a banner on the carrier's bridge proclaimed MISSION ACCOMPLISHED. At that point, 139 of our troops had lost their lives, far fewer than the Pentagon's most optimistic prewar projections.

In the bloody occupation years since, the Powell doctrine has proven its validity, our national objectives and strategy remain at best unclear and ambiguous, and our exit from Iraq uncertain. Our troops have now been in Iraq for more than four years, with almost four thousand young Americans killed and nearly thirty thousand wounded. We've spent a half-trillion dollars fighting terrorists and insurgents in the midst of sectarian violence and outright civil war, sending our forces on multiple tours of duty and exhausting our National Guard and reserves, yet our best intelligence estimate is that Al-Qaeda in Iraq has strengthened, and that we have not succeeded, to this point, in adequately training Iraqi troops and police. Nevertheless President Bush continues to stubbornly insist, against the obvious wishes of both the American public and Congress, that there will be no American troop withdrawals from Iraq until a weak and unproved central government can provide its own security. Without any sense of incongruity, President Bush defies the will of the people while at the same time asking that we be patient with him, his discredited policies, and the generals who've failed for all these years in Iraq.

It is clear that two men, at least, should have been able to influence a wiser course. One was Secretary Powell, whose doctrine determined success in the Persian Gulf War in 1991, and the other was Vice President Dick Cheney. It was Cheney, serving as President George H. W. Bush's defense secretary, who explained the administration's decision not to attack Baghdad then and hunt down Saddam Hussein. Cheney said, "It would have been a mistake for us to get bogged down in the quagmire inside Iraq. . . . The President has made it clear that we are not interested in a permanent or long-term U.S. ground presence, a garrison if you will, on the ground in the Gulf in the Saudi Arabian area. But we are interested in an enhanced naval presence. We think we can do that safely. We've been operating out of Bahrain since 1949 and will continue to do so. . . . We think there is a greater receptivity on the part of our friends in that part of the world now to an occasional U.S. presence, a tactical fighter squadron, for example, deployed from time to time on a temporary basis to work out exercises jointly with our friends in the region; prepositioned equipment, both for air and ground forces; those kinds of arrangements we think make sense."

So little that the Bush administration has done in the conduct of the war since May 2003 has made any sense. The conflict in Iraq, a battered and broken country of fewer than 30 million people, has now lasted longer than World War II. It is unimaginable that President Franklin Delano Roosevelt and his generals would have dispatched our troops to Africa, Europe, and the South Pacific with no planning, preparation, or strategy. America was then a nation with only about a third of its current population. Yet well in advance of Pearl Harbor, President Roosevelt, his cabinet, and his generals were already preparing for war, and the U.S. military had grown to 1.4 million, about the same size as our military today, serving a nation now of more than 300 million people.

Secretary of defense Donald Rumsfeld blustered for two years about the enemy in Iraq as "dead-enders," "bitter-enders," and "thugs." The Pentagon's general staff, whether intimidated by Rumsfeld or simply inadequate military leaders, has failed to succeed against an insurgency, terrorists, and sectarian violence. Such leadership performance, and political climbing, as we see now, would have left America either a

German- or Japanese-speaking nation after World War II. Why do we the people continue to accept the sacrifice of our troops without demanding a clear articulation of its strategy and goals by our government, and why do we the people of this great nation permit such sacrifice without demanding that we all share in the burden? We must demand more of our leaders, and we must demand more of ourselves.

President Bush, upon taking the oath of office, stated, "I do solemnly swear that I will faithfully execute the office of President of the United States, and will to the best of my ability, preserve, protect, and defend the Constitution of the United States." President Bush, in my opinion, has broken his oath. He has without question broken faith with the people of this country and our national values.

There is no longer any doubt that the Bush administration, at the very least, fostered an interpretation of prewar intelligence that supported military action against Saddam Hussein and Iraq, and that some government officials, including secretary of state Colin Powell, were manipulated to advance the war agenda.

This president and his administration have likewise manipulated data, people, and even legislation to achieve their goals. For example, the administration's wholesale and unprecedented use of presidential signing statements on legislation is a breach of both our traditions and the constitutionally established concept of coequal branches of government. Signing statements are typically statements that a president includes with a bill when it is signed into law. In some cases, they simply state that the bill has been signed, or include an opinion about the legislation in question.

Then there are President Bush's signing statements, which he uses to raise objections to particular elements of bills that he has signed into law, and to define those elements that he will not recognize as lawful and binding upon the executive branch. President Bush has, at last count, added statements to more than eight hundred provisions in more than one hundred laws. That is more than the total number of signing statements made by all the previous presidents combined in the history of the United States. I'll leave it to lawyers and scholars as to whether such behavior is unconstitutional.

The American Bar Association, at least, finds that those signing statements are at variance with the Constitution. The ABA also argues that President Bush has violated his oath of office to "preserve, protect, and defend" the Constitution of the United States by issuing these hundreds of signing statements. A bipartisan panel of the ABA likewise asserts that signing statements cannot be a substitute for a presidential veto, and that using them as Bush has done amounts to a line-item veto, which the Supreme Court has ruled is unconstitutional. Frankly, I hope the courts will concur with the ABA. And I hope that the people demand that our succeeding presidents publicly renounce the practice and the precedent.

The domestic spying program in which the White House skirted the Foreign Intelligence Surveillance Act and the FISA court has been upheld, but is, in my opinion, repugnant to the very ideals of American justice and law. A warrantless wiretap on an American citizen is hardly keeping faith with American traditions and values. The White House opposition to the long-held American ban on torture violates not only American values but is counter to U.S. military law and the wishes of our military to publicly support that ban for the protection of our own troops.

The president and his administration are as exasperating as they are inexplicable. The Bush administration supported the Dubai Ports World deal, which would have effectively turned control of more than twenty U.S. port facilities over to a business owned by the United Arab Emirates. The administration sent troops into Iraq without supplying our soldiers and marines with adequate armor and equipment, and had no intelligent plan for a post-Saddam Iraq. It sent those troops in without provisions for giving them the best medical care possible upon their return to America. Vice President Cheney claimed he was exempt from having to comply with an order to provide data on classified documents to the Information Security Oversight Office because his office is not an "entity within the executive branch." The combination of its incompetence and sheer brazenness in the face of obvious truth is nothing short of breathtaking.

"Brazen" is the very essence of the administration's use of presidential signing statements. President Bush has used this instrument to effectively declare that he has the right to ignore provisions of laws that conflict with *his* interpretation of the Constitution. In effect, he has stated that it is his prerogative to apply whatever interpretation of the Constitution he wishes. Of course, the president's lawyers, who have obviously read the Constitution, know full well that interpretation of a law is up to the judicial branch, and that writing the laws is up to the legislative branch. That's what those checks and balances are supposed to provide for. But remember, this is a president who doesn't think much of checks and balances, if he thinks about them at all.

I find it more than exasperating that President Bush has made wholesale use of signing statements to infringe upon the power of Congress, the Supreme Court, and the Constitution. It's an outrageous and illegitimate exercise of presidential power, and the policy was authored in part by the man Bush appointed to the Supreme Court in 2006, Samuel Alito. Working for Attorney General Edwin Meese in the Reagan White House in 1986 Alito drafted the blueprint for what would become in the Bush administration a common justification for the extension of presidential authority.

Here are a few examples of approved legislation along with the president's signing statements and their effect:

March 9, 2006: Justice Department officials must give reports to Congress by certain dates on how the FBI is using the USA Patriot Act to search homes and secretly seize papers.

Bush's signing statement: The president can order Justice Department officials to withhold any information from Congress if he decides it could impair national security or executive branch operations.

December 30, 2005: U.S. interrogators cannot torture prisoners or otherwise subject them to cruel, inhuman, and degrading treatment.

Bush's signing statement: The president, as commander in chief, can waive the torture ban if he decides that harsh interrogation techniques will assist in preventing terrorist attacks.

November 6, 2003: U.S. officials in Iraq cannot prevent an inspector general for the Coalition Provisional Authority from carrying out any investigation. The inspector general must tell Congress if officials refuse to cooperate with his inquiries.

Bush's signing statement: The inspector general "shall refrain" from investigating anything involving sensitive plans, intelligence, national security, or anything already being investigated by the Pentagon. The inspector general cannot tell Congress anything if the president decides that disclosing the information would impair foreign relations, national security, or executive branch operations.

The chairman of the Senate Judiciary Committee, Patrick Leahy, said, "While this President proudly boasts being the first modern President to have never vetoed a bill, he has cleverly used his signing statements as a de facto line-item veto to cherry-pick which laws he will enforce in a manner not contemplated by our Constitution. . . . The President's signing statements are not the law, and we should not allow them to be the last word. The President's constitutional duty is to faithfully execute the laws as written by the Congress."

Additionally, the Government Accountability Office investigated the use of presidential signing statements, and it found that a third of the provisions about which President Bush expressed concern or objection were either not enacted or were not enforced by the agencies charged with their execution.

When President Bush claims the title of "Decider," he's not joking. And none of us who cares about this nation should be laughing.

This president was aided and abetted in his disregard for the Constitution and our laws by a politicized Justice Department led by his incompetent confidant, Attorney General Alberto Gonzales. The nation's senior law enforcement official, presiding over what has traditionally been an independent and proud branch of the federal government, had the temerity to testify that he wasn't fully aware of the decision making that led to the firing of nearly 10 percent of the U.S. attorneys working for him across the country. Attorney General Gonzales at this writing remains the subject of scrutiny by the Senate Judiciary Committee and there is an investigation into why his Justice Department gave inaccurate or, worse, flat-out false information to the American people. The right of the attorney general to dismiss and replace U.S. attorneys is not in question, but his partisanship and incompetent management certainly are. That partisanship has been practiced to the degree that even the ranking Republican in the Senate Judiciary Committee, Senator Arlen Specter (R-Pennsylvania,) has made clear his displeasure and his preference that Gonzales leave as attorney general.

We as a nation are now confronted with the consequences of the decisions made by this president and this government. We cannot continue to drift as we have for the three decades since the first OPEC embargo and tolerate presidents and Congresses lacking in character and the quality of leadership that can guide this nation. Seven presidents have led America in that period, and each has uttered rhetoric promising new alternative energy policies and reduced dependence on foreign oil. But the power of the presidency is such that rhetoric can pass for performance. Slogans, white papers, and even legislation are accepted by our national media and voters as accomplishment. The fact is that in the thirty-four years since the first OPEC embargo, we are more—not less—dependent on foreign oil. Our presidents stand each year before Congress and deliver their State of the Union messages. In 2005, President Bush pushed through the Energy Policy Act of 2005, promising alternate energy initiatives based on hydrogen; again, it was rhetoric with little regard for reality.

President Bush and his father, both of whom have strong ties to America's energy industry, were seemingly fated to go to war in the Middle East. Two men who should have been able to comprehend the need for energy independence and its implications for engagement in the Middle East failed to do so. Instead, Americans are once again engaged in combat there, and our government is no closer to energy independence. Instead, the current president and his vice president have sought to placate Big Oil and our energy industry.

There is no question that oil is critical to our economy and will be for some time. But there is no excuse for the energy policies pursued by the last seven presidents—policies that have left us weaker, more vulnerable, and more dependent on the very nations who have supported terrorism against us and our allies. Our troops are paying in their blood for the failure of politicians who hold the world's most powerful political offices, our taxpayers are paying for the overwhelming cost of supporting the war in Iraq, and American consumers are paying more than ever before for heating oil and gasoline because of the turmoil in the Middle East. The beneficiary of that turmoil and those higher prices and, yes, that blood is our energy industry.

In 2006 ExxonMobil reported the largest profit in history for an American corporation—just under $40 billion. Lee Raymond, its now retired CEO, led the company to those mind-numbing figures. Raymond, by the way, made more than $140,000 a day while he was running the oil giant, just about three times what the average American worker earns in a year. It is impossible to say how much lower ExxonMobil's profits would have been if not for failed American energy policy and foreign policy in the Middle East, but one thing is certain: Lee Raymond was rewarded for being in the right place at the right time. He walked away from ExxonMobil with a $400 million retirement package.

But Raymond has not been just sitting on his laurels or his pile of cash since retiring. He is now the chairman of the National Petroleum Council, one of Washington's most influential lobbying groups. Here is how the NPC defines its mission in our nation's capital: "The purpose of the NPC is solely to represent the views of the oil and natural gas industries in advising, informing, and making recommendations to the Secretary of Energy with respect to any matter relating to oil and natural gas, or to the oil and gas industries submitted to it or approved by the Secretary."

Lee Raymond is not only one of the oil industry's leading lobbyists, but President Bush has named him an adviser to his administration on—you guessed it—energy policy. In late 2005, energy secretary Samuel Bodman commissioned Raymond and the NPC to help the White House determine future energy policies via an "independent" study—specifically, "What oil and gas supply strategies and/or demand-side strategies does the Council recommend the U.S. pursue to ensure greater economic stability and prosperity?"

Raymond and the NPC are conducting that study and will "assess the potential contribution of conservation, efficiency, alternative energy sources, and technology advances under various economic and policy scenarios." In addition they will also "assess the *broad* potential for technology advances to increase petroleum and natural gas supply by 2030." The italics are mine, and I think they're indicative of which potential is likely to find favor with the NPC. Only an American president could without any public flap get away with naming a big oil man and a big oil lobby as the best people to help America wean itself from Big Oil.

In 2007 the president laid out his plan for his Twenty In Ten program in his State of the Union speech. (That was the nifty title that the White House conjured up to describe the goal of cutting U.S. gasoline consumption by 20 percent over the next ten years.) By increasing the supply of alternative fuels and making motor vehicles more energy efficient, the president promised that his Twenty In Ten plan would address energy security and reduce greenhouse gas emissions from motor vehicles and off-road engines and equipment. Want to bet?

We've heard this nonsense from administration after administration. Obviously this president and a Democratic-controlled Congress are not willing to take the bold steps necessary that would genuinely cut energy consumption, create alternative energy sources, and make the nation energy independent. The money involved in the status quo is too big, the lobby is well funded, and the corporate interests are simply overwhelming. The oil industry alone spends nearly $80 million a year lobbying in Washington. Big oil companies could spend a lot more lobbying our elected officials, and likely will, should the need ever arise. So far, the return on these outlays has been handsome: record profits and assured business as usual for years to come.

Several years ago Lee Raymond told a Senate committee that was conducting an energy hearing that the oil business was tough for everyone, producers and consumers. As he said, "We're all in this together, everywhere in the world." Now let's see: record profits for oil companies, record-high gasoline prices for consumers. I'm not sure that's togetherness, and I'm a little nervous about that "all over the world" comment.

International trade, big business, and this president have indeed found true togetherness, and invariably to the exclusion of the interests of working Americans and their families. Until the summer of 2007 the U.S. Congress had ceded to President Bush—as it had to previous presidents for the past three decades—its own constitutional authority and responsibility for trade through a device known as trade promotion authority, or "fast track authority." With that authority Mr. Bush has pursued free-trade-at-any-cost deals all over the globe more energetically than any president before. In so doing he has incurred record trade deficits and a record trade debt of $6 trillion—a figure that is rising faster than our record $9 trillion national debt. The current account deficit in 2006 reached almost $857 billion, yet another new record achieved by the Bush administration, and now represents 6.5 percent of our total GDP.

We have sustained thirty-one consecutive years of trade deficits, and those deficits have reached successively higher record amounts in each of the past five years. The trade deficit has been a drag on our economic growth in eighteen of the twenty-four quarters of President Bush's presidency.

By an interesting coincidence, the United States has run a trade deficit in each of the years following the creation of fast-track authority for the president. The only good news on trade is that in 2007 this Congress refused to extend the president's fast-track authority, and it appears ready to assume its constitutional responsibilities on trade. Let's hope and pray. That body never should have given up its authority or voided those responsibilities for international commerce and trade, but the action of the 110th Congress to end such practices restores some hope that our government will return to the balance of coequal branches envisioned by our founders.

The examples of imperious presidents' extending their powers beyond the boundaries of the Constitution are regrettably numerous, but fast-track authority is one of a smaller number of instances in which Congress has voluntarily diminished both its power and its constitutional role as the representative and protector of the interests of the people and the common good, this time in the negotiation and governmental approval of international trade and commerce agreements. Further, the treaty clause of the Constitution states that the president "shall have Power, by and with the Advice and Consent of the Senate, to make Treaties, provided two thirds of the Senators present concur." Many Americans, if not most, are unaware that many international trade agreements that extend well beyond commerce, and which subordinate both our laws and the Constitution to such agreements (including the North American Free Trade Agreement, which is clearly a treaty) have never been approved by two thirds of the Senate as required by our Constitution. And why has the Senate, under the leadership of both Republicans and Democrats, not approved these treaties and demanded the exercise of their constitutional authority? Because the last three presidents have, without resistance, claimed these deals are "executive agreements" rather than treaties.

Corporate America, special interests, and establishment elites in these instances succeeded in denying working Americans and their families adequate representation in the negotiation and approval of those agreements, and have, in my opinion, committed egregiously unconstitutional acts in breach of both the treaty clause and Article 1, Section 8. To my knowledge there has never been a court challenge to such agreements on constitutional grounds, which is simply incomprehensible, given their profoundly negative consequences.

Barry in Illinois: "Congress complains the president is not listening to them. Now they know how we feel." (April 6, 2007)

6

Debtor Nation

It is incumbent on every generation to pay its own debts
as it goes.

—Thomas Jefferson

America is now the world's largest debtor nation. Our national debt
has risen to nine trillion dollars, a new record high. Our trade deficit
stands at six trillion dollars, also a record and a sum that is rising even
more rapidly than our national debt.

The quality of life for the vast majority of Americans is being
assailed by a host of forces unleashed by the elite establishment in the
pursuit of ruinous free-trade policies, costly wars in Iraq and Afghanistan and against global radical Islamists, and unchecked expansion of
federal entitlement programs. The U.S. trade deficit is approaching $1
trillion a year, and our government is spending almost $200 billion
annually on war. The cost of federal entitlement programs has risen
to $1.2 trillion per year, an increase of more than 2,000 percent since
1970. The federal budget deficit is more than $200 billion. Quite simply,
our runaway government and consumer spending is bankrupting our
nation and millions of Americans.

Not only are more Americans living at or below the poverty line,
but the number of personal bankruptcies and mortgage loan foreclosures has risen to record levels. Personal bankruptcies reached a new
high of more than two million in 2005. Foreclosures on homes in Los
Angeles alone jumped 799 percent between 2006 and 2007.

Most Americans pay little attention to the usually stultifying intri-
cacies and trends in the bond market, stock market, and currency

markets. But recent developments in those markets are sufficiently ominous to give all of us cause for concern. Corporate earnings and stock prices are declining from recent highs, interest rates have risen, and the American dollar is rapidly losing value against the currencies of other nations. In fact, the dollar has fallen to lows against the British pound not seen in a quarter century. The once denigrated euro, meanwhile, has risen to historic highs against our declining dollar. Even the Canadian dollar has reached parity with our currency. These troubling developments are clear symptoms of an economy struggling against massive amounts of American corporate, government, and private debt. Even as investor anxieties and economic dislocation tremor through the markets, our nation's leaders hold steadfast to the public policies and corporate business practices that have produced our uncertain state. Both Republicans and Democrats in our Congress and White House pursue proposals and legislation that are unsustainable and will only worsen the condition of our political economy.

The Bush administration continues to press free-trade agreements that are disadvantageous to the national economy and disastrous to the interests of working Americans. Our government has recently passed energy, bankruptcy, and transportation laws that could hardly be more wrongheaded. Individuals and families who go broke because of overwhelming medical bills are punished rather than supported by the Bankruptcy Abuse Prevention and Consumer Protection Act of 2005. Half of the individual bankruptcies in this country result from the high cost of medical care for critical and catastrophic illness. Parts of that bankruptcy law were literally written by the credit card companies, which benefit at the expense of people who through no fault of their own have fallen on hard times.

The Energy Policy Act of 2005 provided billions of dollars of subsidies and incentives to oil and natural gas companies and did almost nothing to spur development of alternative energy sources. Our dependence on foreign oil is greater than ever before. The 2007 energy legislation driven by the Democratic leadership would only marginally create incentives for alternative energy development and constrain fossil fuel consumption. Whether Capitol Hill is controlled by Republicans or Democrats, the powerful lobbies of big oil and big business continue to dominate in our nation's capital.

While the almost $300 billion Transportation Act passed in 2005 did deliver funding for road and bridge construction, it was one of the most pork-laden pieces of legislation ever signed into law, and included the well-publicized and notorious earmark of Alaska's Ted Stevens to build a $200 million "bridge to nowhere."

Despite the declaration of the overwhelming numbers of Republicans and Democrats who approved it, the transportation bill barely addresses the need to invest in our nation's infrastructure. The American Society of Civil Engineers issues a report card every few years on the state of our nation's infrastructure. This document, which should be required reading for every citizen in this country, outlines how our public policy has ignored the very basic maintenance of such critical national resources as roads, bridges, waterways, the energy grid, and drinking water. Here are highlights of the most disconcerting failures to invest in our infrastructure, as identified by the ASCE:

- We need to spend $94 billion every year to improve the state of our roads and highways, yet we spend less than $60 billion. Poor road conditions cost U.S. motorists $54 billion a year in repairs and operating costs, which comes out to $275 per motorist.
- 27.1 percent of our nation's 590,750 bridges are rated structurally deficient or functionally obsolete.
- America faces an annual shortfall of $11 billion just to replace aging drinking water facilities and to comply with safe drinking water regulations. Annual funding for drinking water is less than 10 percent of the total national requirement.
- Outdated and overworked wastewater management systems discharge billions of gallons of untreated sewage into our surface waters each year. The EPA estimates we must invest $390 billion over the next twenty years both to replace existing systems and to build new ones, yet the government has continually reduced funding for these projects.

- Maintenance expenditures for our power transmission facilities have decreased 1 percent per year since 1992 while demand has skyrocketed. In the wake of the massive power outage of 2003, we can expect more blackouts in the future.
- In 2005 federal funding for Superfund cleanup of the nation's worst toxic waste sites reached its lowest level in two decades. There are 1,237 contaminated sites on the National Priorities List, with 10,154 more that should conceivably be added.
- In 2002 the United States produced 369 million tons of solid waste of all types. Only about a quarter of that total was recycled or recovered.

It has been obvious to officials of both political parties in federal and state government that attention to the structural and environmental needs of the nation has been required for decades. Their inaction has resulted in an extraordinary deficit in the investment to restore and maintain that infrastructure. The ASCE estimates $1.67 trillion will be required over the next five years to merely bring our infrastructure up to good or at least acceptable levels. An unacceptable number of our highways, bridges, and tunnels are literally crumbling while government spending is not even keeping pace with maintenance costs. There should be no question that our next president and our next Congress must, regardless of party, commit themselves to funding this essential public investment.

While that level of public investment is daunting even to a nation with a $12 trillion economy, it is almost trivial when compared to our federal unfunded liabilities. These include our taxpayer liabilities for government retirement plans and programs—Medicare, Medicaid, and Social Security. Social Security and Medicare are not included in the U.S. federal budget, an omission that obscures the staggering rising expense of entitlements and the trillions of dollars in taxpayer IOUs that are piling up all but unnoticed. The total amount of unfunded liabilities is now so large as to be almost unfathomable by the human mind: $59 trillion, a figure that is rising by more than $1 trillion every year.

While it may be impossible for us to comprehend a number that large, we can put it in some context. That $59 trillion is about five times the value of all the goods and services created in our economy each year and would finance the operation of our federal government (except for such off-budget items as Social Security and Medicare) for the next quarter century.

Our elected officials, Republican and Democrat alike, refuse to account for the full impact of entitlement spending in the reporting of the government budget. That refusal obstructs the public view of the impact of these public programs and the irresponsibility of every administration and Congress for the past forty years. And success in keeping the true scale of government spending deficits and liabilities from public notice allows our politicians to ignore and defer the tough, stark policy choices necessary to restore balance to both our government and our national economy.

America is a superpower with a military that is the world's most technologically advanced and is possessed of the greatest destructive power ever known to man. But make no mistake: We are a superpower on the edge. I fear that our business and political leaders have learned neither from history nor from the experience of the Soviet Union less than two decades ago. Then the world's only other superpower, the Soviet Union collapsed under the weight of a central government that exceeded all bounds of reason in its budget excesses, primarily defense spending in the arms race with the United States. The Soviet Union quickly disintegrated, as the "evil empire" could no longer maintain both its global geopolitical economic reach and the production capacity necessary to meet the needs of its society and sustain the living standard of its citizens. American leaders who doubt the certainty of consequences and the sometimes surprising onset of such consequences are utterly delusional and derelict in their guidance of our nation.

The irresponsibility of both political parties and our establishment elite is simply inexcusable. What have decades of heedless government policy and corporate business practices wrought? We are now a people and government grown accustomed to deferring responsibility and action and insistent upon immediate consumption and instant gratification. When the Bush administration contemplates a federal budget, its proposals delay the possibility of achieving a balanced or even surplus budget until 2012, four years after Bush leaves the White House. And how realistic is even that goal? The Congressional Budget Office has concluded in its estimates that if tax breaks and credits for corporations and the wealthy aren't rolled back, a balanced budget in 2012 is unlikely.

Our leaders and lawmakers have pledged since the first oil embargo against the United States in 1973 that America would pursue alternative energy sources and eliminate our dependence on foreign oil for energy. Through the administrations of seven presidents, the result of those pledges is an even greater dependency on foreign oil. We as individual citizens have been just as irresponsible as our government, buying ever bigger homes, and buying cars and appliances with little consideration of their energy consumption.

Our behavior as consumers mirrors that of our government. Americans live on the installment plan and think too little of the consequences of our buy now, pay later culture. The record foreclosures and bankruptcies the are currently afflicting working men and women and their families will have repercussions felt for years throughout our economy and our society. American consumers have amassed a record $2.4 trillion in installment debt and are paying what would have once been called usurious rates, and much of middle-class America's mortgage debt is now based on adjustable loans that will continue to rise throughout 2008, creating more economic pressure on our working families.

Auto loan debt has risen dramatically, as has the total volume of auto leases. Nearly two thirds of automobile loans have payment periods of at least five years, with some lasting as long as eight. And the rising popularity of car leases has been driven by both sticker shock and extended lease terms that reduce monthly payments. The typical car lease runs anywhere from sixty to ninety-six months.

Our credit card debt has more than quadrupled since 1990, from just under $200 billion a year to nearly $900 billion. Credit cards constitute only part of the $2.4 trillion of consumer debt that we had as of the middle of 2007, which also included $880.1 billion in revolving debt and $1.5 trillion in nonrevolving debt such as auto loans.

We are now a debtor nation in every sense. Today the *average* household has $8,000 in credit card debt alone, while the average household income before taxes is $46,326. The typical American family is carrying the equivalent of one-sixth of its gross income on credit cards, and of course paying monthly installments with after-tax income. More than $1.8 trillion worth of goods and services were purchased with credit cards in 2005, and the average household has an outstanding balance of $2,500 on each of its cards. Some credit cards charge interest rates of more than 30 percent on unpaid balances, yet we keep paying more to the credit card companies so we can continue to use their services and, in some cases, go ever deeper in debt.

American are spending as much on meals outside the home as we do for health care—a little over $2,600 per family. We spend almost as much to buy and operate our cars as we do to pay for our homes—about $8,000 per year on each. We're spending more on cars than we ever have, thanks to gas prices, but we still don't use public transportation very often. Only about one-twentieth of all the money we spend on transportation goes to using buses, subways, trains, and other forms of mass transit. Our entertainment spending has gone up as well, rivaling the amount we spend on health care and going out to eat.

Total household debt in 2007 was $2.4 trillion, and more than a third of that is credit card debt. That is what you and I owe to banks, credit card companies, and other financial institutions that loan us money.

As we demand more responsibility of our national leaders in both government and business, I believe that all Americans should at the same time focus on responsible consumption. Credit cards and installment debt are incredibly convenient and make accessible many goods and items that millions of us could not otherwise afford. But the price of instant gratification and deferred payment is lower disposable consumer income, lower to nonexistent personal savings, and a load of personal debt that is often crushing. In July 2007 the House Judiciary Committee held hearings on the practices of the credit card industry, which included testimony that Visa, MasterCard, and the banking industry have worked together to maintain high fees and to disguise those costs to consumers. Penalty fees have nearly tripled in the last ten years, from thirteen dollars in the mid-1990s to as much as thirty-nine dollars now. And credit card users who exceed their credit limits can end up paying 30 percent interest on their cards.

There were once national usury laws that protected consumers against these exorbitantly high interest rates. Some states, such as Delaware and South Dakota, have eliminated usury caps to attract the business of credit card companies and financial institutions, which accounts for why New York–based Citibank headquarters its credit card business in Sioux Falls, South Dakota.

Credit card companies inflict a host of additional charges on users, such as transaction fees, stop-payment fees, delinquency fees, ATM fees, over-the-limit fees, annual fees, and cash advance fees. If you sign up for a credit card, you can easily incur these additional costs on top of the basic principal and interest charges. The more fees, the more debt.

Consumer debt is a huge economic issue—anything that amounts to trillions of dollars should be—but the U.S. government doesn't get involved in it because credit card and personal finance are the domain of big business, which translates to "hands off" as far as politicians are concerned. That policy changes only when the situation becomes unseemly, as it did in January 2007 when Congress looked into especially egregious hidden fees. Our elected officials really couldn't ignore the fact that some credit card companies were charging customers interest on balances that had already been paid.

As American consumers spend more, debt rises, and fewer and fewer are saving money and preparing for retirement. Only a third of us are actively saving for retirement. Many of us will have to work longer—into what used to be considered our retirement years—because we don't have a choice in the matter. Some 30 percent of Americans in their late sixties are working today, nearly double the number just twenty years ago. And what about Social Security? Those trillions of dollars in unfunded liabilities, in my opinion, simply won't be available to many of our retirees over the next twenty years. By some estimates the Social Security system won't be taking in enough money to pay for retirement benefits by 2017. This fund will only be able to cover 75 percent of benefits twenty years after that, and the Social Security fund will be depleted shortly thereafter.

We desperately need a change of direction in public policy, a change in culture and consumption, and elected leaders who can address these issues honestly and forthrightly. In just the last generation the income of the wealthiest Americans—the top 1 percent—has risen by 200 percent, while median family income has risen by only a tenth of that. Not only have the wealthiest benefited disproportionately from the economy at the expense of stagnant wages for working Americans, but they have also benefited from reduced taxes. But income tax cuts alone haven't fully satisfied the wealthy, who also deeply desire the elimination of the estate tax, or so-called death tax. The Senate disappointed them by killing efforts to eliminate the death tax in the summer of 2006, and thereby preserved some $20 billion in tax revenue. But the amount saved by the Senate is paltry compared to the benefits gained by the wealthy and corporate America since President Bush took office: an estimated $1 trillion in tax revenue that might otherwise have been applied against the federal budget deficits over that period. Considered from another perspective, our national debt could have been reduced from $9 trillion to $8 trillion, which would have had the effect of reducing federal government expenditures to service that debt by about $50 billion each year, or reducing the current federal budget deficit by 25 percent a year.

Astonishingly this nation's trade debt is rising at an even faster rate than our national debt, which now amounts to more than $6 trillion. The U.S. current account deficit, the broadest measure of our current trade deficit, rose 8 percent in 2006 to hit a record high of $857 billion, and that deficit continues to worsen because of the misguided and destructive free-trade policies followed by this nation over the past three decades.

I've already pointed out that free trade in recent years has been the most expensive trade policy in this nation's history. There is nothing free about ever-larger trade deficits, mounting trade debts, and the loss of millions of well-paid American jobs. The term "free trade" sounds benign, even positive, but as practiced by the last two administrations free trade has been outrageously costly and destructive. Since the beginning of the new century, the United States has lost more than three million manufacturing jobs. Three million more jobs have been lost to overseas labor markets, as corporate America campaigns relentlessly for "higher productivity," "efficiency," and "competitiveness," all of which have proved to be nothing more than code words for the cheapest possible labor in the world.

Corporate America and our country's political elites have joined forces to put this country's middle-class working men and women into direct competition with the world's labor market. Salaries and wages now represent the lowest share of our national income at any time since 1929. Corporate profits, meanwhile, represent the largest share of our national income at any time since 1950. Today many of our CEOs are being paid four hundred times more than front-line employees.

The Bush administration's pursuit of so-called free trade has resulted in granting wide-open access to the world's richest consumer market to foreign competitors without negotiation of a reciprocal opening of world markets to Americans goods and services. This isn't free trade by any definition, whether that of classical economists like Adam Smith and David Ricardo or that of current propaganda ministers who use the term to promote continuation of the trade policies followed for the last three decades.

More than six years ago Federal Reserve economists warned of what would likely happen when the trade deficit of a developed nation exceeded a critical amount: "We find that a typical current account reversal begins when the current account deficit is about 5 percent of GDP. . . . In general, these episodes involve a declining net international investment position that levels off, but does not reverse, a few years after the current account begins its recovery." That study established 5 percent of GDP as the trade deficit threshold for action by both policymakers and monetary authorities. Our current account deficit is now 6.5 percent of GDP, or 30 percent beyond the Fed's theoretical threshold.

Also troubling is a recent development in investment flows. In 2006 the United States for the first time experienced negative investment flows. The cumulative effect of more than three decades of trade deficits and mounting external debt has resulted in our first investment income deficit since 1946, when the Commerce Department began keeping such records, and it is the first time that Americans have earned less on investments abroad than foreigners earned on their investments in the United States.

Amazingly even our own top trade officials admit that U.S. free-trade policies aren't working, unless they consider trade surpluses for our trading partners to be the desired outcome. While U.S. Trade Representative Susan Schwab appears to understand the consequences of the past few administrations' free-trade policies, she has shown little willingness to change them. Schwab said, "Our trade deficits are too high. We can't . . . pretend that the trade imbalance can just keep getting bigger with no cost." Ambassador Schwab's deputy trade representative, Karan Bhatia, has said outright, "From Chile to Singapore to Mexico, the history of our [Free Trade Agreements] is that bilateral trade surpluses of our trading partners go up."

I've been called a lot of names by the establishment elite and their mouthpieces in the media because of my stance on a wide range of issues of national concern. But some of the silliest denunciations originate with the "free trade" crowd. Because I seek balance and reciprocity in U.S. trade policies, I am a "table-thumping protectionist." The Bush administration has hurled at me its favorite public epithet, "economic isolationist." Donald Luskin, a contributing editor to *The National Review*, added to the litany in a piece provocatively titled "Isolationist Ignorance in Action: Watch Lou Dobbs Ascend to the Pinnacle of Protectionist Prevarication." Luskin claimed, "The advocates of free trade have on their side over 200 years of settled science in economics, going all the way back to Adam Smith. The advocates of protectionism have Lou Dobbs. With his nightly harangues on CNN and through his books, Lou Dobbs has become the public face of today's dangerous movement toward economic isolationism." None of Luskin's claims could be further from the truth. I believe in the importance of an international system of trade and finance that is orderly, predictive, well-regulated, mutual, and fair.

Reciprocity in no way connotes protectionism. Mutuality does not connote economic isolationism. But both terms, when applied to our trade policy, would require a pragmatism and a commitment to the domestic and national interests of this country on the part of U.S. trade negotiators in all international agreements.

It's been twenty-six years since an American president demanded any form of meaningful reciprocity in a trade negotiation, when in 1981 President Ronald Reagan required that Japan restrict its automotive exports to America. In return for its voluntary restraint, Japan was permitted to build car factories in the United States, factories that employed American labor. The result has been increased sales for Japanese car companies and regular employment in America for American workers, and Japanese cars built in America and sold to American consumers. In that scenario, everyone doing business in America wins. However, when an American car manufacturer sets up a factory in Mexico, employs local workers at a fraction of the wage paid to American workers, and then sells those cheaply made cars back to American workers, who benefits? The manufacturer and the workers in Mexico. American workers lose their jobs.

Reagan's trade policy certainly wasn't perfect, but it was a wise policy choice for American labor and consumers. Succeeding presidential administrations have not been as wise. Japanese car companies have built more new factories in the United States, but without reciprocal opening of the Japanese market to U.S. goods and services.

American automakers are losing, not gaining, international market share, and 2007 was the first year that more Americans bought foreign-brand cars than U.S.-brand cars. Meanwhile, foreign car factories in the United States are hiring while Detroit's big three are laying off their American employees.

President Bush and his trade representatives have signed a record number of free-trade agreements, and our trade deficits have set new record highs for five consecutive years. Reciprocity and mutuality are not part of the Bush administration's trade strategy: The United States imported 700,000 Korean-made automobiles, while the Koreans imported a whopping 3,900 American-made cars. By my math, Korea bought roughly one-two-hundredth the number of cars from us that we did from them. Our trade deficit with Korea in 2006 was $13.5 billion, which is only a fraction of the almost $230 billion deficit with China and more than $50 billion deficit with Mexico. It is as if the Bush administration has no concept or understanding of the need for balance in our international trade relationships.

David in California: "Lou, when Bush's term is up, do you think he will open up his presidential library in Mexico City or Beijing?" (May 24, 2007)

President Bush has built his legacy on unfortunate slogans of hollow bravado: "Mission accomplished," "Bring it on," "Wanted: Dead or alive," "You're either with us or against us." Don't forget "I'm the Decider," and of course, "I earned . . . political capital, and now I intend to spend it." The topper was, of course, "I'll see you at the bill signing," referring to his own ill-considered push for so-called comprehensive immigration reform legislation.

This president desperately needs to be told that he is the president of every American and not just of corporate interests and socioethnocentric special interest groups. Someone he trusted and respected should have convinced him that his tortured reasoning and disregard for the working people of this country should never have been exposed before cameras and microphones.

The candidates from both parties seeking the presidential nomination, and politicians seeking election and re-election to the Senate, will be stepping up to those microphones and cameras more frequently in the days and months ahead. I hope every voter will make his or her choice at the ballot box based at least in part on the position the candidates take on the necessity of establishing balanced, mutual, and reciprocal trade agreements. And any candidate, whether liberal or conservative, who says he or she is in favor of free trade should be as discredited by the voters in 2008 as free-trade policies have been over the course of the last thirty years of history.

7

Shadow Government

> [T]here are more instances of the abridgment of freedoms of
> the people by gradual and silent encroachments of those in
> power than by violent and sudden usurpations.
>
> —James Madison

The presidency, as I've discussed, has assumed not only imperial powers and an imperious attitude toward our citizens, but also toward Congress and the Constitution. The president of the United States can now send the military to invade a foreign nation such as Iraq or Afghanistan without a declaration of war, as constitutionally required. The Constitution does not require the people to merrily acquiesce or Congress to simply approve a resolution supporting the use of our military, no matter what interpretations, practices, or conventions have grown up over the past half century. Article 1, Section 8, of our Constitution is direct and explicit, giving only Congress the power to declare war. Waging an undeclared war, like military adventurism, was not part of our Founders' vision and ideals.

While George Washington, Thomas Jefferson, James Madison, and other Founders did foresee many of the perils and threats that would face us throughout the nation's existence as a democratic republic, they could not imagine many of the internal and external forces that are now altering the shape, nature, role, and effectiveness of the federal government they created.

Divisive partisan politics, an imperious presidency, and a Congress that has mutated into an often grotesque bazaar brokering vested interests and factions—all of these have combined to allow the gradual creation of new and unforeseeable social, political, and commercial elements throughout our society. In the aggregate they perform roles and services that had originally been contemplated as the sole purview and responsibility of local, state, and federal governments. They are neither elected nor transparent to society at large, and while most certainly legal, I consider them to be hardly legitimate, or only marginally so. They form collectively what has become a government in the shadows.

This shadow government has come about as the result of political, ideological, and even religious forces driven by such varied motives as financial self-interest, economic philosophy, altruism, religious faith, and idealism. In and of themselves, these reasons for being can be compelling, even laudatory. In practice, their role abridges and impinges on government at all levels and operates beyond the influence of the will of the people, as expressed by the policies created by our representative republican government. I believe we need to discuss and reflect carefully on the impact of this shadow government on our society. That discussion will likely be noisy, but it is a discussion our democracy should begin.

Privatization of government services at all levels, in many if not most instances, has been rationalized as an effective way to reduce the cost of government. While there is a cacophony of contesting views and opinions on the conduct of the war in Iraq, there has been almost no reference to the presence of private contractors sent there by the U.S. government to perform functions and services that have traditionally been the responsibility of the government. Large corporations such as Halliburton and Blackwater USA are among the many that have won noncompetitive bids to do the work once done by the navy's Seabees, Army engineers, and our soldiers and Marines. In fact, there are almost as many private contractors in Iraq today as there are American troops. Those private contractors are beyond the oversight of the U.S. government, and in some instances, such as security contractors, have no accountability for their actions under U.S. law or the Geneva Conventions.

The Iraqi police force, for example, is being trained by a private U.S.

firm called DynCorp, but not all security contractors in Iraq are American by any means. The protection of Iraqi oil wells is handled by Chileans hired by the American security firm Blackwater through a subcontractor, and a Seychelles company called Pilgrims Group is helping to guard the media in the region.

Domestically, the U.S. Supreme Court has recently handed down a decision that supports the funding of faith-based organizations selected by the Bush administration to perform social services that have traditionally been the responsibility of state and local government, and more recently, the federal government. Many civilians are shocked and surprised when they approach U.S. military bases and government facilities throughout the country to find that the gates and entrances are manned not by the U.S. soldiers, Marines, or sailors stationed there, but instead by private security guards.

American taxpayer money is now flowing to corporations, private contractors, special interest groups, churches and faith-based groups, nonprofit organizations, and nongovernmental organizations (NGOs) as the shadow government continues to grow, and in many respects has become competitive rather than complementary to traditional government.

Privatization is reaching across our society and economy, nationally as well as within our communities. Major airports and expressways are owned and operated by quasigovernmental port authorities and transit authorities that are unaccountable to citizens and voters. The three major airports in the New York City area—JFK, LaGuardia, and Newark Liberty International—are governed by the Port Authority of New York & New Jersey. As an example of the extension of privatization and the replacement of traditional government services, the Port Authority decided to turn over operation of one of the principal terminals at JFK not to a consortium of private companies, but to a company owned by the Dutch government. The Port Authority of New York & New Jersey also has jurisdiction and control over the bridges, tunnels, and seaports in the area.

In fact, 80 percent of U.S. port terminals, most under the control of local port authorities as opposed to local governments, are leased and operated by foreign companies. More than six hundred publicly owned drinking water systems and plants and waste facilities, serving more than fourteen million people across the country, are operated by a French-owned company. Increasingly public services are being privatized or outsourced, and the accountability of duly elected government for delivering those services is rapidly diminishing.

It is a government's job, responsibility, and duty to protect its citizens and keep them safe, and educate its children. It is also charged with maintaining the national infrastructure, including the roads, ports, public buildings, airports, schools, public libraries, and a host of systems, services, and organizations that taxpayers rely on every day. That's what we have a government for.

One of the most respected local and state elected officials in New York's history, and a Democratic luminary, Mario Cuomo, was a supporter of the privatization and outsourcing of government services. In 1985, while serving as governor, Cuomo told the *New York Times*, "It is not government's obligation to provide services, but to see that they're provided." Few elected officials are as artful as the former governor in the English language, and I respect him—greatly. But on the question of the government's obligation, I have to differ. While I believe he was being pragmatic, given the economic and political climate at the time he made that statement, in the years since we have seen pragmatism replaced by a sense of expediency, the profit motive, and a waning of both governmental competence and confidence in government.

There is some irony in that fact that an independent populist like me would argue with one of the country's great liberals on the issue of public good, but I strongly believe that the people deserve democracy, transparency, effectiveness, and reliability of government at all levels. The blurring of public and private services and the roles of public and private institutions and organizations diminishes the people's influence over and their power to hold accountable their elected governments. I find the matter of public officials and public servants turning to the private sector to be as confounding as if public agencies and government departments were to suddenly raise their revenues and increase their profits.

Should our port authorities, with unelected officials and unaccountable employees, be superior to officials of local and state governments who must first represent the interests of their constituencies? Should there really be more private security contractors in Iraq than there are American Marines? Is the Defense Department's move to replace soldiers, Marines, and sailors as guards at military bases an effort to save the taxpayer money or a reflection of the fact that our troops are strained to the breaking point in long-running combat, and every service member is needed to fight the wars in Iraq and Afghanistan? Perhaps the American people should consider calling for corporate bids to contract out the jobs of cabinet secretaries directly to private corporations. Perhaps Humana or Aetna should be contracted to staff and run the Department of Health and Human Services. Perhaps Boeing or Lockheed Martin should run our Defense Department, or the Commerce Department can be taken over by contracting with, say, General Electric or Microsoft. I could even imagine the AFL-CIO, in a historic governmental-nonprofit partnership, winning a contract to run the Department of Labor.

The point is, there is a proper and profound role for government in our free society and it is to serve and to protect our people, and to be committed to the common good and the national interest above all else.

While I'm sure big business and even big labor would eagerly accept my outlandish—and, I assure you, facetious—suggestions for what would be the ultimate in contracting out, I believe the American people are being almost as poorly served by the current level of privatization, outsourcing, and absorption of traditional government services by nonprofits, NGOs, and faith-based organizations. What has become our shadow government is encroaching on a system of government that has served this nation so well for two hundred years.

Public-private partnerships and privatization projects are not a new phenomenon. The first efforts at significant privatization of public services occurred in the early 1970s, notably with New York City's decision to put its trash collection up for bid. The transfer of what had been a municipal service to private firms was undertaken by the city's government to halt runaway costs, to restore fiscal prudence, and to cut the city's budget deficit. Cities around the country soon followed suit, but it remains an open question whether competent government management of garbage collection services would have been any less cost-effective.

At the beginning of his administration in 1981 President Ronald Reagan fired every air traffic controller in the nation because they went on strike. What many Americans don't recall is that the Democrat-controlled Congress, which for the most part had opposed Reagan's decision, sided with him on concerns about the right of private contractors working for the military to go on strike. That led Congress in 1982 to stop the Department of Defense from outsourcing DOD jobs and services to private industry and contractors. According to the GAO:

> Since late 1982, Congress has, for the most part, prohibited DOD from contracting for security guards at U.S. domestic installations. According to the legislative history, the prohibition was originally enacted because of concerns about the uncertain quality and reliability of private security guard services, base commanders' potential lack of control over contractor personnel, and the right of contractor personnel to strike.

More than twenty years later our troops were deployed to Iraq in 2003, and fewer soldiers were available for on-site security of American installations. Our representatives decided it was now appropriate to turn to the private sector for military security—despite the fact that any military should by any logic be given the necessary resources to protect and secure itself. In 2003 the Bob Stump National Defense Authorization Act gave the DOD permission to go out and hire contractors. The DOD did so with a gusto it was unable to muster when it was providing equipment for its soldiers. By the end of 2005 the Army had contractors running security at fifty-seven installations, the Air Force had contractors at eighteen installations, and the Navy had contractors at five bases.

The Government Accountability Office immediately found significant, and not unexpected, failings in the military privatization process. These addressed not only the fallacies of "cheaper and more efficient," but also the explicit dangers inherent in outsourcing government functions. The actual wording of the GAO report is astounding:

- The Army's three-phased approach for acquiring contract security guards has relied heavily on sole-source contracts, despite the Army's recognition early on that it was paying considerably more for its sole-source contracts than for those awarded competitively. The Army has devoted twice as many contract dollars—nearly $495 million—to its sole-source contracts as to its competed contracts and has placed contract security guards at 46 out of 57 installations through sole-sourcing. . . . Prior to contract award, the Defense Contract Management Agency assessed these firms' capabilities at the request of the contracting officer and rated one as "high risk" for performance because it was a manufacturing firm with no experience providing security guard services.

- The Army's procedure for screening prospective contract guards is inadequate and puts the Army at risk of having ineligible guards protecting installation gates. The Army found that, at two separate installations, a total of 89 guards were put to work even though they had records relating to criminal offenses, including cases that involved assault and other felonies.

- The Army has given its contractors the responsibility to conduct most of the training of contract guards, and the Army cannot say with certainty whether training is actually taking place and whether it is being conducted according to approved criteria. GAO found that there is no requirement for the Army to certify that a contract guard has completed required training and that Army performance monitors do not conduct oversight of training as a matter of course.

- There is a general lack of government oversight of the guards' training, as well as poor record keeping on the part of the contractors and inconsistent training techniques. We found at 4 installations that government monitoring of the training is not consistently done, if at all. We also found missing or incomplete training documents at each of the 11 installations we visited. At three installations, guards were certified by the contractor before their training had been completed, and one guard was certified before he had completed weapons-qualification training. In early 2005, it was determined that contractor personnel had falsified training records at one installation, and the government paid over $7,000 to the contractor to repeat weapons-qualification training for the guards.

Those statements specifically highlight the major problems that the government faces in relying on the private sector. Outsourcing and contracting to private firms in defense of the nation should give pause to all citizens and to our leaders.

In Iraq it has been estimated that for every two of our troops the United States hires one private contractor to carry out military duties. Their responsibilities range from providing security at reconstruction sites, to serving as supply-line personnel, to participating in combat operations and support. They provide security to foreign dignitaries and the media, and also managed the Abu Ghraib prison; some were involved in the prison's scandal. The estimated number involved in direct military operations alone reaches almost 50,000. In the past these private contactors would have been referred to as mercenaries.

The best known of the private security companies is Blackwater, a defense contractor founded by former Navy SEALS. At the outset of the war, Blackwater was given a $21 million contract to guard the head of the Coalition Provisional Authority, Paul Bremer. According to Blackwater president Gary Jackson, "Nobody had really figured out exactly how they were going to get him from D.C. and stand him up in Iraq. The Secret Service went over and did an assessment and said, 'You know what? It's much, much more dangerous than any of us believed.' So they came back to us. When there is a crisis they have a tendency to call us first."

Most of us can understand that protecting the head of the CPA in Baghdad would not be a job for the Secret Service, but why would high government officials not be protected by U.S. troops? The administration has answered this question to at least their satisfaction, although not to the public's, and they've been very good to Blackwater. Blackwater reportedly pays some of its private security employees in Iraq ten times what any of our troops earn. These private security contractors in Iraq are, of course, paid by private companies, which charge the United States a significant premium for providing private soldiers on demand. According to the latest reports, as of 2006 Blackwater has been awarded more than a half billion dollars in contracts from the U.S. government since 2000—and those were primarily no-bid contracts.

You may be surprised to learn that many of these contracts didn't originate with the Department of Defense, but rather from the State Department and intelligence agencies, including the CIA. The principal benefit of that arrangement? Blackwater employees operating in Iraq are in no way obligated to adhere to the code of military conduct, which would be the case had the DOD originated the contracts. And because Blackwater is a private firm, documents relating to its operations and conduct are not covered by the Freedom of Information Act. The result is that the company can do almost anything it pleases with the taxpayer money that it is awarded, and no one—presumably not even our lawmakers—has the ability to track its business or its behavior.

Contractors operating under their own auspices have created conflicts with U.S. military officials, encountered friendly fire, been responsible for detainee torture and abuse, and killed Iraqi civilians. The secretive nature of much contract work, and the lack of oversight and confusion over legal authority, has finally led some in Congress to ask questions. In January 2007 Congressman David Price (D-North Carolina) introduced legislation that would require oversight and accountability of security contractors. According to Price, "The lack of a legal framework for battlefield contracting has allowed certain rogue contractor employees to perpetrate heinous criminal acts without the threat of prosecution, and has left thousands of contractors working legitimately in support of U.S. missions exposed and at risk." I have to give Price credit for this legislation: His home state, North Carolina, is where Blackwater is headquartered.

Price is not just tilting at windmills. We need look no further than yet another report from the Government Accountability Office about the relationship between subcontractors and the U.S. military:

- Coordination between the U.S. military and private security providers still needs improvement. First, private security providers continue to enter the battle space without coordinating with the U.S. military, putting both the military and security providers at a greater risk for injury. Second, U.S. military units are not trained, prior to deployment, on the operating procedures of private security providers in Iraq and the role of the Reconstruction Operations Center, which is to coordinate military-provider interactions. While DOD agreed with our prior recommendation to establish a predeployment training program to help address the coordination issue, no action has been taken.

- Many private security providers and DOD have difficulty completing comprehensive criminal background screenings for U.S. and foreign nationals when data are missing or inaccessible. . . . Based on its work to date, GAO believes that incomplete criminal background screening may contribute to an increased risk to military forces and civilians in Iraq, and the military would benefit by reviewing the base security measures to ensure that the risk private security contractors may pose has been minimized.

- No U.S. or international standards exist for establishing private security provider and employee qualifications.

- Despite the significant role played by private security providers in enabling reconstruction efforts to proceed, neither the Department of State, nor DOD, nor the USAID—the principal agencies responsible for Iraq reconstruction efforts—had complete data on the costs associated with using private security providers.

From where I sit, the GAO report hardly instills a great deal of confidence in the appropriateness, let alone the effectiveness, of privatization, especially when the American people have no idea of the extent of our government's outsourcing of the war in Iraq.

But most Americans are hardly aware of the extent of privatization in government in general, and the degree to which corporations, think tanks, and lobbying organizations have contracted to perform government functions and tasks.

That changed in early 2006, when *Lou Dobbs Tonight* was the first to report on the Dubai Ports World deal. We revealed that the administration's plan would have allowed seaports in New York, New Jersey, Philadelphia, Baltimore, Miami, and New Orleans to be operated by DP World, a company owned by the government of Dubai. Dubai, one of the United Arab Emirates states, has been used as a base of terrorist operations and financing, and was one of only three countries in the world to recognize the Afghanistan government set up by the Taliban. That our nation was going to enter into a public-private partnership with a country that once supported the radical fundamentalists of the Taliban—at a time when we should have been increasing security at every point of entry into this country—is mind-boggling.

All this occurred just one month after President Bush stated, "Our nation needs orderly and secure borders." Yet he defended the plan by insisting that Dubai was a good friend and ally of the United States. He treated it, as do most fans of privatization at any cost, as a business deal and nothing more. In fact, the president declared that DP World would have nothing to do with security at any of our ports. He was wrong, and we demonstrated that fact on the air. This was clearly a national security issue, but the administration chose to put commerce before safety. Ultimately Congress stopped the DP World deal. But it's an example of both incompetent government and the encroachment of the privatization of functions that are properly the domain of government.

In Indianapolis a wholly owned subsidiary of BAA (which used to stand for the British Airport Authority) operates the city's international airport; the company also runs London's Heathrow. BAA started off its American operations small, running concessions at airports like Newark, Harrisburg, and Pittsburgh, and now has long-term management contracts to operate both the Indianapolis and Harrisburg airports.

British company TBI plc's overseas operations include much of Atlanta's Hartsfield-Jackson International Airport, as well as Burbank's Bob Hope Airport. The company also handles ground and cargo services for Orlando Sanford International Airport. Another British company, National Express Group, has a ninety-nine-year lease on Stewart International Airport just north of New York City. The Port of Authority of New York & New Jersey have stated that plans to relieve New York City airport congestion would involve expanding Stewart and its operations.

The other airports surrounding New York, including Albany International Airport, Tweed New Haven Regional Airport, Westchester County Airport, and Atlantic City International Airport, are managed and operated by AvPORTS, a subsidiary of Australia's Macquarie Infrastructure Company. And Terminal 4 at John F. Kennedy airport in New York, one of the country's busiest and a key international entry point, is operated by a group led by Amsterdam's Schiphol Airport, an organization owned by the Dutch government.

Given the concerns that many Americans have about flying and airports, from increased anxiety over delays and security procedures to the plots against airports like JFK, I think our government should be looking to bolster U.S. control over management and operations, not farming it out to companies whose owners and executives reside in other countries.

The situation at our ports and shipping terminals is even more unsettling. It has been estimated that 80 percent of our port terminals are leased and operated by foreign companies. Among these (some of which are owned by their respective governments) are China's COSCO Container Lines, Singapore's Neptune Orient Lines, Denmark's A.P. Moller-Maersk Group, Japan's NYK Line, The Netherlands's C. Steinweg Handelsveem B.V., Taiwan's Yang Ming Marine Transport Corp., and the United Arab Emirates's Inchcape Shipping Services. According to those proprivatization analysts at the Reason Foundation, this is "largely because federal law requires U.S.-based shipping companies to use American crews, making these firms less competitive." This implies that port management has been reduced to simple economics and the profit motive, and ignores the fact that ports are the primary entry points for products coming into this country every single day. In the process, it also sidesteps concerns over inspection, safety, security, and responsibility to the people of the United States.

One can see (but not justify) how operational control of airports and terminals has fallen into the hands of foreign governments or their holdings, given that foreign businesses from airlines to shipping companies do business with airports and terminals everyday. However, just because these facilities engage in international commerce doesn't mean they themselves should be bought and sold on the international market.

It's more difficult to understand the rationale for putting infrastructure that is purely domestic up for sale to the highest international bidder. But in the search to cut ever more costs and shirk more duties, that's been happening more often than you might imagine—or might like. The latest big play for international companies looking to get a piece of American infrastructure concerns our highway system. All across the country, the government is selling off roads to the highest bidder and claiming to make their states more efficient.

Of course, like many things our representatives say, that claim doesn't always hold water. Take the 91 Express Lanes in California, which opened in 1995 and were built inside the median of an existing freeway (State Route 91) between Orange County and Riverside County. The toll road was constructed at a cost of $130 million by the California Private Transportation Company (CPTC), a consortium led by Compagnie Financière et Industrielle des Autoroutes of France. When the project was completed, CPTC gave the lanes to California, and then leased them back for thirty-five years. Within five years, however, Orange County traffic was in virtual gridlock and the government needed once again to expand the roads. But due to the structure of the lease with CPTC, it was prevented from doing so: In order to build out the roadways, it had to buy out the lease. In 2002 California paid more than $207 million to recover the lanes from the French consortium—almost double what it had originally paid to build the roads just seven years earlier. The Reason Foundation cites Route 91 as one of its success stories.

In 2006 Transurban Group, an Australian business, purchased a ninety-nine-year lease for the Pocahontas Parkway outside Richmond, Virginia. The company acquired the road—which provides access to the Richmond International Airport—for $611 million, and is now in charge of setting and collecting tolls and maintenance and repair. Thus, the state of Virginia is not ultimately responsible for keeping the road in working order; an Australian concern headquartered there is. In an interesting twist Transurban pays the Virginia Department of Transportation to service the roads, a job that VDOT should be doing itself.

In 2005 the Chicago Skyway, which connects the Dan Ryan Expressway to the Indiana Toll Road, was leased to an international partnership for $1.83 billion. The partnership is comprised of Australia's Macquarie Infrastructure Group and Spain's Cintra Concesiones de Infraestructuras de Transporte. These two companies will manage all aspects of the tollway for ninety-nine years. The Cintra/Macquarie partnership sets and collects tolls, is responsible for maintenance and repair, and is allowed to control the allocation of concessions. The city of Chicago got nearly $2 billion in the deal, but it no longer controls a major thoroughfare that carries more than fifty thousand vehicles per day.

A year after securing the Chicago Skyway deal, Cintra/Macquarie was awarded a seventy-five-year lease on the Indiana Toll Road. For $3.85 billion the Spanish-Australian group got complete control of a 157-mile stretch of highway that cuts across the top of Indiana, from Illinois to Ohio. It's worth noting that the toll road is one of the most important transportation links between the Great Lakes and the East Coast. A little bit of trivia that seems relevant here is that of the five final bidders considered for the deal, only one was an entirely U.S.-based organization.

Indiana governor Mitchell Daniels, a former Eli Lilly senior executive and huge advocate of privatization, wrote this about his road: "[A] 40-year-old Indiana Toll Road across the northern part of our state continued losing money and deferring maintenance and expansion, while charging the lowest tolls of any comparable highway. Tolls had not been raised in twenty years; at some booths the charge was 15 cents. As the new governor, I innocently inquired what it cost us to collect each toll. This being government, no one knew, but after a few days of study the answer came back: '34 cents. We think.'" Daniels's solution to these low toll fares? Rather than raise the toll, he sold the road.

Cintra is certainly a very determined company. It recently teamed up with San Antonio–based Zachry Construction to build part of the proposed Trans-Texas Corridor, a gigantic stretch of road running from Oklahoma all the way down to the Mexican border, bisecting Texas along the way. The state of Texas has already hired Cintra-Zachry to develop the plans for the road, and if all goes according to plan, then the Spanish-Texan partnership would also manage it. Cintra-Zachry is supposed to pay for its construction, and then would keep all toll revenue for fifty years. The estimated cost of the Dallas to San Antonio leg alone is $7.2 billion.

However, the deal has hit a number of roadblocks. Terms of the deal have been kept from the public by Cintra-Zachry and its allies over at the Texas Department of Transportation, which sued to keep documents relating to the deal secret. Cintra-Zachry claims that releasing them would give its competitors an unfair advantage in future bids. Nonetheless, the Texas legislature passed a bill to postpone public-private contracts for the corridor for two years, a measure that was promptly vetoed by Governor Rick Perry. Representatives have vowed to find a way to halt the contracts.

The Trans-Texas Corridor may be the most controversial of all the foreign-owned and operated roadways in the United States. Some are calling it the NAFTA Superhighway, and it will be the first leg of a planned ten-lane highway that will cut across the United States and link Mexico to Canada. This would lay the foundation for the Security and Prosperity Partnership of North America, which is the White House's plan to join all of North America into a single union—whether any of us want it or not.

John in West Virginia: "Lou, when the North American Union among Canada, the United States, and Mexico goes into effect, will our flag be red, white, blue and green with a maple leaf in the center? No stars would be needed since the Bush administration will have sold or given all the states to private companies to manage for profit by that time." (March 5, 2007)

Marie in Indiana: "You are the only reporter I've heard mention the North American Union and the NAFTA Highway. Why are the other reporters not talking about it?" (June 22, 2007)

The effort is supported by North America's SuperCorridor Coalition (NASCO), "a non-profit organization dedicated to developing the world's first international, integrated and secure, multi-modal transportation system along the International Mid-Continent Trade Corridor to improve both the trade competitiveness and quality of life in North America." Or so it claims. Founded in 1994 as the I-35 Corridor Coalition, the group incorporated into a nonprofit NGO in 1996 and became NASCO—yet another business-backed group just trying to help out the people of America.

It's particularly ironic that we should be selling off our highways. When Dwight Eisenhower outlined the plan for a national highway system, he said he had been inspired by his years in Europe during World War II. He had seen how munitions and supplies were moved great distances between towns and countries, and how the roads helped in evacuating civilians. He felt a U.S. national highway system would be just as important in helping protect our citizens and keeping them out of harm's way in case of attack by a foreign nation. Now, of course, we're selling the highways off to foreign companies.

The Reason Foundation argues that there is nothing to lose with this plan: "We drive foreign cars filled with imported gasoline. We wear foreign-made clothes. And we use foreign computers and televisions. These toll road companies are building and operating immovable infrastructure in Texas. They can't take the roads back to Spain or Australia. They are spending money in Texas and creating jobs in Texas."

Toll road companies are all these things, certainly. But they are also charged by their investors and shareholders with making a profit from their roads. They are not beholden to the public interest of Americans. Let me ask this: If push came to shove, and these foreign companies had to choose between the interests of their investors and the interests of their client, the American people, who do you think would win out? If you picked "the client's needs" over "the investors' demands," then you haven't been paying attention to the way corporations work in the twenty-first century.

Reason's reasoning here—if I may use that phrase—is laughable. Buying clothes from one company has absolutely no relevance to selling a public road to another company, no matter where they are located. And while the observation that foreign managers can't take the roads out of the country is correct, those managers can block them, barricade them, allow them to fall into disrepair, disrupt traffic flow, allow toll collectors or maintenance personnel to strike, and engage in numerous scenarios that no one wants to think about.

Not that an ethical business would let any of this happen, but it should come as no surprise that even American companies have been known to resort to nastiness to get what they wanted in the recent past. In order to squeeze higher energy prices out of the state of California a few years back, Enron created artificial power outages that resulted in rolling blackouts throughout 2001. "Well, that was Enron," the opposing argument might go. "They were the bad guys." Except that in 2001 Enron wasn't a bad guy; it was one of the largest companies in America, and Wall Street viewed it and its executives as innovative and visionary.

A scenario that highlights the possible ways in which we could lose control of our own infrastructure and not anticipate its long-term effects can be found in the management of our water. Beginning in the 1950s a U.S. company eventually named U.S. Filter Operating Services began managing various water systems across the country, from Pennsylvania to California, handling drinking water and wastewater for a number of municipalities. However, the company was bought in 1999 by French water giant Vivendi, and is now called Veolia Environmental Services. Today Veolia handles the water systems in more than 600 U.S. communities and 115 U.S. industrial facilities. In all, it is responsible for the water needs of 14 million Americans.

When confronted by the concern that water is a public trust, Veolia steps in line with Mario Cuomo and states, "It is the role of government to ensure the quality and economic provision of water, not necessarily to implement that provision."

American Water, which serves some 17 million people in 29 states, was for more than a century a U.S.-based provider of water systems. In 2003, it was bought by Germany's RWE Group. As of 2007 RWE is getting out of the water business and is looking for a buyer for American Water. There is no indication yet of who that might be, but I certainly hope it's a company, or a country, that is friendly to the United States.

United Water, another longtime U.S. water company, was purchased in 2000 by Suez Lyonnaise des Eaux, a French multinational. United Water operates in 20 states and serves more than 7 million people.

Depending on your interest in America's maintaining control of its infrastructure, you may or may not be pleased to learn that these foreign-owned companies constitute three of the four largest private-water management companies in the United States.

Water has recently become a popular investment and operational strategy for overseas companies, and there is no indication that the government has any qualms about establishing these relationships. But customers aren't always so sure. American Water's management of the Felton, California, water system has been under attack for years. It receives more complaints in California than any other water concern, and it charges a premium of 36 percent above what residents pay in surrounding counties. Fed up, the residents of that town approved an $11 million bond in 2005 to buy back their water, but American Water has stated that the system is not for sale. Now residents are pursuing the right of eminent domain to get control over their own water. American Water has run into similar efforts by citizens to return water to public hands in Buffalo, New York; Lexington, Kentucky; and several other California towns—all of which have charged that they are being poorly served by a private entity.

One of those towns, Montara, California, did succeed in buying back its water system from American Water in 2003. However, a follow-up survey presented results alleging that citizens had been happier when American Water ran the system, a finding that ran counter to what many residents and local officials believed. A little bit of digging revealed that the creator of the survey was the Reason Foundation. Guess which water company is a major supporter of Reason and its privatization programs? American Water. It's incredible that these companies not only have the same agenda, but find so many ways to work hand in hand with one another.

The move toward privatization of public works has reached its apex in the Georgia city of Sandy Springs. When the city was incorporated at the end of 2005—it had long been a rural suburb of Atlanta—it voted to outsource public services to get the administration and infrastructure up and running quickly. It also did not want to rely on the same county services it had used before incorporation. According to the city's Web site, the plan was to find a company that could handle "duties such as customer service, human resources, accounting and information technology . . . and provide public services such as public works, transportation, Recreation & Parks, and planning and zoning." A Colorado engineering and operations firm, CH2M HILL OMI, was awarded the contract to manage nearly every public service available in Sandy Springs. The city is just a little over a year into its new life as a hybrid corporate/public entity, so the results aren't in yet. But you can be assured that this project will be worth watching in the coming years.

It is worth watching because our government's success with contractors clearly has not always met with stellar results, as the GAO has pointed out. Part of this is a function of human nature: People are always going to find ways to defraud the government. Part of it is the Pontius Pilate way in which the government washes its hands of involvement in those matters it has assigned to contractors. And part of it is simply that there are some functions the government should handle—or, at the very least, manage—because of the scope and scale of the responsibility.

We have only to look as far as the Federal Emergency Management Agency to see some relevant ramifications. Within twelve months of FEMA's reprehensible response to the Hurricanes Katrina and Rita disasters, estimates of fraud and waste involving the agency and its contractors, along with unscrupulous citizens, was estimated to have been nearly $2 billion, or 11 percent of what the agency had spent up to that time. FEMA not only didn't handle the actual disaster well, it couldn't even handle the aftermath with any sense of organization and order.

It appears that no level of government responsibility is too big or too small to outsource. As we reported on the show in June 2007, the State Department failed to clear a massive and growing backlog of passport applications. Despite having two years to get organized so that travelers could adhere to new federal regulations, the State

Department was unable to process the passports of more than two million Americans in time for the summer vacation season. This bungling cost many individuals their vacations: no passport, no traveling outside the United States. When Maura Harty, assistant secretary for consular affairs, appeared before the Senate to explain the situation, Senator Bill Nelson (D-Florida) told her, "We want to know who's accountable and why this mess has happened as it is. . . . And don't give me this nonsense that the State Department is saying that it's the contractor's fault, and the contractor's saying it's the State Department's fault. You know, when somebody points a finger, there's three other fingers that are pointing back at the individual."

As we reported on the show, that's exactly what Harty did. She claimed that the backlog was due in part to delays at Citibank, which was hired as a private contractor to process the passports. Despite thousands of people paying a sixty-dollar expediting fee on top of the standard ninety-seven-dollar passport fee, the time it takes to get a new passport is now running as long as four months.

Our government has gone so far as to encourage organizations that have no business being remotely associated with politics to participate in it. These groups serve a dual purpose: They lobby and propose legislation on behalf of their business clients and members and they are also available to assist our elected officials in researching, analyzing, and even writing that legislation. Many of these organizations have the power and influence to create the laws that Americans have to live by.

One of them, which we have already seen is a leading supporter and promoter of so-called public-private partnerships, is the Reason Foundation, a nongovernmental organization politely referred to as a policy institute or a think tank. Founded by Robert Poole in 1978, Reason is a nonprofit agency that conducts research and issues policy papers touting the benefits of privatization. According to its Web site, "Poole's 1988 policy paper proposing privately financed toll lanes to relieve congestion directly inspired California's landmark private tollway law . . . which authorized four pilot toll projects including the successful 91 Express Lanes in Orange County." As we have discussed, the 91 Express Lanes in Orange County wasn't successful for very long.

The Web site also states that "Poole's studies also launched a national debate on airport privatization in the United States. He advised both the FAA and local officials during the 1989–90 controversy over the proposed privatization of Albany (NY) Airport. His policy research on this issue helped inspire Congress's 1996 enactment of the Airport Privatization Pilot Program and the privatization of Indianapolis's airport management." Poole has either advised or been a member of the American Legislative Exchange Council's Trade & Transportation Task Force; the Public-Private Ventures division of American Road & Transportation Builders Association; the Federal Aviation Administration; the Office of the Secretary of Transportation; the White House Office of Policy Development; the National Performance Review; the National Economic Council; and the National Civil Aviation Review Commission.

In addition to these impressive credentials, Poole also gave up running his company in 2000 when he was invited to be a member of the Bush-Cheney White House transition team. But Reason claims not to be affiliated with any political party, even though the woman who succeeded Poole in running Reason is Lynn Scarlett. Ms. Scarlett eventually left Reason and is currently President Bush's deputy secretary of the Department of the Interior. But again, Reason is not affiliated with any political party.

The point here is that this nonprofit organization develops positions in favor of privatization that are being accepted and implemented by the government. It bills itself as an organization that

advances a free society by developing, applying, and promoting libertarian principles, including individual liberty, free markets, and the rule of law. . . . Reason Foundation's nonpartisan public policy research promotes choice, competition, and a dynamic market economy as the foundation for human dignity and progress. Reason produces rigorous, peer reviewed research and directly engages the policy process, seeking strategies that emphasize cooperation, flexibility, local knowledge, and results. Through practical and innovative approaches to complex problems, Reason seeks to change the way people think about issues, and promote policies that allow and encourage *individuals* and voluntary institutions to flourish.

The italic on the word "individuals" is mine.

Where does Reason's funding come from? According to the Web site, "Reason is a 501(c)(3) nonprofit organization completely supported by voluntary contributions from individuals, foundations, corporations, and the sale of our publications." According to past filings, some of those voluntary contributions came from: the American Petroleum Institute, American Airlines, American Water, American Plastics Council, Anheuser-Busch, Bechtel, CH2M HILL OMI, Chevron Corporation, Coca-Cola, DaimlerChrysler, Dow Chemical, Enron, ExxonMobil, Ford Motor Company, General Motors, Eli Lilly, Macquarie, Microsoft, the National Air Transportation Association, the National Beer Wholesalers Association, the National Soft Drink Association, Pfizer, Philip Morris, Procter and Gamble, Shell Oil, and Veolia Water, among others.

There is one more aspect to Reason's reach that is worth mentioning. The *Washington Post* ran a piece on January 28, 2007, entitled "5 Myths About Suburbia and Our Car-Happy Culture." The article argues that driving is a function of national wealth, that our air is cleaner thanks to better regulation, and that public transit really isn't that great of an idea. The authors of the piece were Ted Balaker and Sam Staley, who were described in the *Post* article as coauthors of the book *The Road More Traveled: Why the Congestion Crisis Matters More Than You Think, and What We Can Do About It.* I think it would have been helpful if that biographical statement had included the fact that Balaker is a policy analyst at Reason and that Staley is a Reason Foundation director.

This is a most enviable position. Reason takes money from corporations, convinces politicians to privatize government functions, and then gets the media to print its corporate-funded ideas as if they were independent and unbiased. It's a special interest group with big business, big government, and the media all on its side. The world, or at least America, is your oyster if you're a well-connected NGO.

Privatization is driven by two factors: government's desire to free itself of certain duties or obligations and the desire of business to make more money. Toll-road companies aren't waiting around in hopes that some government agency will come knocking on their door with an idea: They are actively promoting their cause. In this they are helped by those nongovernmental entities known as NGOs.

NGOs are noncommercial entities that exist to advocate for specific causes or provide developmental or charitable assistance to groups in need. They cover the spectrum from the Red Cross to the National Audubon Society to Oxfam to the AARP. They also include groups like the Reason Foundation, NASCO, policy-making think tanks, and thousands of other organizations. This latter class of special interest group is the open yet barely talked about secret in American politics. It advocates for its own interests, lobbies on behalf of industry, and often works much too closely with our legislators.

Quite a few NGOs register as 501(c)(3)s, a categorization usually reserved for tax-exempt charities. Many of these 501(c)(3)s are small organizations and actual charities, involved in everything from Little League to soup kitchens. Others are huge charities like the Bill and Melinda Gates Foundation and the Ford Foundation. It's hard to think of a liberal or conservative think tank as a public charity, but those organizations technically manage to qualify as 501(c)(3)s under existing law. And it offers an attractive exemption: In 1992, there were 516,554 organizations registered as 501(c)(3)s. By 2003, that number had increased to 837,027.

According to the IRS, however, 501(c)(3)s have to meet the following criteria:

> To be tax-exempt under section 501(c)(3) of the Internal Revenue Code, an organization must be organized and operated exclusively for purposes set forth in section 501(c)(3), and none of its earnings may inure to any private shareholder or individual. In addition, it may not attempt to influence legislation as a substantial part of its activities and it may not participate in any campaign activity for or against political candidates.

Organizations described in section 501(c)(3) are commonly referred to as *charitable organizations*. . . . The exempt purposes set forth in section 501(c)(3) are charitable, religious, educational, scientific, literary, testing for public safety, fostering national or international amateur sports competition, and the preventing of cruelty to children or animals. The term *charitable* is used in its generally accepted legal sense and includes relief of the poor, the distressed, or the underprivileged; advancement of religion; advancement of education or science; erecting or maintaining public buildings, monuments, or works; lessening the burdens of government; lessening neighborhood tensions; eliminating prejudice and discrimination; defending human and civil rights secured by law; and combating community deterioration and juvenile delinquency.

Where exactly does the Reason Foundation, as a 501(c)(3) entity, fit into this charitable framework? And what about that section where influencing legislation is strictly prohibited?

The same can be asked of the Cato Institute, the Heritage Foundation, the Brookings Institution, the Center for American Progress, the American Enterprise Institute, and dozens of other influential think tanks. While they all work diligently on public policy matters and seek to influence legislators, they retain their tax-exempt status by operating under the "educational" heading for 501(c)(3)s.

A few 501(c)(3)s are actually brazen about their attempts to influence legislation. Foremost among these is the American Legislative Exchange Council (ALEC). According to its Web site, "The mission of the American Legislative Exchange Council (ALEC) is to advance the Jeffersonian principles of free markets, limited government, federalism, and individual liberty among America's state legislators." It sounds noble, as do most of the mission statements from those attempting to make sure that legislation serves their needs and those of their supporters. They really do have their mission statements and their promotion down to a science.

ALEC is a think tank whose core members include more than twenty-four hundred state legislators, which amounts to about a third of all of our state reps. Ostensibly, these legislators get together and chat about how to make America a better place for their constituents. The group's operational strategy is "[t]o promote the principles of federalism by developing and promoting policies that reflect the Jeffersonian principles that the powers of government are derived from, and assigned to, first the People, then the States, and finally the National Government."

However neither ALEC's backers nor its members are "the People." In fact, it has more than three hundred corporate and private foundation members, a list that is truly breathtaking in its scope. Most of corporate America's multinationals and trade associations are involved, including ExxonMobil, Coors Brewing Company, American Express, Allstate, Pfizer, Ford Motor Company, General Motors, Philip Morris, the American Nuclear Energy Council, the American Petroleum Institute, Amoco, Chevron Corporation, Shell Oil, McDonald's, the Chlorine Chemistry Council, Union Pacific, the Pharmaceutical Research and Manufacturers of America, and Waste Management, to name but a few. These companies and lobbying groups provide close to 95 percent of ALEC's financing; the membership dues of the twenty-four hundred state legislators combined add up to barely 5 percent.

What do the corporate members get in return for their support? Quoting again here: "ALEC provides its public- and private-sector members with a unique opportunity to work together to develop policies and programs that effectively promote the organization's mission."

That mission is to get laws passed that are beneficial to its members, be they legislators or corporate America. Make no mistake, ALEC is very good at accomplishing this. It does so by drafting model legislation in its internal task forces at the behest of its public- and private-sector members. Let me quote ALEC again: "Unique to ALEC Task Forces is their public-private partnerships, a synergistic alliance that identifies issues and then responds with common sense, results-oriented policies. Legislators welcome their private sector counterparts to the table as equals, working in unison to solve the challenges facing the nation. The results are the policies that will define the American political landscape well into the 21st century."

This model legislation is then molded, deliberated, and worked over to the point that it's ready to present on Capitol Hill or at state legislative sessions. According to ALEC, "These bills provide a valuable framework for developing effective policy ideas aimed at protecting and expanding our free society. While ALEC provides the resources, our members, long known for their legislative activism, introduced hundreds of bills based on ALEC model legislation."

This group is actually creating legislation on behalf of more than 300 corporations and trade associations, giving that legislation a dry run, and then actively working to guarantee that it becomes law. "In 2004 alone 1,108 ALEC model bills were introduced and 178 were enacted into law." And the group proudly notes this: "During the latest legislative cycle, dozens of ALEC model bills were enacted into law."

The relationship between members has been referred to by critics as "pay to play," indicating that corporate America ponies up the dollars in order to work, and play, with our elected officials in a convenient and mutually beneficial environment. For years the tobacco industry has been a significant benefactor to ALEC's mission, contributing more than two hundred thousand dollars annually and paying for the organization's legal bills. It, like other members, sponsors parties, retreats, and other junkets for state legislators who are key to getting legislation passed.

This is all a very efficient and promising method to get issues in front of the appropriate politicians. However, the process is not open to the working men and women of this country. All the memberships are offered either to legislators or to private-sector organizations. If you represent a company willing to pay at least five thousand dollars, you can join right online.

Not only do organizations like Reason and ALEC work specifically for the benefit of corporate America and special interests, they're taking money out of your pocket. Donors to these organizations get a write-off; they don't have to pay taxes on their donations. But the 501(c)(3)s themselves don't have to pay taxes either, putting them in a category with churches. Since any think tank worth its salt brings in millions of dollars a year, that's a lot of money that's not getting taxed. It's a double shot to the American people: The money is effectively used against us, and its tax-free status means that the shortfall is probably going to have to come out of our pockets at tax time.

It's bad enough that our government is actively trying to privatize its duties in areas related to commerce. That's shirking one very important duty. However, the fact that our federal government is increasingly relying on NGOs, not-for-profits, and foundations to provide it with policy research and the drafting of legislation means that it is not generating the knowledge base and the empirical foundation for the laws that it is enacting, and that its proper functions and tasks have been encroached upon by the shadow government.

8

God and Politics

I have no doubt that every new example will succeed, as every past one has done, in shewing that religion and Government will both exist in greater purity the less they are mixed together.

—James Madison

There is no issue over which I've struggled more, emotionally and intellectually, than the role of religion in our society, whether it involves questions of the separation of church and state, or, depending on one's point of view, the engagement or intrusion of churches and religious organizations in partisan politics. I've debated these topics on the air; argued with preachers, priests, and rabbis; and found myself in opposition to the political positions usually taken by religious organizations on such issues as gay rights, illegal immigration, and the war in Iraq.

At the same time, I'm a devout believer in the importance of religion in our society and culture. Religion is the most critical compass of the moral and ethical questions that bedevil us in these complex and conflicted times. I likewise fully recognize its profound historical role and influence in the founding of our nation and our government. I strongly support the preservation of religion in our society and culture and, like most Americans, support at the same time the doctrine of separation of church and state, and the constitutional right to freedom of religion.

I am also adamantly opposed to those who would remove the words "In God We Trust" from our currency or "under God" from our Pledge of Allegiance, and to those who would deny prayer in our public schools because, as atheists or secularists, they take offense at the practice. And

I don't like the idea of removing nativity scene displays and Christmas trees from town squares and public property because I believe them to be powerful cultural icons.

I have absolutely no fear of any prospect that our government will interfere with religion, nor do I think anyone should have such concerns. I *do* think, however, we should all be concerned that religion could potentially become a too powerful influence in partisan politics, and that we should be wary of the rising influence of religion on public policy. Ours is not only the most racially and ethnically diverse nation, but also the most diverse in representation of religion and denomination. But in terms of political influence, there is no question that three religions dominate: Protestant, Catholic, and Jewish. And their sway in partisan politics and Washington is rising.

For instance, I consider Cardinal Roger Mahony's support of illegal immigration to be a step too far, especially when he, as archbishop of Los Angeles, called upon his parishioners to disobey federal law. Apart from the fact that the Catholic Church's involvement in the illegal immigration issue is transparently self-serving, given that most illegal aliens are Catholic, church leaders should be a guide to the faithful, exemplary in their public conduct, and respectful of this nation's legal system, which has hardly been the case with Cardinal Mahony. The cardinal's intrusion and that of the U.S. Conference of Catholic Bishops into our illegal immigration crisis prompted me to write a column in March 2007 in which I noted that "this is the same Cardinal who fought all the way to the Supreme Court to keep secret all documents related to pedophilia among priests. But the Cardinal and other Catholic leaders are quick to embrace the laws of bankruptcy protection in order to not compensate victims of sexual abuse by members of the clergy and keep them out of the U.S. judicial system."

Cardinal Mahony subsequently agreed to pay $660 million as settlement of the claims of hundreds of victims of sexual abuse by priests. He also succeeded, however, in preventing those priests from being brought to court and tried for their crimes.

The leadership of the Catholic Church is hardly alone in its political activism. The involvement of a number of Protestant organizations in the illegal immigration debate also troubles me greatly, in part because I look upon them as taking a position antithetical to the interests of the American people and of our nation, and at variance with the views and opinions of their church members on the issue of illegal immigration. In fact, church members disagree by an overwhelming margin with their church leaders on this subject.

Domestic issues are not the only area in which churches have taken a stand. I consider the Land Letter, signed by Richard Land and Charles Colson, an unnecessary and unwarranted religious rationale for the president and the U.S. government to go to war in Iraq. I'm no less concerned about the role of AIPAC, the American Israel Public Affairs Committee, in American foreign policy. This Jewish lobbying group works tirelessly to represent the interests of Israel in America. On his show, Charlie Rose asked me if I thought the Jewish lobby had too much influence in Washington. We were taping live in Manhattan and a large number of Rose's studio audience audibly gasped when I replied yes. They exhaled comfortably when I said that I believed that the Saudi Arabian embassy also had too much influence in Washington.

I have at various times reminded various church leaders of Romans 13, where it is written: "Everyone must submit himself to the governing authorities, for there is no authority except that which God has established. The authorities that exist have been established by God. Consequently, he who rebels against the authority is rebelling against what God has instituted, and those who do so will bring judgment on themselves."

Religion has an important role in our society, even our political culture, and I don't believe there are clear, bright lines of any kind that make it easy for the sectarian and the secular to achieve proportion and balance. As I said, I believe in the critical importance of countervailing positive influences in society, a system that complements the architecture of checks and balances in our representative republican government. The truth is, however, that the influence of our traditional institutions—that is, churches, schools, and government—is in decline as those institutions themselves fail in their primary social role.

Churches of every denomination have been essential elements in nearly every community in this nation. They have served as both places of worship for the faithful and gathering places for community events. With their leaders they have met the needs of local citizens and ministered to their own congregations, who in turn supported the church. They have known the individuals and families who were their parishioners and members. And while they have expressed concern for the spiritual state of the nation and the world, their focus has been on the people in the community. But as religious organizations have turned their attention to matters of national concern, their time and resources have been diverted from their own congregations. And it is the people in the community who have been underserved and in many cases neglected.

We must restore these institutions, support them in their traditional roles, or find new influences to counter the forces that are now disrupting and dividing American society. Ours is a nation in pain, as evidenced by the almost unlimited flow of illegal drugs, the rising number of unwed mothers and single-parent homes, and the worsening violence in our communities, not to mention its glorification in the media. Sex and violence are among the most dominant forms of negative imagery that assaults us all. I think our children and their families need as much help as they can get in this fast-moving and increasingly unsettled twenty-first century.

Schools, parents, and families cannot be realistically expected to compete successfully with and counteract the social and multimedia assault on our young. While our churches and religious organizations could be a stronger and more relevant force in our society than they are now, even in decline, they remain a key influence in a society racked with negativity, immorality, and often unethical and ineffective leadership in nearly all of our major institutions.

It is disheartening to consider the current state of churches and religious organizations, which are supposed to nurture faith and guide the faithful in their ethical, moral, and spiritual lives. Over the past decade some religious leaders have trumpeted their own righteousness while breaking trust with their followers, while churches have undergone wrenching and dispiriting episodes that have shocked everyone who respects religion.

That includes most Americans, for nearly all of us believe in God, and most of us practice our faith. Approximately 60 percent of Americans say that religion plays an important role in their lives, which is twice the number who make that assertion in Canada or Italy, nearly three times that in Germany, and five times that claimed by citizens of Japan. More than 60 percent of people over the age of thirty believe that the strength of American society stems from the strong religious faith of its citizens. Only 12 percent of Americans claim to be unaffiliated with any organized religion.

While our Constitution declares that "Congress shall make no law respecting an establishment of religion, or prohibiting the free exercise thereof," it does not directly speak to the politicization of religion and religious involvement in community and nation politics. Religious organizations are not supposed to be political organizations; it's why they enjoy the freedoms they have, freedoms not always available to religions in other countries. As entities separate from the state, they also enjoy the benefit of tax-exempt status, a status they maintain by refraining from endorsing political candidates as well as any attempts to influence legislation. Yet increased religious involvement in the political process has attracted the attention of the Internal Revenue Service, which is beginning to address the issue of separation of church and state more aggressively.

During the course of 2004 the IRS discovered a disturbing amount of possible intervention by religious groups in national politics, and determined that more than five dozen churches and charities violated federal laws against political activity by religious organizations. During the midterm election campaigns in 2006, the IRS sent out warning letters to more than fifteen thousand churches and tax-exempt non-profit organizations throughout the country serving notice that engagement of churches in partisan politics would not be tolerated, and that maintaining their tax-exempt status was contingent upon their political neutrality. In the final month before the midterm elections, forty active investigations were being conducted into the political activities of various churches.

Tony Perkins, president of the Family Research Council, unequivocally maintains that churches are absolutely free to take stands on political issues. He strongly believes that the national dialogue is enriched and better informed through the participation of pastors, ministers, priests, and rabbis, and the churches and religious organizations they serve. All religious leaders acknowledge that the Internal Revenue Service code presents a clear limit on the ability of churches to support political candidates and prohibits their endorsement.

Barry Lynn, executive director of Americans United for Separation of Church and State, fears that churches and religious organizations are pressing for the unrestricted ability not only to aggressively take part in partisan politics, but to be able to use the power of the pulpit to actually endorse or oppose candidates:

"There is no doubt that the tax laws do permit people to talk from the pulpit about the great moral issues of the day. That's pretty much been happening for a very long time in the United States. Almost from the beginning of the founding of the country. However, now we've got people . . . who would like to make tax-exempt organizations able to literally endorse candidates from the pulpit and use the powerful resources of the church not just to talk about moral issues, but actually to endorse candidates. That would be a terrible idea. We've already seen the Internal Revenue Service investigating and hearing about more and more of these intrusions by religious groups into the promotion of partisan political candidates. It's got to stop. . . . [I]n America, the Constitution provides the values that we all share. We don't go to someone's sacred text and someone's interpretation of that sacred text and decide what the policy of the United States should be."

There is no constitutional prohibition against churches' taking a position on particular candidates, and until recently election-day sermons were commonplace. In 1954 Lyndon Johnson, then serving as senator from Texas, created an amendment to the tax code (specifically, section 501(c)(3) of the federal Internal Revenue Code) that mandates that institutions with tax-exempt status not engage in political activity. That amendment was introduced to provide religious organizations, charities, think tanks, foundations, and NGOs with guidelines for keeping that status. The provision specifically states such organizations are prohibited from "participat[ing] in, or intervening in any political campaign on behalf of any candidate for public office." Should a 501(c)(3) organization undertake such involvement in political affairs, its tax-exempt status can be revoked.

Johnson's support of the amendment was viewed as a personal response to the nonprofit organizations that opposed his bid for reelection to the Senate, by, as he claimed, "producing Red-baiting radio shows, television programs and millions of pieces of literature." Johnson was not alone in his disdain for nonprofits' railing against his politics; committee records from the time showed a growing congressional desire to limit the political influence of nonprofits nationwide.

Deterred but not defeated, churches have been rebuilding their political musculature since the late 1980s. Leading that effort is the Christian Coalition of America, founded by televangelist Pat Robertson and spearheaded by Ralph Reed. The CCA made a concerted effort to organize Protestant churchgoers, primarily evangelicals, around a profamily platform that coincided with their beliefs on a number of social issues, including abortion, anti–gay rights, pro–school prayer, and the teaching of creationism in public schools. It sought out and supported politicians who were sympathetic to their agenda and became a significant source for their campaign funds. In fact, Reed and his organization were so strongly mobilized that during the 1990s they were considered the seventh-most-powerful lobbying group in Washington, just behind the National Rifle Association and ahead of the American Medical Association.

The Christian Coalition successfully got voters to back their candidates on profamily issues and played a critical role in the successful Republican victories in the House and Senate in the 1994 midterm elections. For the first time in forty years, the Republicans had control of Congress. Only two years after Bill Clinton had won the presidency, the Christian Coalition had helped restore Republican power in Washington. Reed's knack for creating grassroots campaigns among fed-up religious voters put him in high demand: He consulted on eighty-eight federal and state campaigns, an indication of how important the religious vote had become in politicians' election strategies.

Although the influence of the Christian Coalition itself waned, the religious right turned out the evangelical vote in both 2000 and 2004. President Bush was, and is, their man: an ally who publicly extolls and shares their values. President Bush repaid the favor by creating the Office of Faith-Based and Community Initiatives in his first year in office. Religious organizations were now encouraged to bid on government contracts, notably for social services, and to offer those services under the banner of their particular beliefs and denominations. The doctrine of the separation of church and state, or at least its illusion, was to be maintained by requiring a division between overt religious activities and contracted services. In 2006 the Government Accountability Office found that many faith-based programs honored those instructions only in the breach. In June 2007 the Supreme Court ruled against a challenge to federal funding of faith-based organizations.

Religious groups are also organized to influence and occasionally pressure corporations that stray or are perceived to stray directly into the political arena. James Dobson's evangelical organization, Focus on the Family, and Donald Wildmon's conservative American Family Association have boycotted companies like Disney, Procter & Gamble, and the maker of American Girl dolls for their perceived endorsement of gay rights. There's no law against boycotting a company; it is one of the rights we are granted as citizens. But when churches urge candidates to behave a certain way, or make demands for political favoritism, then their activity goes against the law.

Some of the nation's religious leaders nevertheless remain hell-bent on political involvement. A coalition called Christians for Comprehensive Immigration Reform has intensively lobbied Congress with advertising and direct mail campaigns in support of amnesty for illegal aliens. James Dobson injected religion into the 2008 presidential election campaign by declaring that Fred Thompson wasn't sufficiently Christian to connect with the conservative base and win the GOP nomination.

Cardinal Roger Mahony is likewise still at it, threatening Catholics with being denied heaven if they don't support amnesty for illegal aliens. As the Cardinal warned: "Anything that tears down one group of people or one person, anything that is a negative in our community, disqualifies us from being part of the eternal city." And nobody in the federal government seems too concerned that the Catholic Church has repeatedly lobbied on behalf of millions of illegal aliens and their supporters for wholesale amnesty and open borders. Ironically, Mahony is now spearheading a drive to register a million new voters by 2008.

Catholics in my audience were unimpressed by the cardinal's threat.

Albert in Georgia: "Lou, All my life I was under the illusion that I was an American and a Catholic. Now I'm told I'm neither because I don't support amnesty for illegal immigrants. Thank you, President Bush and Cardinal Mahony, for setting me straight." (June 15, 2007)

Paulette in Maryland: "If the Catholic Church wants amnesty for illegal immigrants, they should take full responsibility for them. They should provide health care, housing, and jobs." (May 11, 2007)

Occasionally ministers, preachers, and priests even call down damnation upon their critics in the national media. The Adalberto United Methodist Church in Chicago has been providing sanctuary for more than a year to Elvira Arellano, an illegal alien, and her son, Saul. Elvira Arellano had been deported as far back as 1997, but was arrested in the United States again in 2002 for using a fake Social Security number. She also gave birth to Saul in the United States, which makes him an American citizen. I criticized the church for what was clearly illegal behavior and participating in what was pure political theatrics.

In July 2007 an Adalberto United Methodist minister was among those demonstrating on the steps of the U.S. Supreme Court to stop immigration raids on employers and halt all deportations of illegal aliens. The Reverend Walter Coleman said, "There is no redemption for Lou Dobbs. That's a fact. I hope he hears this, because he's in serious trouble." I have to admit that the good minister doesn't make it easy for me to be too enthusiastic about religious participation in the usually secular debate on issues of national importance. Nonetheless, I support Reverend Coleman's First Amendment rights, all of them, even when he's hurling hellfire in my direction.

The heavily Mormon state of Utah embraces illegal aliens, and its population has exploded over the past ten years. In May 2006 the state government and church leaders rolled out the red carpet for Mexico's then-president Vicente Fox, who openly encouraged millions of his impoverished citizens to enter the United States illegally, find work, and send remittances of an estimated $25 billion each year back to Mexico. The Mormon Church also helped proamnesty incumbent congressman Chris Cannon win reelection with a get-out-the-vote campaign.

Bobbi in Nevada: "Lou, I'm surprised that so many people are missing your point on the church-state issue. The real issue here is that the church is endorsing something that's clearly illegal. Religion is good, but when it's used for political purpose, then we're in trouble." (May 16, 2007)

We possess religious beliefs, we practice our religion, and our Constitution protects our religious rights. What, then, is the appropriate role of religion in our political lives? That question merits close examination, and I believe the debate is only beginning. As I mentioned earlier, religious faith is cited by nearly two thirds of respondents as the basis for a strong American society. Nearly two thirds of us are members of a church or synagogue, and more than one third of us attend church or synagogue at least once a week.

Reverend Lynn sees clear limits to how far religion should extend: "What houses of worship cannot do, under federal law, is to endorse or oppose candidates for public office. They may not use their resources to intervene in a partisan race. Houses of worship cannot become cogs in anyone's political machine." James Dobson, Pat Robertson, Cardinal Mahony, and most church leaders, in contrast, believe it is entirely appropriate that churches and nonprofits have become extensions of both Democratic and Republican political message machines at the local and national levels.

Churches have, of course, long taken public and political positions on the issue of war and peace. Some religious organizations today oppose the war in Iraq, while others support it, and both base their judgments in scripture and articles of faith. Before the war the president received theological endorsement for the invasion of Iraq from five evangelical leaders. The so-called Land Letter was sent to President Bush in October 2002, stating, "[W]e believe that your stated policies concerning Saddam Hussein and his headlong pursuit and development of biochemical and nuclear weapons of mass destruction are prudent and fall well within the time-honored criteria of just war theory as developed by Christian theologians in the late fourth and early fifth centuries A.D." The letter goes on to outline why these religious leaders believe that Bush was taking the correct course of action, and basically letting him know that from a religious perspective, he was justified in doing so.

The letter was authored by Richard Land, president of the Ethics & Religious Liberty Commission of the Southern Baptist Convention, and signed by, among others, Charles Colson. Colson, you may recall, was President Nixon's counsel and once advised the president to fire-bomb a liberal think tank and helped cover up Watergate. Colson was convicted of obstruction of justice after Watergate and sent to prison, where he became a born-again Christian. After his release Colson emerged not only a Christian but a commentator and spokesman for the far right. He also created Prison Fellowship, which advocates prison reform through religious ministry. Colson has become such an influential element of the religious right that Florida governor Jeb Bush restored all the rights that Colson had lost with his felony conviction, including the right to vote and practice law.

Meanwhile, churches and religious organizations are finding themselves challenged in maintaining their hold on the faithful. A Pew survey found that in 1994, 72 percent of all respondents had no doubt in the existence of God. By 2007 that number had dropped to 61 percent, the first significant decline in America's faith in God in decades.

Congregations have been sorely tested by some of their church leaders. The sexual abuse scandal that has rocked the Catholic Church and the efforts of church leadership to shield their priests from prosecution, have shaken the church and public perception of its moral authority.

Cardinal Mahony refused to cooperate with local and state law enforcement officials investigating priests accused of sexual abuse and relented only when the Supreme Court ordered him to. He and other church leaders claimed to be protecting the church and its members, which obviously they had failed to do. A series of lawsuits have bankrupted five American dioceses since 2004—San Diego, Tucson, Portland, Spokane, and Davenport—and Los Angeles may well be next, with the trend showing no sign of abating.

In July 2007, two days before the start of a clergy sexual abuse trial in which Cardinal Mahony would have been forced to testify, he suddenly announced the largest diocesan settlement to date in the sex abuse scandal: $660 million to be paid out to 508 victims. It is estimated that 40 percent of that money will go to the attorneys representing those victims; the other principal beneficiary of the plan is, of course, Cardinal Mahony.

At a time when the American people would be better served by a Catholic Church that is strong, stable, and guided by principled leadership, it is confronted by a host of challenges, including the fact that it now has far fewer priests. The median age of diocesan priests is now fifty-seven; in 1975 it was forty-seven. The average age of new priests being ordained is thirty-five, and one in three of them is foreign-born. Of the 42,307 priests in the United States, fewer than 300 are under the age of thirty. And while the number of priests dwindles, the ratio of priests to Catholic practitioners has risen to approximately 1 to 1,200. In 1950 the ratio was approximately 1 to 650.

Other churches and religious organizations wrestle with their own demons. Pastor Ted Haggard, founder of the New Life megachurch in Colorado, was head of the 30 million strong National Associations of Evangelicals. In the wake of the Christian Coalition, the NAE has arguably become the most influential and active religious lobbying group since President Bush was elected in 2000. Haggard and the NAE were credited by some for rallying the significant support that helped President Bush defeat Senator John Kerry in 2004. Haggard's backing and loyalty garnered him invitations to the White House, and by some accounts he talked to President Bush or his advisers weekly.

Reverend Haggard was an outspoken critic of gay marriage and liberal ideology right up until the moment in November 2006 when he was accused of drug abuse and paying for sex with a male prostitute. He was forced to give up his leadership position at the NAE and his ministry at the New Life Church. Church leaders sent Haggard to therapy to cure his homosexuality, yet made scant mention of drug therapy or rehabilitation. Haggard was not charged with the use of illegal drugs, or the illegal hiring of a prostitute. The amount of lying he did to his family and his church members seems to have been of little or no concern.

Religious leaders of all denominations are severely tested to lead their flocks with integrity, to serve their spiritual and moral needs, and to practice—not just preach—their faith. While the divide between the appropriately secular and the sectarian is not always evident in our modern society, the need for stronger and better leadership in both is abundant.

9

Crossing the Line

> You cannot dedicate yourself to America unless you become in
> every respect and with every purpose of your will thorough
> Americans. You cannot become thorough Americans if you
> think of yourselves in groups. America does not consist of
> groups. A man who thinks of himself as belonging to a particu-
> lar national group in America has not yet become an American,
> and the man who goes among you to trade upon your national-
> ity is no worthy son to live under the Stars and Stripes.
>
> —Woodrow Wilson

The Bush White House has not only accelerated the privatization and outsourcing of many of its governmental responsibilities, but has also chosen to not enforce a substantial number of federal laws. And Congress, whether led by Republicans or Democrats, has failed to demand enforcement of those laws. No wonder that most Americans believe their government has broken trust with the people, or that opinion poll after opinion poll shows that Americans disapprove of the leadership of both the White House and the Congress. Most of us can't begin to justify why, after six years of a global war on terror, our federal government has failed to take every measure necessary to secure our borders and ports. Most of us can't understand why Transportation Security Administration screeners at our nation's airports insist that elderly people in wheelchairs take off their shoes and submit to strip searches, while another Department of Homeland Security agency, Customs and Border Protection, is compelled to allow as many as one million illegal aliens to enter our country each year. How can the executive officers of the Department of Homeland Security even pretend they're doing their job when only 5 percent of the cargo entering our country's ports is inspected? Are President Bush and DHS secretary Michael Chertoff simply hoping that radical Islamist terrorists won't notice that our borders are wide open and our ports unprotected? Why has Congress not demanded that they be secured? How is it possible that most of our elected officials act as though they were possessed of a higher responsibility than serving the national interest and the safety and welfare of the American people?

The answers to those questions are found in the twenty-first-century orthodoxy that is without question the most powerful force in Washington, D.C. It is embedded in lobbying firms, think tanks, and special interests that have as either their direct or indirect objective the suppression of the rights and will of the citizens of this country. This new orthodoxy is composed of political and governmental, business and media, and academic elites who have intellectually replaced America's traditional "free enterprise democracy" philosophy with one of "free markets," unfettered by governmental representation, regulation, or law.

You and I might believe there's no higher duty of government than to serve the common good, but it is now patently obvious that most of our elected officials of both major political parties disagree. They have chosen to subordinate their duties and responsibilities to the people and our nation in order to serve the new orthodoxy and its Washington agenda, which is driven by multinational business and socioethnocentric special interest groups. That agenda has in a matter of years become not only un-American, but anti-American: Corporate America seeks cheap labor whether by outsourcing or illegal immigration, by the elimination of borders, and, necessarily, by subsuming national priorities to international ones. Socioethnocentric special interest groups, meanwhile, join in the assault on our borders, demanding multiculturalism rather than assimilation into American society. America's elites have embraced corporatism, globalism, and multiculturalism as the unholy trinity of a twenty-first-century orthodoxy that is now at work to deny our traditions, values, and way of life and to render impotent even the idea of

America's national sovereignty. But the arrogance of this program has become so obvious and transparent that the American people are beginning to see and comprehend what confronts us all.

I believe the American people realize more each day the enormous stakes in what has become an all-out political engagement between the elites and our citizens in the struggle to define who we are as both citizens and a nation, and to determine our nation's future. Nowhere has that orthodoxy been more vigorous, more transparent, or more arrogant in pushing its agenda than in America's border and port security and illegal immigration crisis. I've been at the forefront of the debate on that crisis for four years now, during which immigration proponents have expended massive amounts of money, energy, and effort to either obfuscate or distort the essential facts underlying the situation. The truth is straightforward: Had the United States secured its borders and ports after September 11, not only would the American people be better protected against terrorism, but illegal immigration would not now be a national crisis. Had corporate America not chosen to import illegal aliens, not chosen to employ and exploit them in defiance of U.S. law, there would be no illegal immigration crisis. Had the federal government enforced existing immigration law against both illegal employers and illegal aliens, there would be no crisis.

Instead, the president, Republican and Democratic congressional leaders, lobbyists for corporate America, and socioethnocentric special interests united in their drive to legalize illegal aliens and to leave our borders wide open. Through their creation and support of the McCain-Kennedy "comprehensive immigration legislation," they sought to grant amnesty to all illegal aliens and establish a new guest worker program, while giving only lip service to the issue of border and port security. While the Senate passed the legislation in 2006, the Republican leadership in the House managed to turn it back, and the bill died.

Undeterred, President Bush and the new Democratic-led Senate took up the cause of "comprehensive immigration reform" and amnesty a year later. This time, the effort in the Senate was led by a small group of senators of both parties, meeting in secret with representatives of the orthodoxy, including the U.S. Chamber of Commerce and the National

Council of La Raza, to assure agreement on the legislation before they put it before all of the Senate for discussion. This little band of senators became known among their colleagues as the "Grand Bargainers" or the "Masters of the Universe," and neither title was meant as an honorific or term of respect. The Grand Bargainers were a bipartisan collection that included Senators Ted Kennedy, Jon Kyl, Dianne Feinstein, John McCain, Bob Menendez, Lindsey Graham, Ken Salazar, Arlen Specter, John Cornyn, Mel Martinez, Saxby Chambliss, and Johnny Isaacson; ultimately, Senators Cornyn, Menendez, and Chambliss withdrew. Although Senate majority leader Harry Reid charged ahead to push what was now officially Senate bill number 1639 through the legislative process with hardly any debate, the bill met strong resistance, and Senator Reid felt compelled to pull it. But within days the president and the Grand Bargainers had prevailed upon Reid to reintroduce the legislation. After only a few acrimonious sessions of debate, Reid put the bill up for a final procedural vote.

On June 28, 2007, the Senate defeated bill 1639 in a cloture vote by a margin of 53 to 46. Despite arm-twisting and pleas from President Bush, Homeland secretary Michael Chertoff, and commerce secretary Carlos Gutierrez, 37 Republicans voted no. Unmoved by repeated declarations from Senators Harry Reid, Ted Kennedy, and Jon Kyl that the "time is now" and that "a bad bill is better than no bill," 14 Democrats broke with their leadership and likewise voted against it.

That critically important vote was a result, I believe, of engaged citizens' finally making their voices heard in the corridors of the Senate and of their elected officials' responding to their constituents. The senators were inundated by e-mails and phone calls, which were so numerous the Senate switchboard actually shut down for a few hours at one point. The outcome of the cloture vote was the result of the 2006 midterm elections, which turned over control of the Senate and House to Democrats. Freshmen senators who voted no on cloture (in opposition to the bill) include John Tester, Jim Webb, Bernie Sanders, Claire McCaskill, Bob Corker, and Sherrod Brown. But only one senator among the announced and likely presidential candidates, Sam Brownback, voted no. Senators Obama, McCain, Hagel, Dodd, Clinton, and Biden all voted yes.

The contrast between the majority of new senators who voted against the legislation and the overwhelming number of presidential candidate senators voting for it represents an interesting divide on these issues. With recent polls showing popular opinion opposed to the legislation and supporting border security, it is possible that the six presidential senators, including Clinton and Obama, may pay a significant price at the polls for their support of Senate bill 1639. Better they pay that price, however, than Americans citizens and taxpayers be burdened by another four years of presidential leadership indifferent or even antagonistic to the common good and national interest.

I hope that the national debate on illegal immigration and border security does move to the presidential campaign, and that each candidate will be called upon to state fully his or her positions and disclose to the voters his or her full views and how those views align with a vision for a twenty-first-century America. Illegal immigration and border security have become top-tier issues among Americans polled over the course of the past year, having emerged from the shadows of American politics—and just in time. While most of the candidates will try to avoid taking a position and speaking directly and emphatically on these issues, the 2008 presidential campaign offers us the best opportunity to reach a meaningful consensus and to align the interests of our leadership with our citizens.

President Bush has been fond of saying that we cannot secure our borders without a guest worker program. Such an assertion is palpable nonsense not only because of its tortured logic, but also because eight such programs already exist. Several of them are appropriate to meeting the needs of the labor market, if corporate America could demonstrate the need for the additional workers. Homeland Security secretary Michael Chertoff suggested immediately after the defeat of the immigration bill that he would now not have the tools to secure our borders and ports—a measure this administration has actively resisted and refused to adopt since taking office in 2001, which has permitted millions of illegal aliens to enter this country. And the administration has outright lied about the underlying facts of this national crisis.

There are as many as twelve million to twenty million illegal aliens

IMMIGRATION FACTS

Legal Permanent Residents (LPRs)

- Total number of legal permanent residents (LPRs) admitted to the United States in 2005: 1,266,264. Of these:

  —14% were born in Mexico.

  —7% were born in China.

  —6% were born in the Philippines.

- 65% of individuals who became LPRs were already living in the United States.

- 63% of individuals who became LPRs were granted the status based on a family relationship with a U.S. citizen or LPR.

Source: DHS, Office of Immigration Statistics

Naturalized Citizens

- Total number of foreign nationals who became naturalized citizens in 2006: 702,589. Of these:

  —12% were born in Mexico.

  —6.8% were born in India.

  —5.8% were born in the Philippines.

  —5% were born in China.

Source: DHS, Office of Immigration Statistics

Wages

- Wages in the overall construction sector have fallen almost 2% since the start of the decade.

- Wages have fallen nearly 4% since 2003 (which was the peak time for wages in this sector).

- Construction workers made the same hourly rate as they did in 1965 (measured in 1982 dollars).

- Wages have fallen by nearly 4% for landscaping workers.

- Landscapers are making the same hourly rate as they did in 1972.

Source: Bureau of Labor Statistics

Visas and Admission

- Last year, the United States granted 1.3 million people legal permanent residency.

- 14% are from Mexico.

- A total of over 2 million people are legally admitted to the United States each year.

- More than 400,000 skilled foreign workers and their families received H-1B visas last year.

- Nearly 900,000 other legal foreign workers were admitted on some type of employment visa.

- 660,000 student visas were issued.

- 455,000 people were given temporary employment transfers.

  Source: DHS, Office of Immigration Statistics

Arrests

- ICE agents make an average of:

  —279 administrative arrests daily

  —55 criminal arrests daily

- ICE detention facilities house approximately 19,729 aliens daily.

- ICE screens more than 547 visa applications a day.

  Source: U.S. Immigration and Customs Enforcement: "ICE Fiscal Year 2006 Annual Report, Protecting National Security and Upholding Public Safety."

Border Apprehensions

- Total number of border apprehensions in 2005: 1.3 million (at northern, southern, and coastal borders)

  —The border patrol made up to 94% of all apprehensions from 1996–2005.

  —98.5% of all apprehensions occurred at the southern border.

  —86.19% of all apprehensions were of Mexican nationals.

- Total number of southern border apprehensions in 2005: 1,171,428.

continued

Of these:

—86.8% were Mexican nationals.

—81.5% were male.

—90% were age 18 and over.

Source: DHS, Office of Immigration Statistics, "Border Apprehension: 2005," November 2006 .

ICE Annual Detention and Removal (Fiscal Year 2006)

- Since May 26, 2006, Fugitive Operations Teams have administratively arrested almost 24,000 criminal aliens, illegal alien gang members, fugitive aliens, sexual predators, and other immigration status violators as part of a nationwide interior immigration enforcement effort. This is a combination of criminals, illegals, fugitives, illegal alien gang members, and people who have ignored or violated a deportation order.

- Of all the aliens arrested by ICE fugitive operations, more than 14,000 were fugitive aliens, of whom more than 2,000 were criminal fugitive aliens (charged with criminal offenses and then discovered to be fugitives). The remaining more than 9,000 arrests were composed of nonfugitives (undocumented immigrants), of whom almost 2,000 were criminal aliens.

- In fiscal year 2006, ICE investigations resulted in more than 2,000 criminal arrests and more than 100,000 administrative arrests.

- 9,874 criminal arrests and 6,763 convictions for immigration-related activities including financial enforcement, human smuggling and trafficking, general and criminal alien enforcement, identity and benefit fraud, and compliance and worksite enforcement.

- Total apprehensions of foreign nationals detained by ICE in 2005: approximately 238,000

- 208,521 foreign nationals were formally removed from the United States in 2005. Of these:

  —69% were from Mexico.

  —7% were from Honduras.

  —6% were from Guatemala.

Source: DHS, Office of Immigration Statistics, "Immigrants Enforcement Actions: 2005," November 2006.

living now in the United States, the vast majority of whom have arrived over the past twenty years, as many as half of them since President Bush was elected. In its first four years the Bush administration was responsible for bringing 318 fines against employers of illegal workers. By contrast, during the eight years of the Clinton administration, immigration enforcement agencies issued an average of nearly 700 such fines each year. From 1995 to 1998 immigration agents carried out an average of 15,000 worksite arrests of illegal aliens. In the Bush administration, there were just 159 worksite arrests during all of 2004.

The Government Accountability Office has determined convincingly that workplace enforcement is in general a low priority for the government. The agency found that in 1999, the INS devoted only 240 agents to this task, or about 9 percent of its staff. Shockingly, seven years later, only 100 agents, or just 4 percent of the staff, were assigned to the matter. As David Walker, head of the GAO and the nation's comptroller general, told me, "We have a serious problem with illegal immigration. The fact of the matter is we are not enforcing existing laws adequately. We are not dedicating enough resources to it. We're not leveraging technology enough. And as a result, we have a lot of situations where people who are not legal are able to gain employment and that is serving to draw more people into the United States because of the economic implications. . . . [W]e'll have to use a lot tougher enforcement mechanisms if we want any system to work. We were supposed to have tough enforcement after the last reform act in 1986 but haven't had it."

President Bush and Secretary Chertoff have not only been negligent and derelict in their duties to protect this nation, but have refused to fulfill those duties. In my judgment, neither man has any credibility on these important issues, and history will hold them accountable. Not once has the president or any member of his administration acknowledged that we admit more than two million foreign citizens to enter, reside, and work in the United States legally each year, while at the same time allowing an estimated one million illegal immigrants to enter the country annually. To suggest, as advocates of amnesty and open borders have, that America must be a welcoming society ignores the fact we accept more legal immigrants than any other nation. These advocates should be asked what other nation is more tolerant of abuses of its immigration system and of the utter disregard of its borders and laws.

These advocates should also be told that this is a new America, and that their agenda can no longer be hidden from the American people. Their specious charges of racism, nativism, and xenophobia against proponents of secure borders and enforcement of our immigration laws make no sense, given that the United States is the most racially and ethnically diverse nation on the planet. But that hardly matters. The open borders and amnesty coalitions of big business, ethnocentric special interests, and the political elites of both parties are fully aware that their day is drawing to a close.

The defeat of Senate bill 1639 has in no way dissuaded those special interests from seeking to advance the open borders and amnesty agenda. My conversation on the air with the head of La Raza is illuminating:

Dobbs: The pro–illegal alien lobby, just as we suspected, isn't giving up. President Bush, proamnesty senators, corporate America, socio-ethnocentric groups all working hard to salvage their amnesty legislation. . . . Certainly among those groups is La Raza and its leader, Janet Murguia. What is clear to me, Janet, is that you talk about comprehensive immigration reform, the president talks about it, Senator Kennedy talks about it, for crying out loud, Senator Kyl is talking about it. But you know what? They're not talking straight, are they? Because if you're going to have a comprehensive immigration legislation, wouldn't you want to have a comprehensive legislative process? Public forums, public hearings, research, and rigorous, rigorous fact-finding? This nonsense of bringing people out of the shadows is precisely the language of 1986 and the advocates of that amnesty bill that got us into exactly this situation, right?

Janet Murguia, President, La Raza: Well, Lou, I think you and I disagree in some respect because . . . I want you to understand that, you know, the Senate did bring up a bill last year. This is their second effort. . . . There's been a lot of discussion, a lot of debate. We need to finish the job.

Dobbs: Debate? Debate?

Murguia: Yes.

Dobbs: Debate? They rammed that bill through last year with this president and the Republicans and the Democrats and the Republican leadership and the Democrat last year. This year they were told to go stick it effectively. Let me just show you one thing. . . .

Murguia: Look . . . this is a bipartisan bill. It's not a perfect bill and it's been a very difficult process. . . . We're on the track here. We need to get the job done.

Dobbs: Janet, give me a break. Janet, you and I have known each other too long to talk by each other. You said bipartisan.

Murguia: That's right.

Dobbs: It's difficult. It's not perfect. My gosh, we know that. What I ask you about is where is the research? Where is the Congressional Budget Office? Where in the world is this administration's commitment to truth and fact-finding on the impact, the fiscal, societal impact of this legislation? You and I both know this administration and this Congress is hiding from the truth. And they don't want the American people involved. There hasn't been a single public hearing on this legislation.

Murguia: Well, I think there's been a lot of discussion, a lot of debate . . .

Dobbs: Among whom? The secret authors of this legislation?

Murguia: We've got a consensus on the fact that this needs to be a comprehensive solution.

Dobbs: I'm sorry. Who . . . Whoa. Wait. I missed that bulletin. Who agreed to that? What consensus are you talking about?

Murguia: Well, when you can bring Senator Kyl and Senator Kennedy together, two people on the opposite extremes, a Democrat, a Republican, when they can come together and say, look, we need to make sure that there is a comprehensive . . .

Dobbs: Well, forgive me. There is another view here, Janet.

Murguia: Uh-huh.

Dobbs: I mean, there are 280 million middle-class Americans in this country, 300 million Americans who are saying, what are you talking about?

Murguia: Well, there is support among the American people to get a solution. They want a comprehensive, rational, fair, and orderly solution for this. And this bill is our best chance for moving forward and not accepting the status quo. We know that the current system isn't working, Lou. We have got to move forward.

Dobbs: OK. Let me give you an idea of what happens with this not-perfect bill and the debate that you're talking about. Here's what Senator Trent Lott had to say about amendments to the bill. You remember there were killer amendments last week and a real heartfelt bipartisan effort there. Well, the Mississippi Republican, Senator Trent Lott, Senate whip . . . said amendments to this bill will simply disappear once that bill goes into conference, quote, "No big deal. You pitch those before you get to the Rotunda." You want to sit there and tell the American people that this is meaningful debate and this isn't political theater arranged by the elites in both parties and socioethnocentic groups? Come on.

Murguia: Lou, we need to let the legislative process move forward and we have to make sure that as it moves forward that we take into account all of these perspectives. . . .

Dobbs: How about the perspective of the American people? . . . They're the only people not represented in this. You were there. The U.S. Chamber of Commerce was there in those secret meetings as the Senate is authoring this. . . . Where in the heck were the American people?

Murguia: I don't know what you're talking about in terms of secret meetings. That wasn't anything we were a part of.

Dobbs: You weren't involved in any part of the crafting of this legislation? Your input wasn't . . .

Murguia: There have been a number of voices that have been . . .

Dobbs: I know, but I'm asking about yours, Janet. La Raza's.

Murguia: There's a broad coalition that's involved. Bipartisan, representing a lot of different voices and they're all trying to . . .

Dobbs: OK. Give me one example of working men and women in this country and their representation and their families. American citizens.

Murguia: Well, I happen to represent a number of working families through our organization. The Chamber of Commerce represents business. The Catholic Church . . .

Dobbs: Pardon me. I would like to see someone that committed just to those folks and not to, if you will, open borders and amnesty.

Murguia: Well, I don't support open borders, and our organization does not support open borders.

Dobbs: Good. So would you accept border security as a condition precedent to any attempt at reforming existing U.S. law?

Murguia: Border security must be a part of this solution, and it is a part of this equation. In this bill. But it cannot stand alone.

Dobbs: Why? Why? . . . You and I both know that comprehensive is just another way to bury border security and port security.

Murguia: No. Lou, border security and enhancements around the border and interior security are all part of this bill that's on the Senate floor. We need to move forward in a balanced way that just has border security and enforcement alone. We've quintupled efforts to help in border security the last ten years. That alone won't work. We need to have a comprehensive solution that addresses the current undocumenteds that are here, the future flow of workers, and the employer worksite enforcement. All that has to be a part of this if it's going to be a workable equation. That's in the Senate bill. It's not perfect, but we need to move that legislation forward.

Dobbs: Janet, you get the last word and I appreciate you being here. Good to talk with you.

On one side of this issue are the people of the United States, who are concerned that our national borders cannot be secured, who are concerned that our laws are not being enforced, who are concerned about what is happening to American jobs, and who are concerned about what their government plans to do with as many as twenty million people who are in this country illegally.

On the other side are special interest groups, led by corporate America, who are interested in a nearly unlimited supply of cheap labor, who are interested in reducing their business costs, who do not want to pay a fair wage or provide employee benefits, and who see human beings as nothing more than a means of production.

The common good is pitted against the self-interested few, and as our elected representatives have been demonstrating for the last few years, the self-interested few are getting preferential treatment. By now it's probably foolish for us to have expected anything different. In what other country would citizens be treated to the spectacle of the president and the Senate focusing on the desires of twelve million to twenty million people who had crossed the nation's borders illegally, had committed document fraud and in many cases identity theft, had overstayed their visas, and had demanded full forgiveness for their trespasses?

As the only remaining superpower in the world, we should by any logic seek to keep our borders secure and get a handle on what or who is making its way into this country. Only 5 percent of all the cargo brought into our ports from other countries is actually inspected. Thousands of tons of drugs from anti-American countries like Afghanistan make their way across our borders and through our ports every year. U.S. authorities seize more than one hundred tons of cocaine a year, most of which comes across our border with Mexico. Other than what is written on cargo manifests, we literally have no idea of what is actually transported into this country every day from all over the world.

Not even *legal* imports are adequately inspected by agencies of the federal government, an oversight that places the American consumer at the mercy of the marketplace and the luck of the draw. Recently there are few agencies where this has been so obvious as in the Food and Drug Administration. Tainted spinach, peanut butter, and pet food resulted in sickness and even death over the course of 2006 and 2007.

The government spent weeks trying to pinpoint the source of the contaminations, but as we reported on the show, the FDA has known for years of the potential dangers in spinach and peanut butter. Documents showed that the FDA was aware of potential E. coli contamination of spinach and grains as far as back as 1995. However, the agency was too overwhelmed to conduct follow-up investigations in the following decade. The result? Tainted greens killed three people and sickened two hundred others in twenty-six states. FDA inspectors investigated complaints of salmonella contamination at a ConAgra plant in Georgia in 2005. The FDA didn't follow up on that, either, and salmonella found in two of ConAgra's peanut butter brands sickened four hundred people across the country. It is incumbent on the FDA to act on these investigations for the good of every consumer in America.

Joe in Pennsylvania: "I think I know what FDA stands for. Fails to Do Anything. Keep up the good work." (June 6, 2007)

Lois in California: "Let me get this straight. We can buy poisoned food from communist China, but we can't buy a good cigar from Cuba. God help us." (May 30, 2007)

Tim in Wisconsin: "The Bush administration doesn't allow prescription drugs from Canada because they could be unsafe. However, they do allow poison food additives from China. I think I prefer Canadian drugs." (May 10, 2007)

U.S. food makers have more than doubled their business with other countries, including China, over the past five years. Throughout 2007 the news out of China was that corrupt officials had allowed the export of tainted products; the country was ultimately identified as the source for the tainted pet food in the United States. And although Chinese products were found to be responsible, the FDA has no provision for testing the ingredients that come from there. For example, over 80 percent of vitamin C consumed in this country is produced in China, whether in vitamin tablets or as an additive in a variety of products, including soups and beverages. U.S. manufacturers of vitamin pills have an obligation to consumers to make sure the vitamin C they import and put in their products is safe, but federal guidelines for testing are voluntary, not mandatory. And the FDA only investigates if there is a problem, by which time, of course, it's too late.

Too many products are finding their way onto our shelves without proper examination and oversight. A look at the number of products that have had to be pulled off the market is extraordinarily telling. The year with the highest number of recalls by the FDA was 2005, when 5,338 products were involved. By May 2007, 3,079 products had already been recalled, and that figure doesn't include the pet food, which was estimated to involve close to a thousand separate items.

This country now imports more than 80 percent of its seafood, and most of it originates in Asia and Latin America. Less than 2 percent of imported seafood is physically inspected, and only 0.5 percent is subjected to a lab test. Fish that were fed contaminated ingredients from communist China have already entered the U.S. food supply. Interestingly, the European Union inspects a minimum of 20 percent of imported seafood. If a problem is found, they inspect 100 percent of the seafood from the exporting country. The FDA has said it can only do what its budget will allow.

The Chinese government has decided to attend to the lax oversight of the food products it exports. To show the world it was serious about taking strong measures to address the problem, on July 10, 2007, it executed the chief of its state food and drug administration.

Our problems with China and toxins aren't limited to food. The U.S. Consumer Product Safety Commission states that China is the largest exporter of toys and baby products to the United States, and that category, too, has the largest number of recalls. China's state agency has admitted that 20 percent of toys and baby clothes made in China are unsafe. Inspectors found that toy animals were stuffed with low-quality materials, and even garbage. And toys were so badly made that loose parts could be easily pulled free. Baby clothes, as well as milk powder, were also found to contain chemicals that could be a health hazard. We are bringing these products in without any inspection, without any sort

of consumer protection whatsoever. Our government agencies are actually permitting corporate America to import this junk.

Chrysler, newly freed from its Daimler parent, is looking to cut
costs in its subcompact car line by importing cars built by China's
Chery Automobile Company. In July 2007 the two companies signed
a deal that will bring the Chinese vehicles to the American market
within the next couple of years.

> *Barbara in New York*: "Hi, Lou. Unbelievable. We continue to receive
> inferior, unsafe, and downright dangerous products from Red China
> and now Chrysler wants to market a car made there. They'll deserve
> every lawsuit that comes their way." (July 10, 2007)

That about sums it up.

You should know that one of our own leading exports to China is
waste products. Now that they're coming back in the form of children's toys, we have certifiable proof that what goes around comes
around.

This lax attitude toward goods coming into the United States also
applies to how we deal with people entering this country. Though the
United States permits some two million foreign citizens to legally
come and work and reside here every year, there are still an estimated
million more who come in illegally. There may be more than twenty
million illegal immigrants living in the United States, although our
government cites a smaller number of about eight million to twelve
million, a figure that includes six million unauthorized workers, representing about 5 percent of our total workforce.

Illegal immigration and its impact on our society tend to be discussed in purely social and empathetic terms by our political leaders
and the media: Illegal aliens are already here, so give them legal status
and citizenship, regardless of the fact that they have entered the country unlawfully.

They are paid to work, but pay few taxes. In many states they are
provided with free services, such as schooling and emergency medical
care. The Bush administration and many of our elected officials would

like to offer these people a permanent home and even more benefits, including driver's licenses. The rationale for this amnesty is that it is a humanitarian gesture. Such misdirection obscures the real reason that politicians want to allow illegal immigrants to remain: because corporate America relies on this cheap labor force to help keep its costs down. If businesses, especially those in agriculture and construction, had to pay fair wages to American citizens, along with benefits and Social Security payments, their profit margins would suffer. In a business culture that slavishly responds to Wall Street's demand for more profits, that just won't do. When profits are the only goal, employees, customers, and communities are largely ignored.

Our national media, while claiming "objectivity" in its coverage of illegal immigration, is almost uniformly allied with business, socioethnic special interest groups, and political elites. The *Washington Post* and the *New York Times* seldom differentiate between illegal and legal immigrants in their reporting, and they report almost exclusively on the plight of illegal aliens but seldom on the taxpayer costs of illegal immigration or the impact on our society. The language of our national media doesn't describe those who are in this country illegally as illegal aliens, but rather as undocumented immigrants, immigrants, migrants, or, my personal favorite Orwellian term making its way into reporting, "entrants." Obviously, such language is intended to blur the distinction between legal and illegal immigration, to engender sympathy, and to further obfuscate the reality of our illegal immigration crisis.

For example, the *Arizona Republic*, the largest newspaper in a state that is on the front lines of illegal immigration and border security crises, used the term "undocumented immigrant" more than eighty times in thirty-six separate stories in April 2007; the term appeared as many as twelve times in a single article on "migration." At the same time, "illegal alien" appeared a total of only nine times during that span, with seven of the references coming from readers' opinions, one from a quotation, and one from an editorial. How's that for objective reporting and a neutral editorial policy?

I especially liked Fareed Zakaria's piece that appeared in *Newsweek* just before the 2006 election, "Time to Solve Immigration." Zakaria wrote: "This compromise package has the potential to be realized after the elections. After all, how many issues are there today on which George W. Bush, Hillary Clinton, John McCain, Ted Kennedy and Rudy Giuliani all agree?

"The great obstacle to immigration reform has been a noisy minority. . . . Come Tuesday, the party will be over. CNN's Lou Dobbs and his angry band of xenophobes will continue to rail, but a new Congress, with fewer Republicans and no impending primary elections, would make the climate much less vulnerable to the tyranny of the minority."

It must have been very distressing to Mr. Zakaria when the new Congress acted on behalf of American citizens rather than at the media's behest.

The media cannot talk about illegal immigration without buffering its language or blunting its reporting. Instead of asking and answering important questions about why our immigration laws aren't being enforced and why we're permitting pervasive document fraud, the national media seems hell-bent on trying to confuse the issue, shamelessly playing with language, equating legal immigration with illegal immigration while obviously trying to preserve the illusion of objectivity.

The national media almost without exception refuses to acknowledge that the economic benefits of illegal immigration accrue to those who employ illegal immigrants, not to the nation, and that this flawed system results in an actual cost to our economy. This cost takes the form of social benefits, retirement programs, and wage pressure, all of which comes at a very steep price, paid by American citizens and taxpayers. Benefits like Medicaid, Medicare, and Social Security will accrue to illegal aliens under all of the so-called comprehensive immigration proposals, and our elected representatives don't want you to even consider the overwhelming expense involved.

Robert Rector of the Heritage Foundation wrote that "it seems likely that if 10 million adult illegal immigrants currently in the U.S. were granted amnesty, the net retirement cost to government (benefits minus taxes) could be over $2.6 trillion." That number could rise substantially if the number of illegal immigrants has been underreported. Does anyone really believe that all of the people who would be given amnesty would foot the bill for their future benefits?

California congressman Ed Royce revealed another unacknowledged cost when we spoke on the show: "[O]n top of all of this, we can also look at the consequence of bringing such low-skilled immigration into the United States. It is going to push down wages, it's going to import an awful lot of poverty into this country, and these individuals on average pay one dollar in taxes for every three dollars in public benefits they receive. Figure out what it means for Social Security in the future as a consequence of this act."

When it comes to illegal workers in the United States, wage pressure always forces wages down, never up. If corporate America can pay a bare-bones wage without any benefits, it will do so. Illegal immigrants are willing to accept just such a deal.

During the nationwide 2006 May Day demonstrations in support of illegal immigrants, meat-packing businesses like Cargill and Tyson closed many of their plants. Why? Because these companies rely on illegal immigrants to do jobs they're not willing to pay very much for. In 1980 a meat-packing job paid nineteen dollars an hour, but today that same job pays closer to nine dollars an hour, according to the Labor Department. That's entirely consistent with what we've reported on the show: Illegal aliens depress wages for U.S. workers by as much as $200 billion a year, in addition to placing a tremendous burden on hospitals, schools, and other social services.

"The meat packers are confirming what we know," says University of Maryland economics professor Peter Morici, "and that is that this large group of illegal aliens in the United States is lowering the wage rate of semiskilled workers, people who are high school dropouts or high school graduates with minimal training."

Then there is so-called chain migration. This involves extending citizenship to the families of legal immigrants who are now citizens. Each year a quarter of a million immigrants are allowed to enter the country legally this way, a number that includes parents, adult siblings, and children.

The proamnesty groups tried to figure out how to apply chain migration eligibility to illegal immigrants eligible for amnesty. Should they give the extended families of people who crossed our border illegally the same rights as legal immigrants, now that they're pardoning these illegals for their crimes? The potential numbers are astronomical: The office of congressman Phil Gingrey (R-GA) estimates that, based on current legal immigration trends, each newly approved illegal alien could bring in as many as 273 relatives.

The big thinkers in Congress only got around to taking into account this ramification of the proposed amnesty in May 2007—after our elected officials had already drafted much of the legislation they were trying to jam down our throats. In an effort to address this issue, and save the "grand compromise," the White House scrambled to make adjustments that would allow in only those who had demonstrable skill sets beyond the immediate family of those receiving amnesty.

Such oversights only underscore the fact that Congress has refused to conduct a national dialogue on this legislation or acknowledge critically important issues related to it, whether chain immigration or the skills and the educational levels that this nation seeks in its immigrants. To have them come to the fore only days before the initial deadline should have caused considerable embarrassment in the Congress and in the Senate, but it did not. The display was breathtakingly short-sighted, but it didn't stop the charade of congressional leadership trying to create a plan while coordinating with the White House while trying to keep members from defecting and doing the will of the people.

Just as he did when he was on the verge of losing the CAFTA vote, President Bush dragged out his "national security" card to turn the issue away from amnesty. Trying to avoid further confusion about his amnesty plans—the president said at one point, "Amnesty means that you've got to pay a price for having been here illegally, and this bill does that"—he pledged $4.4 billion for what he called "direct deposit on enforcement measures." The White House then had the gall to claim, "Security first is still the byword of this legislation."

Among the "security first" measures offered by the administration were operational control of 100 percent of the international land border with Mexico; the hiring of 20,000 trained border patrol officers, ready for duty; 370 miles of physical fence coupled with 300 miles of vehicle barriers; and some 31,500 detention beds. Department of Homeland Security secretary Michael Chertoff joined the fray, saying that he expected that 150 miles of border fence would be completed by September.

For the most part, these are hollow promises. As we pointed out on our broadcast, that 370 miles of fence was less than half the 854 miles of double fence signed into law by the president the previous fall. And Chertoff's promise to have 150 miles of fence in place by September was amazing, given the fact that, by the end of June, not only had fewer than 13 miles of fence actually been completed, but it was not the double fence that had been mandated.

There are lots of ways to put this, but the fact remains: When the president of the United States and the Democratic leadership of the U.S. Senate say that the proposed immigration legislation is all about border security and not about amnesty, it's a lie. There are a few on Capitol Hill willing to admit it. Ed Royce pointed out that the emperor had no clothes when he said, "We have . . . concocted here in the Senate, unfortunately, a plan which serves only the interests of the special interests and only the interests of the open border lobby, not the interest of the American people."

The Senate did have one impressive moment when it sought truth and justice in the midst of the immigration crisis, and for that they deserve credit and thanks.

The Senate Judiciary Committee hearing, led by Dianne Feinstein, focused on the reasons for the prosecution of two Border Patrol agents now serving long sentences in federal prison. Ignacio Ramos and Jose Compean were given terms of eleven and twelve years respectively on their convictions for shooting an illegal alien drug smuggler. Senator Feinstein, along with Senators Jeff Sessions, John Cornyn, Jon Kyl, and Tom Coburn, demanded answers of U.S. attorney Johnny Sutton, who had chosen to prosecute Ramos and Compean while giving the illegal alien drug smuggler blanket immunity to testify against the agents. Ramos and Compean had pursued the smuggler in a high-speed chase, and ultimately wounded him when he ditched his van, loaded with hundreds of pounds of drugs, and tried to escape.

The agents were serving their nation in a war zone along our southern border. The fact is, Mexico remains the primary corridor for drugs entering the United States, and is the principal source of heroin, cocaine, marijuana, and methamphetamines in this country. Between 70 and 90 percent of cocaine entering the United States from South America passes through mainland Mexico or its waters; heroin brought in from Mexico accounts for about 30 percent of the U.S. market, despite Mexico's relatively small percentage of worldwide production. Mexican traffickers dominate drug distribution in the United States, controlling most of the primary distribution centers. The federal government has treated Ramos and Compean with contempt rather than gratitude for their service on the front lines of a critical war.

I have maintained throughout their case that the prosecution of these two agents was unwarranted, that sufficient facts were in dispute that should never have been brought to trial. The two Border Patrol agents received excessive sentences by any reasonable standard of justice. But reason did not prevail, and the Senate Judiciary Committee has begun the process of righting this wrong.

At the committee's hearings, Border Patrol chief David Aguilar testified that from February 1, 2005, to June 30, 2007, there were 1,982 incidents in which Border Patrol agents were assaulted. These assaults included rock throwing, physical and vehicular attacks, and shootings. In response, Border Patrol agents retaliated with the use of deadly force on 116 occasions, with 144 agents discharging their weapons during these 116 incidents.

Aguilar also testified that 13 assailants died as a result, and 15 incidents ended with the assailants being wounded. Of the 144 agents involved, comprehensive investigations were formally conducted, and not a single agent had been criminally prosecuted for his actions. Why, then, did Sutton choose to prosecute agents in this case? The senators did not like U.S. attorney Sutton's answers.

T. J. Bonner, president of the National Border Patrol Council, the union that represents Ramos and Compean, expressed anger at the sentences and said the Border Patrol was suffering as a result: "The ramifications of this case [will be felt] by the Border Patrol." Bonner added an anecdote about a former Border Patrol recruit who eventually declined joining the organization, explaining, "You'd have to be crazy to join this outfit, because you eat your own."

Senator Feinstein and Senator Cornyn announced on our broadcast that they have decided to request that President Bush commute the sentences of Ramos and Compean. The family of Ignacio Ramos watched and listened to the senators make their announcement in our Washington, D.C., bureau, and they were moved to tears. They weren't alone.

Patrolling the border is an increasingly dangerous job, as the nearly two thousand attacks against our agents prove. Not surprisingly, the Border Patrol is having a hard time filling its ranks, and is spending almost a million dollars trying to recruit six thousand new agents. To get the word out and improve its visibility in the marketplace, the Border Patrol signed a twenty-five-race sponsorship deal and placed its emblem on a race car, in hopes of finding potential candidates among the NASCAR audience. Not everyone thinks this is a particularly good idea or use of taxpayer dollars; the Border Patrol union and other agents are furious that those funds aren't going toward strengthening law enforcement. In its first race the Border Patrol NASCAR racer finished twenty-fifth, an inauspicious beginning and an irony not lost on anyone. I only hope that justice soon prevails for Ramos and Compean.

While the federal government is seemingly eager to prosecute federal agents protecting our borders, it appears determined to leave those borders wide open and our immigration laws unenforced. Across the country states and municipalities have stepped into the breach, trying to fight back against the impact of illegal immigration and the federal government's abrogation of its responsibilities. More than 140 relevant laws and ordinances were passed at the state and local level in 2007. The open borders and amnesty special interests are fighting those efforts in court, led by the American Civil Liberties Union.

No case attracted more national attention than that of Hazleton,

Pennsylvania. In the summer of 2007 a federal court ruled that Hazleton's Illegal Immigration Relief Act, which aimed to hold landlords and employers responsible if they did business with illegal aliens, is unconstitutional. More than 120 communities across the country have passed similar legislation and local laws.

The court ruled that Hazleton had no right to enact any ordinances dealing with illegal immigration because they interfered with or violated federal law. Federal District Court Judge Munley wrote: "Whatever frustrations . . . City of Hazleton [Pennsylvania] may feel about the current state of federal immigration enforcement, the nature of the political system in the United States prohibits the city from enacting ordinances that disrupt a carefully drawn federal statutory scheme. . . . Even if federal law did not conflict with Hazleton's measures, the city could not enact an ordinance that violates rights the constitution guarantees to every person in the United States, whether legal resident or not." The ruling cheered the plaintiffs, who immediately claimed that it sent a clear message to other communities across the country.

That ruling, however, only inspired Hazleton mayor Lou Barletta to fight back. As he said on our broadcast the night the decision was handed down: "I'm very disappointed . . . that Judge Munley has ruled against all legal residents of the City of Hazleton. This fight is far from over. I have said it many times before, that Hazleton is not going to back down." Barletta said he wasn't at all surprised by the decision: "The judge has really shown throughout the course of this trial that he was not in favor of what the City of Hazleton was doing. And I say that just by the fact that some of the illegal aliens who were suing the City of Hazleton who have gone by the name of John and Jane Doe, their identities were protected by the judge. They did not have to show up for the trial. I never saw the people who were suing us. And, obviously, I feel that this was an injustice not only to the city, but to those around the country." Most state legislatures have subsequently begun considering or have acted to curtail the impact of illegal immigration, and the court battles are only beginning.

Our illegal immigration and border security crisis has been building for more than four decades. In signing the Immigration and Nationality

Act of 1965 into law, President Lyndon Johnson promised it would not be revolutionary or affect the lives of millions, even as it overturned sixty years of U.S. immigration policy of national origin quotas and led to the creation of explosive chain migration.

Twenty-one years later, President Ronald Reagan signed into law amnesty for more than three million illegal aliens who had entered the country. President Reagan then promised that new employer sanctions would "remove the incentive for illegal immigration by eliminating the job opportunities," and that the law's amnesty provision would allow millions who were hiding in the shadows to "step into the sunlight."

And now, after another twenty-one years, we hear the same language, as the proamnesty and open borders advocates demand that American citizens ignore history, reason, and the national interest. They are again marketing the same false assurances about border enforcement and insist there will be no social or economic cost to the taxpayer or the nation. A record of more than four decades of disruptive and destructive immigration policy initiatives should be a sufficient history lesson for all Americans.

Illegal immigration has, in fact, the potential to change the course of American history. Demographers at the Brookings Institution and the Population Reference Bureau paint a troubling picture of the future of our democracy. As more illegal aliens cross our borders and settle in large states like California, Texas, and Florida, congressional seats will be redistributed to these bigger states following each decennial census. States with low levels of immigration will ultimately lose seats as a result. Unfortunately for American citizens, this seismic shift in political representation will be decided by noncitizens who cannot vote.

There's no question that this type of mass immigration would have a calamitous effect on working citizens and their families. Carol Swain, professor of law and political science at Vanderbilt University and author of Debating Immigration, would like to see more people speak up for the sectors of society most affected by illegal immigration.

When I talked to her on the show, she asked, "How many African-

American leaders have you seen come out and address the impact that high levels of illegal immigration [are] having in the communities when it comes to jobs, when it comes to education, when it comes to health care? And often, these low-skilled, low-wage workers compete in the same sectors for jobs."

President Bush's repeated exhortations that "the American people" need to get behind his plan reveal, on some level, his awareness that the American public is united against his legislation. Yet his rhetoric, and that of so many of our country's elites, makes it sound as if the working people of this nation are in conflict with one another over this issue. President Bush stated that "America should not fear diversity." These are the words of neither a leader nor a uniter. Senate majority leader Harry Reid referred to an amendment to make English the official language of the country as an act of prejudice, stating bluntly that "this amendment is racist." Even though 84 percent of all Americans and 71 percent of Hispanics say that English should be the official language of government operations, Reid used his position to make a divisive statement. Nonsense like this from national leaders is unworthy of their offices and fails to elevate the American spirit.

Divisiveness begins in Washington, not in the hearts of Americans. Are we as a nation well served by a Congress that created the Albanian Issues Caucus, the Congressional Asian Pacific American Caucus, the Congressional Black Caucus, the Organic Caucus, the Caucus on Indonesia, the Caucus on Swaziland, the Congressional Israel Allies Caucus, or the Congressional Caucus on India and Indian Americans?

Five decades ago, there were only four congressional caucuses. Today there are approximately two hundred, most of which are dedicated solely to particular countries, regions, races, ethnicities, specific issues, and special interests. We would be better served if we rid Congress of these spurious and divisive caucuses that serve narrowly focused special interest groups and instead create the "We the People" Caucus.

The American people are in danger of being relegated by the establishment orthodoxy to irrelevance, and our national sovereignty to history's dustbin. The American people would likely rise up in revolt if our political and business leaders were to publicly and openly express their desire to integrate the economies of Mexico, the United States, and Canada, and effectively remove our common borders. In fact, the so-called Security and Prosperity Partnership officially aims to do just that by the year 2010. The Security and Prosperity Partnership was launched in March 2005 and is designed to harmonize regulations in North America; the word "harmonize" appears frequently. This is, no matter what anyone claims, a very serious and unprecedented challenge to the sovereignty of our nation. And it's happening without the knowledge, and certainly without the approval, of the American people or the consent of Congress.

According to the SPP's official Web site, "The SPP is a White House–led initiative among the United States and the two nations it borders—Canada and Mexico—to increase security and to enhance prosperity among the three countries through greater cooperation. The SPP is based on the principle that our prosperity is dependent on our security and recognizes that our three great nations share a belief in freedom, economic opportunity, and strong democratic institutions." Unofficially the SPP is about creating a North American Union, and diminishing the sovereignty of each of the three countries involved.

In May 2005 the Council on Foreign Relations published a report titled "Building a North America Community." Among the goals it expressed was to break down trade regulations between the United States and Canada, between Canada and Mexico, and, of course, between Mexico and the United States. All this has been explored without congressional approval and certainly without congressional oversight or voter approval. In the report, the president of the Council on Foreign Relations, Richard Haass, states, "The Task Force's central recommendation is establishment by 2010 of a North American economic and security community, the boundaries of which would be defined by a common external tariff and an outer security perimeter."

In June 2005 we reported on the show that a task force was already proposing a way to unify the three countries of North America into a European Union–style coalition. You may be thinking, *Wait a minute, we didn't approve that*. You would be right. No one else has, either, and very few people in the media outside of our broadcast are reporting on this topic.

I invited Robert Pastor, a longtime proponent of North American community, and one of the primary architects of the plan, to appear on the show in 2007. He told me, "The United States, Canada, and Mexico now are already the largest free-trade area in the world. We have $800 billion worth of trade. This is a source of comparative advantage for the United States. But the council report feels that we could take greater advantage if we were [to] deepen economic integration, if we can secure ourselves better, not only at our borders, but also by thinking about continental security perimeter as well." When I asked why a common security perimeter was viable when the United States does not have secure ports nor does it have anything approaching secure borders, he responded, "It's precisely because our ports are not secure and our borders are not secure that we need to find not only better ways to do that, but also better ways to turn our two neighbors into partners to enhance our security and to enhance our prosperity, as well."

This goes far beyond border security or continental security. Pastor has proposed a North American Trade Tribunal, which in practice would take precedence over the Supreme Court in certain cases pertaining to the union; a North American Customs and Immigration Force, which would have authority over the U.S. Immigration and Customs Enforcement agency; and a North American Inter-Parliamentary group, which would be able to act without interference from the U.S. Congress in setting up the union. As he told a Senate subcommittee, "The North American Council should develop an integrated continental plan for transportation and infrastructure that includes new North American highways and high-speed rail corridors." That sounds suspiciously like the blueprint for a NAFTA Superhighway, doesn't it?

Pastor was one of the speakers at a conference called the North American Forum, which convened in September 2006 in Banff, Canada. Discussions there included an integrated energy and transportation structure, a standard North American tariff on imports, and the beginnings of a plan to prop up parts of Mexico's infrastructure with

U.S. taxpayer money. Members of each government held meetings—which the press was not allowed to cover—to discuss the benefits of a possible union. I found it rather curious that the organization Judicial Watch could obtain information about this gathering only by going through the Freedom of Information Act, but what they found was more than a little disturbing. One of the notes from the conference contained this incredible sentence: "While a vision is appealing, working on the infrastructure might yield more benefit and bring more people on board, evolution by stealth."

Stealth? I'm not a big fan of stealth when it comes to the public's right to know and the issue of our national sovereignty. I prefer sunlight and public debate on issues of national policy and the potential integration of the United States with other countries. It's messy that way, but then, it's the American way. Elitists like quiet evolution of policy created in the dark, where it will remain away from the prying eyes of the press and the public. When individuals start taking on supergovernmental initiatives without either the approval or the direction of elected officials, it becomes more than a little problematic. The fact of the matter is that government relations are defined by our Constitution, while this is an attempt to integrate economies without the approval of the elected officials of the country and without transparency of any kind.

Why should anyone in this country, Mexico, or Canada, presuming they're interested in the sovereign rights and power of their respective nations, tolerate this kind of elitist nonsense?

Cliff Kincaid, the editor of the "Accuracy In Media Report," had this to say on the show: "Lou, I have been here in Washington, D.C., for almost thirty years, and this story about the submersion of U.S. sovereignty to this emerging trilateral entity, the North American community, the North American Union, whatever you want to call it, seems to be the story of our lifetimes. It is simply incredible.

"I've seen literature out of the people behind us who even envision a North American Supreme Court with the ability to overrule our own Supreme Court . . . this started, really, under President Clinton. It follows from NAFTA. It's been continued and expanded under President

Bush to the Security and Prosperity Partnership. So you have a bipartisan consensus in favor of it.

"The Democrats like eliminating the borders between the three countries because they see potential voters coming out of Mexico. The Republicans see benefits because big business, one of their big constituencies, sees cheap labor and resources from Mexico and even Canada to be exploited.

"So both parties, in other words, Lou, have a vested interest in keeping this all hushed up."

While Congress has done nothing to investigate the forces at work behind the SPP and the North American Union, more and more states and concerned citizens are fighting back. Fourteen states have already proposed legislation against the SPP and are introducing bills to prevent the United States from participation in the SPP at all.

Americans face substantial challenges and rising threats, and too many of those challenges and threats are not external, but come from within our own society and political system. We need to assert ourselves as citizens now, demand that our elected officials act to fully secure our borders and ports. Without that security, there can be no control of immigration and, therefore, no meaningful reform of immigration law. We need to enforce existing immigration laws, and that includes the prosecution of the employers of illegal aliens. As Senator Claire McCaskill (D-Missouri) put it, illegal employers are the magnet that draws illegal aliens across our border. Enforcing the law against illegal aliens at large in the country, and against those who employ them, will mean bolstering, in all respects, the Immigration and Customs Enforcement agency.

Our government should fund, equip, and hire the people necessary to man the Citizenship and Immigration Services to ensure that the agency is capable of fully executing and administering lawful immigration into the United States and eliminating the shameful backlog of millions of people who are seeking legal entry into this country.

Those three steps are necessary to assure the security of the nation and the effective administration and enforcement of existing immigration laws. They should be considered nonnegotiable conditions precedent to any change or reform of existing immigration laws.

At the same time, the president and Congress should order exhaustive studies of the economic, social, and fiscal effects of the leading proposals to change or reform immigration law, and foremost in their consideration should be the well-being of American workers and their families. Any thoughtful redrafting of our immigration laws should include public hearings held throughout the nation and a robust investigation of all the important issues that surround our illegal immigration crisis, with fact-finding that is both rigorous and thorough. The process will be time-consuming and will demand much of our congressmen and senators, their staffs, and relevant executive agencies.

The importance of securing borders and ports and reforming our immigration laws is profound, and that security is fundamental to the future of our nation. That future can be realized only with a complete commitment to a comprehensive legislative process of absolute transparency and open public forums in which our elected officials hear the voices of the people they represent. American citizens deserve no less.

10

Eating Our Young

Let us think of education as the means of developing our greatest abilities, because in each of us there is a private hope and dream which, fulfilled, can be translated into benefit for everyone and greater strength for our nation.

—John F. Kennedy

We have acted for too long as if the miserable state of public education is someone else's problem. It is not; it is a problem that all of us face as a nation, and we must confront it together.

The essence of the American Dream is the reasonable expectation of parents that their children will have the opportunity to build a better life. But for millions of American parents that expectation either no longer exists or is no longer a reasonable one. I wish I could say that their concern is misplaced, but again, the facts are irrefutable. For the first time more Americans are expressing uncertainty about the future of their children and the opportunities that await them. A Pew Research study in 2006 revealed that only a third of all Americans believe that their children will be better off. The American Dream is dimming for millions of American families.

I believe that a number of factors explain the stagnation of working wages and a rising sense of anxiety and frustration in our middle class. Corporate America is undeterred in its determination to outsource middle-class jobs and to import cheap foreign labor, while our government is representing neither the interest of our people nor that of our nation. The divide between the wealthy and privileged and the middle class and those who aspire to it is widening. A 2007 Pew Research study found not only that the American family's income has failed to keep up with productivity growth since 2000, but that working men in their thirties today earn less than men in their thirties did in 1974. As recently as a decade ago, young working men were earning more than their fathers.

When American families can no longer be assured of their children's opportunity to build better lives than their parents, when the encroaching economic reality denies hope and optimism to our nation's working men and women and their families, the success of the very nation is in doubt.

Today we invest far more money in our elderly than in our young. We spend far more on nursing homes and Medicare than we do on our public schools and universities. Our Congress and president create laws such as No Child Left Behind and then not only leave hundreds of thousands of our students behind, but make it impossible for them ever to catch up. Teaching our children is no longer a priority to which our nation is committed.

Many, if not most, communities have simply lost control of their public schools and the young people who are their students. Millions of us have not only neglected our roles as citizens and failed to participate in school board and city council meetings, but also allowed our roles in the lives of our children to be diminished. Too many of us have allowed our sense of responsibility for our children to end at the doors to our homes. And too many of our children lack either respect or regard for family, for one another, for their teachers, or for society. When it comes to our youth, our society is more permissive than tolerant, and more neglectful than involved, and not only our children, but our society and the nation will bear the consequences of our failure to meet our responsibilities.

The danger signs are all around us, and yet we are not responding to the obvious need to prepare youths for the many tests and challenges that await them as adults and as citizens. Whether in our conduct as parents or in our conduct as citizens, we are more than failing our young people, we are devouring their potential and their promise to live the American Dream.

I don't know a single person who doesn't want our children to inherit a nation that is better than the one we grew up in. I have two sons and two daughters, now all but grown, who mean the world to me. My wife and I did our best to bring them up with good, traditional American family values, to be responsible and respectful, cooperative and passionate, to tell the truth and work hard, and to be independent. We didn't always succeed, and like most parents, we've shared plenty of late nights wondering why one of our kids took up our lesson of independence better than he did our lesson of responsibility.

Most parents try, as the saying goes, to give their kids roots and give them wings. But millions of young people are being denied the opportunity to realize their potential and build lives of which they can be proud. They need us to provide guidance and support, yet we are failing them on many levels: as parents, fellow citizens, and educators. We are allowing the lowest common denominator to become the standard of behavior for too many of our youth and failing to prepare them for a responsible, productive life in American society.

Too many of our homes and schools are no longer a safe refuge for our children from drugs, violence, and vulgarity. Schools are not only failing to educate many of our children but are also unable to teach civility and require discipline of students as a simple condition of their attendance. Many of our public schools, whether elementary or high school, out of a warped sense of political correctness fail to even prepare their students for competition in the real world.

An increasing number of schools have done away with valedictorians, salutatorians, and class rankings. Schools in Annapolis, Maryland; Minneapolis, Minnesota; Toledo, Ohio; Palm Beach, Florida; and Burlington, Vermont, are among those that have all chosen to honor groups of students instead of individuals. Why would school boards, superintendents, and principals fail to honor excellence? Administrators explain that they don't want to single out any particular student for achievement and success, concerned that it would be an emotional affront to students who weren't at the top of their class. Those students shouldn't have to be reminded that someone else worked harder and accomplished more than they did. I'm afraid that the reason so many schools have decided not to recognize achievement is that the school itself is not committed to providing the best possible education, and is not committed to the highest standards in teaching. I hope I'm wrong.

Life is competitive, and our schools should be as well. Educational administrators should be saluting outstanding students, praising them and supporting them, and they should be held up as outstanding examples. Honoring excellence, hard work, and accomplishment is, in my opinion, one of those important countervailing influences to the base and the negative, which are unfortunately also part of the reality that our children are inheriting.

Our public schools are too often guided by school boards that are not engaged by the parents of students, who should be demanding better of themselves, school administrators, and teachers, and certainly our children. The poor performance of public education in this country will require tremendous investment to prepare and train a new generation of administrators and teachers who are better equipped and certainly far better paid for their performance in their critically important social role.

While educators blame parents in large measure for the failure of public education, it is important for all of us to understand that parenting, always a tough and demanding responsibility, is an all but impossible task for many. The sad fact is that America's traditional family structure is collapsing. More of our kids are the product of divorce and are often raised by only one of their parents. The number of households headed by single parents has nearly doubled in less than forty years. Almost ten and a half million of those households are single-mother families, while another two and half million are families headed by a single father. Those single parents are usually working full-time, often with second jobs just to make ends meet, and are hard-pressed to give sufficient attention to their children and to their children's schools.

Also disturbing is just how many children are born out of wedlock and have never had the benefit of a two-parent family. More than a third of all babies in America are born to unwed mothers. That's one and a half million children each year. Forty years ago, just over 3 percent of white infants and 24 percent of black infants were born to single mothers. Today, those rates have risen to almost 25 percent of white infants born out of wedlock, more than 46 percent of Hispanic babies, and 69 percent of black infants. These statistics reveal nothing less than a national tragedy, because birth out of wedlock is a consistent predictor of both educational and economic achievement.

Unfortunately the children of unwed mothers are not only denied the nurture and support of the traditional family but they are almost invariably poor. Only 8 percent of married households with two or more kids under eighteen are poor in this country, while 52 percent of never-married households are impoverished. It's even worse for younger kids. In those married households with children under the age of six, 11.5 percent are living in poverty. An astounding 62.4 percent of the homes with never-marrieds raising children under the age of six are living below the poverty line. Nearly two thirds of the babies born to unwed mothers are likely to live their lives in poverty. Our 2008 presidential candidates, Republicans and Democrats in Congress, or for that matter, the national media, are not focusing on the profound societal impact of these single-parent families and the impact of their children in the public school system.

In the late 1960s it became politically correct to refer to the poor as "disadvantaged." But I believe we have to be honest enough to describe the children of single-parent families and impoverished households as both disadvantaged *and* poor. And as Americans we should be urgently undertaking an examination of the root causes of such societal and economic dysfunction and doing whatever is necessary in our communities and nation to end what is nothing less than a shameful waste of young American lives.

There is additional troubling evidence of our society's failure to come to terms with the reality of twenty-first-century America. Not only are more of our children growing up in single-parent families, but more of our young adults are living longer with their parents. Today, 56 percent of men and 43 percent of women ages eighteen to twenty-four live with their parents. An estimated 65 percent of recent college graduates moved back in with their parents, and 11 percent of adults between twenty-five and thirty-four live in their parents' households.

These statistics reflect a number of factors, including economic hardship, inadequate education and preparation for the workplace, and our failure to promote traditional ideals of self-reliance and independence. I believe we need to invest far more in education, because it is the great equalizer in our society. While I also believe we need to spend far more on the training and education of our teachers, there is no doubt that money is neither the principal problem nor an automatic solution.

We are now spending nearly $9,000 per student each year in our public schools—more than twice what we spent as recently as thirty years ago. That is more than countries like Germany, France, Japan, and the United Kingdom spend—all of whose students outrank Americans in educational testing. Canada spends only $5,947, Japan spends $5,913, and Finland spends barely $5,000 annually on each student— and their kids are better educated than ours. Spending itself is clearly not a guarantee of educational excellence: Based on international reading tests, Ireland, Iceland, and New Zealand also outperformed America while spending far less per student. The United States is ranked seventh in education, tied for that less-than-stellar position with Australia, Belgium, and Denmark.

Too often the money that we *are* spending on education does not accurately reflect what is actually earmarked to teach our students. In fact, typically less than half the amount spent on education in the United States goes to the classroom or teaching. Too much, unfortunately, goes directly to sustaining an already bloated bureaucracy. We are wasting not only the educational opportunity of our young, but much of the money we're spending on their behalf.

Unfortunately, the money that actually does make its way into the classroom is not being put to good use. Our eighth-graders receive lower science and math scores than their peers from fourteen other nations and lower science scores then their peers in eight other nations. Our high school seniors perform below the international average for twenty-one countries on general knowledge in math and science. Our proud nation ranks twenty-fifth out of forty-one industrialized nations in math and science. That puts us squarely in the lower half of rankings.

Less than 40 percent of our public school math teachers have an academic degree in the field they are teaching. More than half of middle school math teachers have never even had a calculus course. How are these teachers supposed to help students learn the fundamentals of mathematics—let alone instill a sense of passion or excitement in the subject—if they've never been thoroughly trained in the subject themselves?

A Business–Higher Education Forum report from 2007 highlights the dire need for mathematics and science teachers at the middle school and high school levels. That report projects a national shortfall of more than 280,000 math and science teachers by 2015. The group recommends creating a comprehensive package of incentives including scholarships, signing bonuses, and differential pay to attract these teachers.

We need better compensation for schoolteachers, and we need better school environments for our children. School buildings themselves are in a sorry state of disrepair, part of a larger problem with crumbling infrastructure that we're facing in the United States. The American Society of Civil Engineers, in its 2005 Infrastructure Report Card, gave the state of our schools a D. According to the ASCE, "The Federal government has not assessed the condition of America's schools since 1999, when it estimated that $127 billion was needed to bring facilities to good condition. Other sources have since reported a need as high as $268 billion. Despite public support of bond initiatives to provide funding for school facilities, without a clear understanding of the need, it is uncertain whether schools can meet increasing enrollment demands and the smaller class sizes mandated by the No Child Left Behind Act."

Our schools need more than a quarter of a trillion dollars worth of maintenance to bring them up to "good" condition and a B grade—not even an exceptional or excellent B-plus or A. How can we say that as a nation we take education seriously when our officials haven't taken the time, and we haven't spent the money, to make sure our kids are getting decent facilities? As a nation, we must understand that the deterioration in our public school system must be reversed, that there is no more urgent domestic policy issue, and that all levels of government must take the initiative to restore our public schools to meet our simplest obligations to our children.

School budgets are determined by local property taxes and bond issues. In many communities an increasing number of the residents are baby boomers moving into their "empty nester" phase. It is estimated that there are about 30 million empty nesters in America, and once their kids have left the school system they are typically not interested in public education. In addition, many of the oldest baby boomers—and certainly their parents—are dependent on fixed incomes. They don't want higher property taxes, nor do they want to pay for a new school bond issue. Since older and retired people vote with a fair amount of consistency—and more than three quarters of citizens sixty-five and older are registered, giving them the highest registration rate of any age group—they're almost certain to vote against anything that eats into their income.

Such short-sightedness on the part of our citizens ensures that the next generation will be underserved, as will the generations to follow. In addition students who do not receive the educational resources they need will be facing a corporate culture in America that is increasingly hostile to American workers. The nation's business elites claim that they cannot find enough skilled Americans to do the specialized jobs they require, and thus they insist on ever more immigration visas. Those elites do not, however, talk about ways in which increasingly profitable big business might offer assistance to underfunded public education.

Nearly every educational authority in whom I have confidence points to three essential reforms that must take place in our public schools: 1) We must eliminate classroom overcrowding, 2) we must reestablish strict discipline in our schools and our classrooms, and 3) we must better educate, motivate, and provide incentives for the teachers of our children in every grade from K through 12.

Even achieving those goals, however critically necessary, is not sufficient. One out of every three students drops out of our public high schools each year. For blacks and Hispanics, the dropout rate is 50 percent. A high school degree no longer assures preparation for our competitive twenty-first-century workplace, but high school drop-outs are almost four times as likely to live a life of poverty as high school graduates.

Once we allow a student to drop out of high school, we are consigning him or her to a life that seldom gets better and typically gets worse. The Alliance for Excellent Education estimates that each high school dropout earns about $260,000 less than a high school graduate over his or her lifetime. The alliance also reports that dropouts not only earn less money but also drain state and federal budgets through their dependence on social and welfare programs. Increasing the male graduation rate a mere 5 percent would add $2.8 billion in earnings to the U.S. economy. Those students who drop out make up nearly half the heads of households on welfare, and Justice Department data show high school dropouts make up 75 percent of America's state prison inmates, almost 59 percent of federal inmates, and 69 percent of those in jail. The overall cost to our society is overwhelming.

A June 2007 report by *Education Week* revealed that more than 1.2 million students failed to graduate high school this year. The same report indicates that Detroit's public high schools will graduate only 25 percent of their students. Cleveland and Baltimore will graduate less than 35 percent; Dallas, New York, and Los Angeles about 45 percent. In fact, ten of our nation's biggest cities will graduate fewer than half their students. This is nothing less than a national crisis. We are deluding ourselves if we view it as anything less.

About forty thousand kids drop out of Los Angeles high schools each year. Los Angeles has as many students dropping out of its schools as the entire student body of the schools in Buffalo, New York. Nowhere is the futility of simply spending money more apparent than in Los Angeles. The L.A. school budget has risen more than 50 percent in the past four years, from $8 billion in 2004 to an estimated $13 billion, and its graduation rate continues to fall.

Christopher Swanson, director of the Editorial Projects in Education Research Center and supervisor of the *Education Week* national dropout rate report, said of these findings: "I think that really speaks to the challenge of getting students to graduate from high school at a time where it's more important than it's ever been . . . to provide opportunities for our young people to have a successful career and for the United States in general to be competitive in the world." I believe that quality elementary and high school education is essential in preparing our young people to be decent, responsible, and productive members of our society. And we are failing miserably.

Nowhere is the situation worse than in Detroit, Michigan, and nowhere is the high cost of so-called free-trade policies and incompetent corporate management more glaring. Detroit's economy and community have been devastated by the loss of tens of thousands of jobs, and the disappearance of too many mothers and fathers from the lives of their children. Detroit is a city in pain, and the city's future is uncertain. And despite the best efforts of local and state leaders, hope is in short supply. When I talked to Detroit's mayor, Kwame Kilpatrick, about the challenges he and his community faced, he acknowledged, "We need immediate national action, similar to the way that we went out and went into action, sprung into action in the Middle East. We need the same kind of national effort with American schools. There's no reason why we're not coming in and diversifying how we teach children. We have jobs in Detroit: nursing jobs, computer technology jobs, jobs in many fields. But how do you move a family that's been in the plant for twenty years into that type of field? How do you change the way education is taught? . . . I don't argue with the [graduation] number. I mean, sure, we think it is slightly higher, but this is a problem. It's a crisis. And we need America and the state to respond as such. No longer can we use excuses like we're teaching to the tests. Come on now. We have to teach our children and create a way to get them to where they need to be. . . ."

Mayor Kilpatrick is trying to lead his city in the worst of circumstances and times but is committed to progress. Admitting that there is a problem is a big step; too many school districts have been reporting misleading numbers or denying that problems exist.

Partisan politics and ideology have subsumed both intelligent analysis of and public policy proposals to deal with our failing public schools. The little dialogue that does exist about the public school crisis is given over to loud discussion of the No Child Left Behind Act, school choice or vouchers, and the merits and inadequacies of magnet and charter schools.

Charter schools are similar to public schools but have some notable differences. While they are funded by taxpayer dollars, they have an average enrollment of less than three hundred students per school, use innovative teaching methods to help those students (especially those who have not performed well in traditional public schools), and feature longer days, longer school years, strict discipline, and customized curricula. Parents can select which school they send their children to based on the school's mission or curriculum. A high percentage of students in charter schools are considered at-risk kids or have dropped out of the public school system.

Most important, charter schools are accountable to either the local school boards or government for both their financial and their academic performance. If they do not live up to stated goals, which are usually set higher than those for traditional public schools, the charter of these schools can be revoked. And charter schools offer something that public schools cannot—parents can withdraw their child from the school if they are not happy with the education their student is receiving.

Though charter schools have met with support from elected officials in both the Democratic and Republican parties, including Presidents Clinton and Bush, the schools face criticism from those who believe all public education money should go to traditional public schools and the teachers who work in them. There is also the concern that those charter schools that are run for profit will, like Corporate America, operate with a singular focus on the bottom line and sacrifice the needs of students in order to attain financial goals. However, since these schools have specific standards to meet in order to continue their operations, their regulation would appear to be more stringent than that applied to the vast majority of public schools. Accountability in our schools, be it at the administrative or the teacher level, is, to my mind, sorely lacking.

In evaluating our schools, we also need to look more closely at the benefits of magnet schools, which offer specialized curricula as part of the public school system. Students with exceptional aptitude or interest in particular subject areas attend magnet schools and receive focused and intensive instruction in those subjects. Such schools, often found in large urban public school systems, provide students with the opportunity to excel in disciplines such as science, engineering, or even vocational skills, which might receive only cursory coverage in their usual classrooms. Magnet schools also enable exceptional students, those who are least served by large classes and standardized lesson plans, to move at a pace that will encourage and inspire them. Overcrowded classes cannot advance at the speed of exceptional kids, because others would get left behind. Magnet schools provide a solution to nurturing those kids who are not given the attention they need, ironically enough, because they are moving faster than other students in their class. Not paying attention to their unique classroom needs is as much of an educational failing as not attending to those kids who need help and attention in order to keep up.

In my opinion school choice is the only rational policy response to our public education crisis. And by school choice, I do not mean vouchers. I do mean that we must choose to make our public schools work for our students, we must inspire students and offer incentives for them to learn, and we must raise both the quality and the pay of teachers to educate our youth. Every single political candidate for election, whether for the office of president or the local school board, should be required to address our national public education crisis and declare his or her proposals for reversing our educational decline. But there must be a commitment on the part of all of us to become engaged with our schools and our school boards, by attending meetings or making our voices heard at the ballot box.

11

Nation in Denial

Let us not forget who we are. Drug abuse is a repudiation of everything America is. The destructiveness and human wreckage mock our heritage.

—Ronald Reagan

The war on drugs has cost more American lives than our wars in Iraq and Afghanistan, the war on terror, and the Vietnam War combined. The number of our dead and wounded in this struggle increases each day. But there is no government department or agency responsible for reporting its daily casualties, and there is no U.S. government strategy to win this bloody conflict. Our establishment elites apparently consider the staggering loss of American lives to be acceptable, and the mounting financial and economic costs to be a reasonable price for the nation to pay to preserve open borders and ports and to assure unimpeded international commerce and trade.

America's war on drugs has been waged by our federal government as little more than a holding action, and federal, state, and local law enforcement are forced to fight as a rear guard in our national retreat from the fearsome assault on our children, schools, neighborhoods, communities, and nation.

America is battling not only drug dealers, distributors, traffickers, and cartels, but also ourselves. We are permitting the destruction of millions of American lives because we also lack the knowledge and understanding to treat and to cure addiction and the social forces that not only permit but often encourage drug and alcohol addiction. We are losing the war on drugs on both fronts, and a new threat in that war has been opened by legal pharmaceuticals, which are increasingly prescribed to millions of us as painkillers and antianxiety and antidepression drugs. The consumers of those drugs are increasingly America's youth. Our drug dependence is truly becoming a national dependency of frightening proportions.

Pharmaceutical companies are now one of the country's largest advertisers in all forms of media. Prime-time television is saturated with their advertising for panacea drugs for everything from restlessness, insomnia, anxiety, and attention deficits to depression. The drug companies once relied on extensive networks of salesmen to sell and distribute their products to physicians, hospitals, and pharmacies, and marketed those products primarily with advertisements in trade and professional magazines, health care journals, and conferences and conventions. But that all changed a decade ago. In 1997 the FDA offered the pharmaceutical industry new options for advertising on broadcast media. Up until that point, if a drug company named a drug and what it was used for during a TV or radio ad, the law required that the company also cite the drug's potential risks, as was done in print ads. The drug makers sidestepped that condition by running ads without mentioning the actual purpose of the pill. Because ads for drugs like Claritin were being aired without telling viewers and listeners what the drug did—usually just a caution to "check with your doctor"—consumers were confused about their use and what they should be asking their doctors about.

Seeking to clear the air, the FDA loosened the advertising rules and required only minor mention of side effects and risk. This decision thrilled the pharmaceutical companies, and soon words like Viagra and Lipitor became part of the American lexicon and were firmly established in the public consciousness. And for good reason: according to the Government Accountability Office, "Drug company spending on DTC [direct-to-consumer] advertising—such as that on television and in magazines—of prescription drugs increased twice as fast from 1997 through 2005 as spending on promotion to physicians or on research and development." The number of TV ads for prescription drugs run between 1994 and 2000 increased forty-fold. The pharmaceutical industry, with a budget of hundreds of millions of dollars to influence Congress and government policy, employed two lobbyists for each representative and senator in Congress, and their investments and efforts were handsomely rewarded.

The federal government gave the pharmaceutical industry basically free rein to market to consumers, and the overwhelming message it conveyed is that there is a single pill, or a cocktail of pills, that can cure whatever ails Americans. Consumers are inundated with these messages to the point that doctors can barely keep up with even the names of all the new drugs their patients are asking about and often demanding.

The Government Accountability Office states that "DTC advertising appears to increase prescription drug spending and utilization. Drugs that are promoted directly to consumers often are among the best-selling drugs, and sales for DTC-advertised drugs have increased faster than sales for drugs that are not heavily advertised to consumers. Most of the spending increase for heavily advertised drugs is the result of increased utilization, not price increases."

We may not be a nation of hypochondriacs, but we are quickly becoming a society that is accepting the media message that the normal pains, disappointments, fears, anxieties, and even depression that are part of any normal life are unacceptable burdens that the right prescription of the right pill can remedy or remove. Big Pharma encourages us to self-diagnose and urges us to seek out medication to the point that we are quickly becoming, in the judgment of many, an overmedicated society and a drug-dependent nation. Americans are popping pills to brighten their outlook, to calm themselves, to lose weight, and to manage the behavior of our children.

Almost half of all Americans are taking at least one prescribed medication. I'm not suggesting in any way that we shouldn't be grateful for the many scientific advances in the pharmaceutical industry that prolong and improve the quality of our lives. But it seems to be almost unimaginable that our society has become so infirm that fully half of us require treatment with drugs. A decade ago fewer than 40 percent of us were taking any prescription drugs. Now, nearly 20 percent of us are taking three or more prescription drugs—an increase of 50 percent in the last decade. It's a wonder we can even get through our days without all these drugs making us loopy.

We are also ensuring that the next generation of Americans will be even more drug dependent. The number of kids now on medication is staggering. Today, 24.2 percent of kids under eighteen are on meds of one kind or another. That's about 20 percent more than a decade ago. As the appropriateness of drugs to control hyperactivity among ever larger numbers of our children is being examined, some doctors are actually also using those drugs to treat overweight children. For example, CNN reported the story of an Illinois doctor who prescribes Adderall, an amphetamine intended to treat ADHD, to help children lose weight. The drug was neither designed nor intended for that purpose, but the doctor has prescribed Adderall to some eight hundred young people with their parents' full approval.

Television, newspapers, magazines, and the Web constantly document the high life of the rich and famous, which typically involves drinking and partying, and of course, these personalities are always glorified for their behavior. Hardly a day passes without a media story or a news report of an actor, singer, or some other celebrity driving drunk or stoned, having drugs found in their possession, entering rehab for treatment of drug and alcohol addiction, exiting rehab, or simply fleeing rehab.

Many celebrities have also been charged with using phony prescriptions to obtain prescription drugs, leading to a whole new culture of drug abuse: the illegal purchase of legal medication. It seems that no painkiller, antidepressant, or sleep medication is too obscure to be cited as a reason for celebrities to check into rehab or explain away bad public behavior.

While the abuse of prescription drugs is growing faster than alcohol and drug abuse, illegal drugs remain by far the greatest threat to our society. A longstanding war against illegal drugs that has been fought only halfheartedly and ineffectively has permitted what could easily be interpreted by our youth as a tacit acceptance and implied approval of America's drug culture. For many of our adolescents, in particular, the use of illegal drugs has become commonplace, a practice that either escapes the attention of their families or is indulged with the hope that it will end with maturity and an adult sense of responsibility. And the hopes of those parents and families are often not realized. In 2005, of adults ages eighteen to sixty-four who were employed full-time, 10.6 percent were classified as having a substance use disorder, and 2.4 percent had a substance use disorder accompanied by serious psychological distress. According to the Department of Labor, current illegal drug use almost doubled between 2002 and 2005 among people aged fifty to fifty-nine. Why? A significant percentage of the baby boomer generation hasn't escaped its addictive vices and is bringing them along into their later years.

A U.S. surgeon general's report found that underage drinking "is deeply embedded in the American culture, is often viewed as a rite of passage, is frequently facilitated by adults, and has proved stubbornly resistant to change." Even more shocking is the fact that the first drink almost never is taken in a bar: Only 7 percent of underage drinking occurs where alcohol is legally sold. Instead, it's happening at home, usually without the knowledge of parents, but too often with their acquiescence, and occasionally even with their complicity. We all know that parenting can be challenging, frustrating, and gut-wrenching, especially when we are uninformed, negligent, or worse, oblivious and indifferent.

Substance abuse and addiction are epidemic, and most of the victims of that epidemic are our youth. The number of teenagers now using illegal drugs is more than twice the level of the early 1990s. Nearly all of our kids are exposed at some time to marijuana, cocaine, ecstasy, crystal meth, and a host of other drugs, along with alcohol and cigarettes. The National Center on Addiction and Substance Abuse at Columbia University estimates that four and a half million teenagers have abused prescription drugs such as OxyContin, Vicodin, Ritalin, and Adderall.

Methamphetamines have become a national scourge. In a 2005 survey of five hundred law enforcement agencies, 48 percent stated that meth was their biggest drug problem. Twenty-two percent of the agencies cited cocaine, another 22 percent cited marijuana, and 3 percent reported heroin as their primary drug concern. Almost 90 percent of these agencies reported increasing numbers of arrests related specifically to meth beginning in 2002. Almost half of the counties surveyed claim that one in five inmates is locked up due to meth-related crimes, while 17 percent say that half their lockups are in for meth crimes.

One element of adolescent drug use has become so familiar as to barely register with us, and that's the abuse of alcohol. Teenage drinking plays a part in three of the leading causes of teen mortality: accidents, homicide, and suicide. More than two thousand kids between the ages of fifteen and twenty die every year in alcohol-related automobile accidents. Seventeen hundred college kids die each year of alcohol-related injuries. Nearly six hundred thousand more college students are injured in alcohol-related incidents.

Joseph Califano, chairman of the National Center on Addiction and Substance Abuse, has written an extremely important book that I think every parent and young person in the country should read. *High Society* is an outright call for this nation to wake up and sober up and recognize that substance abuse and addiction have become America's number-one serial killer and crippler. I've spoken with Califano many times about our society's failure even to acknowledge the war within and our inability to deal intelligently and effectively with drug and alcohol abuse, and the treatment and prevention of addiction. Califano put college drinking into perspective. While acknowledging that college kids will predictably drink, he notes that there has been a deadly change in drinking behavior on college campuses: "The troublesome thing is [that] there's been an increase in the intensity of drinking by college students. I mean . . . almost a quarter of our college students meet . . . the clinical medical criteria for alcohol or drug abuse addiction. And, you know, this is wasting the best and the brightest in this country and playing Russian roulette with them. I think . . . the atmosphere has got to be changed on college campuses. And our kids have got to come to realize that this is . . . the one thing they can do that can destroy their careers and sometimes destroy their lives."

America's youngest generation is plagued by illegal drugs that are coming into the country almost unimpeded. Our borders and ports remain wide open, while our drug enforcement and border security agencies remain understaffed, underfunded. After almost four decades of fighting the war on drugs, the DEA reports that approximately 65 percent of the cocaine entering the United States crosses our border with Mexico. In point of fact, Mexico's drug cartels are the principal source not only of cocaine, but also of the methamphetamines, marijuana, and heroin sold in this country.

Lack of border and port security is a primary reason that Colombia and Afghanistan, two of the prime exporters of heroin and cocaine, can successfully traffic and distribute their product throughout every state in this country. Despite overwhelming U.S. military force in Afghanistan, and the overthrow of the Taliban, the United States has chosen not to destroy the country's poppy fields, and today Afghanistan produces and exports 92 percent of the world's supply of illicit opium, from which heroin is derived. Opium accounts for just about half of Afghanistan's total GDP. The resurgence of the Taliban in Afghanistan hardly inspires hope that opium production will be curtailed or destroyed. Our "war on drugs" and our "war on terrorism" have converged in Afghanistan, and there is no doubt that U.S. policies in both wars remain separate, and success elusive, at best. Our president and our Congress have much to explain about their inability to deal decisively with both threats to the welfare and the lives of the American people.

While the government has fought a holding action in the war on drugs, our leaders conduct PR campaigns to distract public attention from what is nothing less than a catastrophic failure. John Walters, director of the White House Office of National Drug Control Policy, hails the Bush administration's antidrug policies, which he claims have led to a decline in drug abuse and improvements in our physical and mental health. On February 13, 2007, Walters announced that "President Bush understands that illegal drugs rob our citizens of their dignity, health, and freedom. We owe a debt of gratitude to parents, community leaders, and law enforcement officers who have helped make our national drug problem smaller."

While he focused on a marginal decline in drug use, Walters did not mention a shocking rise in drug overdoses. The Centers for Disease Control and Prevention reported in 2007 that the number of unintentional drug overdoses nearly doubled over the course of five years, rising from 11,155 in 1999 to 19,838 in 2004. Fatal drug overdoses in teenagers and young adults more than doubled.

More than twenty-two million Americans were classified with substance abuse or dependence problems in 2005, according to the Substance Abuse and Mental Health Services Administration. Nearly eight thousand people are trying drugs for the first time every day—that's about three million a year. The majority of new users are younger than eighteen, and more than half of them are female.

As is often the case, the Bush administration and I don't appear to be looking at the same statistics. Or perhaps we just have different concerns. Or perhaps I simply have an unrealistic expectation of what our government leaders' responsibilities are to ensure all Americans "life, liberty, and the pursuit of happiness." How can anyone of any ideology, political persuasion, or religion who claims to value each and every American and treasure his or her rights as citizens tolerate our government's failure in the war on drugs?

What explanation or excuse can there be for any of us to ignore our government's failure to halt the destruction of so many young lives?

On *Lou Dobbs Tonight* we regularly cover our national crisis of substance abuse and in addition have featured a series of special reports titled "The War Within," in which we investigate the ways in which illegal drugs are trafficked, the violence of drug cartels, the role of corrupt and ineffective government, and occasionally the successes by law enforcement in the war on drugs.

While hundreds of thousands of our people are in prison for illegal drug use and dealing drugs, the national media does not hesitate to report without context or judgment what has become a routine cycle of celebrity partying, bizarre public behavior, arrests for drug and alcohol abuse, a requisite apology from the desperate star, starlet, or entertainer, and the seeking of refuge from both publicity and law enforcement in rehabilitation.

For the most part the rich, famous, and shameless escape responsibility and consequence for their actions, and nearly always the law. Drugs, pills, and booze claim the lives and potential of not only the poor but also the privileged. But as with nearly all aspects of our society, the divide between the poor and the privileged is wide. Working men and women and their families seldom have the money, time, or ability to parent their children as they would like, and they usually can't afford the rehabilitation clinics or counseling and therapy to help reclaim the lives of the young casualties of substance abuse and addiction.

On our show Congressman Jim Ramstad (R-Minnesota) told the audience that "of the 26 million addicts and alcoholics in the United States, including 3 million young people under twenty-one, only 17 percent . . . have access to treatment. But of the bigger number, the 26 million, about 8 million are on health plans that [are] allowed to discriminate. About 90 percent of health plans are allowed to erect discriminatory barriers to treatment that don't exist for treatment for physical diseases. Artificially high copayments, artificially high deductibles, limited treatment stays. The average treatment stay allowed by 90 percent of the health plans is seven days. Ask any chemical health professional and they'll tell you nobody, nobody can get on the road to recovery in seven days." In fact, most health care authorities say that the minimum period of care and treatment is thirty days. And even then, aftercare is a critical component of recovery from addiction.

The human cost of substance abuse and addiction is as heartbreaking as it is appalling. And the economic cost is staggering. Drug abuse and addiction cost the United States more than $180 billion per year. That estimate includes reduced worker productivity, health care expenses, and resources to address the consequences of drug-related crime. Substance abuse crime is responsible for another $100 billion each year and is rising at more than 5 percent annually. The numbers for alcohol abuse are astronomical: $185 billion per year. The cost of alcohol and drug abuse and addiction amounts to almost $400 billion each year.

In addition, more than 20 percent of the inmates in state prisons—over 250,000 individuals—have been incarcerated for drug-related offenses. At the federal level, more than half of all prisoners are drug offenders.

Incredibly none of our elected officials, whether Republican or Democrat, or the president or Congress, has produced a single initiative for this nation to prevail in our long-running, and losing, war on drugs. And as of this writing, not a single candidate for his or her party's presidential nomination has so much as addressed the war on drugs and substance abuse in this country, nor has any moderator of any of the presidential debates asked a question of any candidate that even touches upon these issues. The war on drugs must be won just as surely as America must win the war on terror, and our next president must commit every resource to ending substance and alcohol abuse and assuring the development of successful, fully accessible treatment of addiction for all Americans, regardless of economic or social circumstances.

This great national tragedy must be ended.

12

Media Madness

A popular government, without popular information, or the means of acquiring it, is but a prologue to a farce or a tragedy, or, perhaps both. And a people who mean to be their own governors, must arm themselves with the power which knowledge gives.

—James Madison

Media saturates our lives. We are bombarded throughout the day with its messages and imagery, whether at home, work, or play. And media sources continue to multiply and overwhelm us, if in no other way than by their sheer number: television, radio, newspapers, magazines, books, the Internet, e-mail, billboards, iPods, BlackBerries, cell phones, closed-circuit programming, video games, movies, advertising at the grocery store and the department store, blue-light specials, and those LCD screens in the seat backs and aisles of the airplanes in which we fly.

There is seemingly no escape from this nonstop barrage. Families trying to teach their children traditional values, and at least constrain the negative influences on their lives, have no way to compete with ubiquitous and irresistible media.

Murder in video games. Misogyny and rape in music lyrics. Implied sex in magazine ads and on billboards. Record companies paying big money to rappers who then tell interviewers that they wouldn't report a crime if they witnessed it. Paris Hilton, whose celebrity status is constructed on her wealth, youth, drunk driving, and a starring role in her own home porn movie, given the red-carpet treatment. The high-profile

191

publication of a hypothetical confession by O. J. Simpson, complete with TV interview. Twenty-four-hour news coverage of the drug-overdose death of Anna Nicole Smith and the paternity of her baby. The desperate news race to feature an accused child molester in a renewed frenzy over the JonBenét Ramsey murder case. Reality shows in which housemates gossip and scheme and lie to win game-show prizes. All are driven by the media's relentless quest for eyeballs and ears, trying to influence us to buy, to watch, to own, to lease, to entertain and amuse ourselves, and apparently only at the margin, to inform and educate.

As media expanded from traditional print to broadcast beginning in the 1920s, the U.S. government sought to ensure that media companies understood that the use of the airwaves was a right granted to them by the public. The frequencies that carried radio and TV programs were considered a limited resource owned by the public, and the privilege of using those frequencies required that the media create programs or allot time that served the public good. As each radio station—and later TV stations—was assigned frequencies in cities and towns all across the nation, addressing matters of public interest was both an obligation and a duty.

Broadcasters aired their programming and news in the communities in which they were based. Issues presented on the air were of both immediate and lasting importance to the audience, and reflected the concerns of the local population. Citizens tuned in knowing that a percentage of what they saw and heard was relevant to their families, neighbors, and towns.

Today, much of the news and entertainment production and programming we receive in our communities is centralized and national rather than local. Not only are most radio and TV stations that we consider local owned and operated by large media groups and corporations, but the content they broadcast is as homogenous and uniform throughout the country as McDonald's franchises.

For better or worse, ours has become a media society in which the technological ability to communicate instantly and all but universally has been less liberating and democratizing than limiting in the values and tastes the media seeks to inculcate and insidious in the values it both consciously and subconsciously denigrates and even destroys.

Political correctness is one of those values promoted insidiously by corporate America and big media, and free speech is the right most threatened by that promotion. Don Imus lost his radio and television shows when both CBS and MSNBC fired him in April 2007 for insulting and offensive remarks he made about the Rutgers women's basketball team. There is no question that Imus, whose job was to entertain his audience, was trying to be funny, and instead offended.

Imus's words went well beyond irreverent and inappropriate to offensive and absolutely unacceptable. A firestorm of public protest ensued, and Reverends Jesse Jackson and Al Sharpton immediately assumed the forefront of that protest, directing the outcry at CBS, MSNBC, and their advertisers. MSNBC, owned by NBC Universal and General Electric, canceled its simulcast of the Imus show on WFAN radio, and issued a statement that said: "What matters to us most is that the men and women of NBC Universal have confidence in the values we have set for this company. This is the only decision that makes that possible."

It took only a week for MSNBC to fire Imus, with CBS following the next day. For an entire week Imus had been front-page news, and the coverage was merciless. But not as merciless as Sharpton and Jackson, who neither accepted Imus's public apologies nor in any way conducted themselves as if they were capable of making a mistake, let alone sinning. Imus lost his job because his critics, his corporate bosses, and the national media lost all sense of proportion.

As critical as I am of Imus's remarks, I believe his punishment was excessive. Both CBS and MSNBC should have suspended him for weeks, a month, or more, with appropriate recompense to the exemplary young women of Rutgers. But his firing was a cowardly corporate response to what appeared to be opportunism on the parts of Reverends Sharpton and Jackson. Both men have done good, and tried to do good, but in this case I believe they lost their way in the emotion of the moment, and could have accomplished much by tempering their demands.

Whether you like, dislike, or are indifferent to Don Imus as a radio commentator, you cannot ignore the good he has done as a man. I know of no other media personality who works as hard and gives as much of himself and his money to charities and causes that benefit children and our wounded troops. Losing all sense of proportion and balance, the news media devoured him.

Imus's career in recent years is particularly instructive, in that it straddled the often competing and nearly always contradictory interests of entertainment and news. News itself represents only a minute portion of media and entertainment, which has become such a massive force in our society and economy that movies are no longer the dominant sector of entertainment. Video games and Internet gaming are a far larger and more lucrative industry than Hollywood, while in television, entertainment shows dwarf news and information programming. There are now fewer than two dozen news and information channels on cable and satellite television—representing about 5 percent of what was to be the five-hundred-channel nirvana of the twenty-first century. And the Internet that a decade ago we thought would be an amazing and wondrous instrument of education and information may one day live up to its promise, but it remains today primarily a distribution network for e-mail, IMs, and pornography.

The media inundates us with images and messages of what it judges to be important in this country—whether the Imus controversy, Britney Spears in rehab, Barack Obama's Indonesian grade-school education—and forgoes investigation into our broader ills, such as drug addiction, illegal immigration, and port and border security. The media selects stories best designed to attract viewers, and when interest wanes, the stories disappear. There is no follow-up, rarely any conclusion. The media used to take pride in its investigative skills. That is no longer true. Investigation has given way to sensationalism and salaciousness.

The truth is that broader issues such as health care, privatization of our government, the miserable state of education, and a national drug crisis do matter to people in their daily lives. American working men and women are as concerned about the well-being of their families as they are about the state of our nation. The decisions made by corporate

America, politicians, and special interest groups have a significant effect on their lives. That's why our show covers these subjects with the same commitment and intensity day after day. Compared to the loss of three million jobs to outsourcing, the trials and tribulations of spoiled Hollywood celebrities are inconsequential. That other broadcasters prefer to spotlight such events over the plight of our nation's middle class is, of course, their prerogative.

I believe my viewers watch our show in order to become better informed about what is going on in this country. Every night we present the facts on an issue and state what we think about them. My colleagues and I do not pander to our audience, nor do we tell it what it should think. I believe the audience who watches night after night is smart enough to do its own thinking and make up its own mind. American citizens are quite capable of deciding what is fair and what is balanced, given the facts and the opportunity.

The Democratic leadership of Congress is now earnestly discussing whether to resurrect the Fairness Doctrine. The Fairness Doctrine faded into history more than twenty years ago as a result of rapidly expanding cable television networks and programming and the deregulatory fervor of both the Carter and Reagan administrations. The doctrine, which had been in place since 1949, stated that broadcasters on both radio and television had an obligation, enjoined by their use of the public airwaves, to present differing views on controversial political issues. Broadcasters and most radio and television journalists embraced the demise of the doctrine, which they considered to be in many respects an intrusion on First Amendment rights. I happen to agree and strongly believe that the so-called Fairness Doctrine is an unwarranted, unjustified, and unconstitutional infringement of freedom of the press.

Under the Fairness Doctrine, the Federal Communications Commission required that television stations, in particular, conduct themselves as public trustees; that significant airtime be devoted to community needs, interests, and controversies; and that the various conflicting points of view within the community on important issues be expressed.

Freedom of expression owes much to the aggressive voices of talk radio. Our national dialogue would be far fainter and impoverished without the voices of my friends Steve Cochran on WGN in Chicago; Joe Madison on WOL in Washington, D.C., and XM Radio; Doug McIntyre on KNBC in Los Angeles; Chicago's Roland Martin; Phoenix's Charles Goyette; and Denver's Peter Boyles. The list of talkers and thinkers goes on, led by WABC's Rush Limbaugh, Mark Simone, John Gambling, and Sean Hannity; New York's Steve Malzberg, Mark Riley, Laura Flanders, and Randi Rhodes; Philadelphia's Dom Giordano and Michael Smerconish; Raleigh's Warren Ballentine; San Diego's Rick Amato and Rick Roberts; Ken Chiampou in Los Angeles; Ft. Lauderdale's Joyce Kaufman; and Washington's Wilmer Leon. There are literally dozens of other men and women who have enriched the airwaves by giving voice to views across the political spectrum and, more important, by giving voice to the concerns and issues that matter to most Americans that receive little or no attention in mainstream national media. There would be nothing fair about any doctrine that would silence such important voices.

For much of the twentieth century, the community determined what was important and would be permitted in and by the media. FCC licenses for television stations were a prime example. It used to be that public service, including offering airtime to members of the community, was part of what the media had to provide to local communities in order to be licensed. Licensees were considered public trustees, serving at the will of the people. Part of that service included presenting news and information on matters of community importance, and allowing for the expression of varied points of view on those issues.

The Federal Communications Commission required television stations, in particular, to conduct themselves as public trustees, with significant airtime devoted to community needs, interests, and controversies and to the expression of the various and conflicting points of view within the community on those issues. A condition of license renewal was that stations actually had to seek out and report such issues in the communities in which they were licensed to operate, which in FCC parlance came to be known as the "Ascertainment of Community Needs."

If you're of a certain age, you can remember when the broadcast day was filled with local news, beginning with farm and crop reports. Features like this may seem quaint and nostalgic in retrospect, but they clearly provided the benefit of communicating and informing the local communities of the issues and political developments in their hometowns, which helped to sustain positive citizen engagement in local, county, and state government.

By the 1980s broadcasters were complaining that the Fairness Doctrine was having a negative effect on their programming. Because they were required to air so-called balanced reporting on news stories and issues, the stations claimed, they could only cover fewer issues of importance, rather than more, because of demands on the airtime. What the broadcasters were actually saying was that the time devoted to public service and community service programming was cutting into their revenue and profits, because the Fairness Doctrine reduced the airtime that could be sold to advertisers.

In 1987 President Ronald Reagan vetoed the bill that would have put the Fairness Doctrine into law. The principles of the Fairness Doctrine are entirely consonant with the principles and tenets of journalism, and in my opinion most journalists would agree that it is our obligation to seek out those issues that affect our communities and states and, of course, the nation. And while I believe that governmental deregulation has gone much too far as a general proposition, government mandates of what constitutes fairness in the news media should always be rejected.

Years later, the Telecommunications Act of 1996 permitted a greater concentration of media ownership and enabled already large and powerful media companies to expand. The telecom act lifted the ownership cap on the number of television stations that a company could own in a single city or market from 25 percent of audience market share to 35 percent. In radio, a single company was authorized to own as many as eight stations in a single market, and the restrictions on national radio station ownership were simply done away with. A single company could now buy as many stations as it wanted.

The result has not been unexpected. Media companies have grown and expanded. As local television and radio stations have become units of national media corporations, they have also become far more homogeneous, almost uniform, and their attention is focused on national issues, with considerably less coverage of their local communities and local issues. The local radio broadcast in San Antonio is likely to sound like one in Des Moines or Portland. In fact, local announcers may not be local at all—they may be situated hundreds or thousands of miles away reading from a prepared script that only makes it sound as if they are part of your community.

One reason that local television station news broadcasts look and sound much the same is that national TV news consultants advise the managements of the nationally owned stations how best to achieve audience growth and ratings. The thirty-minute national newscasts on ABC, CBS, and NBC cover almost the exact same stories each and every night, and are differentiated primarily by the image of the news anchor presenting the news.

The twenty-four-hour cable news networks are relatively differentiated compared to the world, nightly, and evening half-hour newscasts. The Fox News Network is currently leading this field, followed by CNN, and then by MSNBC. Fox's branding is loud and clear, claiming to be "fair and balanced." CNN is "the most trusted." And MSNBC is brought to you by Microsoft and NBC. They are differentiated, as well, in their personalities and programs: Fox with Bill O'Reilly, Brit Hume, and Sean Hannity; CNN with Larry King, Anderson Cooper, and myself; MSNBC with Keith Olbermann, Joe Scarborough, and Chris Matthews. But the cable news network differentiation tends to dissipate quickly during daytime programming, when "breaking news" flashes on television screens and monitors simultaneously at the cable networks. Car chases, petrochemical plant and factory fires, and train derailments are favored features of all three cable networks' extended daytime news coverage. Viewers love it, and seem to have no brand loyalty when a riveting high-speed car chase is under way. I will admit that I, too, have stood stock still in the middle of our newsroom staring at a monitor watching police cars chase speeding fugitives through neighborhoods, down busy city streets, and along interstates.

There's an old axiom in network television news—"Don't ever be above the news"—which reminds us to cover stories that are of interest to our broad and diverse audiences even when we as editors might believe there are far more important if somewhat arcane issues that should be reported. There is another, more powerful axiom in local television news—"If it bleeds, it leads." Both principles tend to push local and national television news editors and managers toward the sensational rather than the substantive. And the downward pressure is building, not lessening, in cable television news.

When I started out as a cub reporter in local news many years ago, I vividly recall a station manager telling our small news team, "You can't preach if the pews are empty." I've found over the decades since that that is the essence of the struggle in news management: to attract a television news audience while maintaining the integrity of the journalism. The struggle goes on, and sometimes we lose the struggle.

This explains why cable news featured almost nonstop coverage of Anna Nicole Smith's death, coverage that ran over the course of an entire week. Her drug-overdose death was the logical, foreseeable conclusion to the life of a woman with a tortured childhood and adolescence, and whose tumultuous celebrity was exploited by the national media for years. Smith's celebrity was established with another death, that of the elderly billionaire who died a year after she married him, and with the public spectacle of his family's legal efforts to prevent her from inheriting hundreds of millions of dollars.

Even in her death, drama and public spectacle followed her: what and who had killed her, where should she be buried, and the richly important question of who among many had fathered her baby.

I found the Anna Nicole Smith story repugnant from beginning to end, filled as it was with characters and personalities who had exploited this woman throughout her life. She, of course, had exploited a very wealthy old man, and in so doing achieved a notoriety that galvanized millions of viewers. Anna Nicole Smith lived and died in a storm of exploitation, her life seemingly devoid of the love, care, or concern of others and perhaps for others. The week after her death produced more media attention and viewer fascination than the funeral of a president, great author, or Nobel Prize–winning scientist.

During the week she died 21 percent of primary cable news programming featured Anna Nicole Smith. This was followed in airtime by the Iraq war, which got all of 15 percent of the coverage. On February 8 and 9, when the news broke, a staggering 50 percent of the airtime on CNN, MSNBC, and the Fox News Channel was devoted to Smith's death—this for a woman who was essentially a caricature of celebrities who are famous for being famous.

Yes, cable news definitely lost that struggle. But we also win some. On my broadcast we did not report the Anna Nicole Smith story because that is not what my audience expects of me. My audience and I are attracted to ideas, issues, and the people in the public arena who influence, for good or bad, our lives, our communities, and the nation. Just as cable news makes it possible to cover Anna Nicole Smith or a car chase, it also makes broadcasts like mine possible. And by the way, it's worthy of note that such broadcasts still, day in and day out, attract a larger share of the audience than car chases. Thank God.

I fully understand the importance of all forms of news, whether entertainment news, sports news, celebrity news, pop culture news, and even business news. But I also believe in the importance of journalists, editors, and their managers maintaining a sense of proportion. Having twenty-four hours of programming time available each day is both a blessing and a burden to cable news networks: a wonderful opportunity to program all kinds of news in all kinds of ways, and an intimidating amount of time to fill with quality content. I believe that, overall, we do a pretty good job, although undoubtedly we could improve considerably.

I am first and foremost an advocacy journalist. Each night my colleagues and I report on the most important and interesting news of the day and on the issues confronting my audience and our government. I report, I debate, and I offer my opinion, and my audience not only expects but demands that I do so. My colleagues and I take pride in the success of our broadcast, and pride in the audience that joins us each evening. Our audience knows where I stand on every single issue, and that I approach neither the news nor the issues with an ideological or partisan bias. I'm not an objective journalist, because the price of objectivity for me would require neutrality on the welfare of the American people and our national interest. I adamantly and passionately place our fundamental national values and interests first in every aspect of our program.

> *Rhoda in California*: "Lou, I believe your journalism and efforts are a large factor in why the amnesty bill has not passed. Americans have a lot of knowledge from their firsthand experience living with the downside of illegal immigration, but we also need a truthful advocate in the media." (June 11, 2007)

The good of the country and our citizens is my motivating concern and consuming interest. That's why I've been drawn to issues-oriented reporting, whether the outsourcing of American jobs, free trade, public education, the war on terror, border and port security, or the fight against drug addiction and trafficking. We are relentless in our reporting of those particular issues because of their importance to our people and our nation. By "relentless" I mean that we do not simply report on one of these important issues and revisit it in a few months. Television news typically features an issue and moves on, fearing that viewers will become bored with the subject irrespective of the content. High story counts, variety, and pacing are critically important in conventional television news programming.

But our broadcast and our approach is quite different. Because I am an advocacy journalist, and my audience is smart and engaged, we are expected to report on issues in-depth and with consistency. Because I am an advocacy journalist and an independent populist, and because I decry the failings of both Republicans and Democrats, liberals and conservatives, establishment elites, and a government that fails our citizens, I'm frequently the object of personal attacks in the national media by partisans, elitists, and mouthpieces for vested interests of all sorts.

I could reduce the number of those personal attacks by at least 50 percent by choosing one partisan side or the other. And if I would just align myself with the interests of one orthodoxy or the position of one of the elites, my public life would quiet considerably. I'd much rather endure the media's slings and arrows than give up sleeping well at night.

Some of my detractors, who can neither refute our empirical reporting nor reasonably oppose the positions I take on issues, choose instead to question my style of reporting or my motives. I've literally laughed out loud at contentions that I've chosen to cover issues like free trade and the outsourcing of middle-class jobs in order to boost ratings. If those issues—which my broadcast has been reporting on for years— are such "sexy topics" that they inspire big ratings, I have to wonder why no other broadcast on television covers them as we do.

Perhaps other broadcasts and reporters get bored easily. In her 60 Minutes profile of me in the spring of 2007, Lesley Stahl chose to call me "Johnny One Note" on the subject of illegal immigration. During the interview she asked if the audience ever got tired of me "repeating the same topics over and over," emphasizing "over and over" as if I were indulging the most audience-tiring and unprofessional practice.

My reply was exactly what I believed: namely, that to continue reporting on important issues is an obligation, and one that my audience expects me to fulfill. Instead of describing what we do as "repetition," I told Stahl that consistent and continuing coverage is neither boring nor repetitious to our audience, but "thorough and ongoing," and I know my audience would expect nothing less. Much of television news condescends, but we never speak down to our audience for two simple reasons: One, it may be a good television news approach, but I think it's bad manners; and two, I know there are lots of people in my audience smarter than me.

Lesley Stahl also suggested that I cover these issues "to inflame" my viewers, and took exception to me for being an advocacy journalist. Advocacy journalism has, in fact, been an important element of American journalism from its earliest days. As to inflaming anyone, I honestly find it inexplicable that any American citizen wouldn't be incensed when fully informed of what is happening in our country and what is happening to our citizens.

> *Pete in Chicago:* "Lou, I am tired of hearing you complain that our federal government doesn't work. In August 2001, I applied for a copy of my citizenship papers with INS. In May of 2007, I received it. You can see for yourself how fast and efficient they are." (June 25, 2007)

While the thrust of Stahl's piece was on illegal immigration, she zeroed in on a brief ad-lib conversation that had taken place on April 14, 2005, between Christine Romans and me during which Christine mentioned that the number of incidences of leprosy, or Hansen's disease, had hit seven thousand. Her comment was an unscripted remark, not a report. Stahl then interviewed an executive at the Southern Poverty Law Center who disputed those numbers, and who claimed that I was using such figures to paint all illegal immigrants as "disease-carrying rapists and thugs."

That was utterly wrong, as I've always expressed my respect for illegal aliens and my understanding of their motivation in crossing our border to make more money and escape corrupt governments and impoverished economies. But then followed a series of events that are symptomatic of the media's tendency to forgo investigation in order to gain momentum with a story, regardless of the facts or underlying truth.

A little more than a week after the *60 Minutes* broadcast, the Southern Poverty Law Center ran advertisements in the *New York Times* and *USA Today* demanding that both CNN and I retract the leprosy statement. I never hesitate to correct a mistake, but the simple fact is that seven thousand is the correct number, and neither CNN management nor I would retract a correct statement. The *New York Times* then published a column titled "Truth, Fiction and Lou Dobbs" that picked up where the SPLC advertisement had left off. The editorial was riddled with errors, all of which I addressed on the air or in my column. The most egregious of the lot was the *Time*'s claim that we had "reported" on leprosy, when the truth was that we did not air a report of any kind on the topic until after the *60 Minutes* story, and did so then only to set the record absolutely straight. The *New York Times*, *60 Minutes*, and the SPLC had taken an eight-second comment and played it to the hilt. Adhering to "he said/she said" journalism, these respected news organizations chose not only to not report the fact that the number of leprosy cases had risen to 7,029 from 1975 to 2005, but also to ignore the simple, straightforward premise of even the few reports we've done on public health concerns created by our government's failure to screen for communicable disease when our immigration system is ignored and defied by those who enter the country illegally.

Because most of the national media is in thrall to a politically correct orthodoxy—usually liberal and "objective" to the point of neutrality on the public interest and the common good—they fail to truly enlarge the body of public knowledge on critically important issues and examine facts that are usually inconvenient to ideology and partisan perspective.

My comments, my positions, and my advocacy are all part of an easily accessible public record. Determining the content of our reporting is simply a matter of reviewing transcripts, videotape, and the Web. So there is no excuse for my media and partisan critics not getting the facts right about that very public record.

Why should readers, listeners, and viewers trust our national news media's coverage of critical events or issues of national importance that substantively affect people's lives when those news organizations and journalists have allowed themselves to become part of the herd and pack orthodoxy?

I realize that not every journalist has the freedom and privilege I enjoy to report and analyze the news independently and to straightforwardly advocate positions and resolutions that I believe support the common good and the national interest. At the same time, other reporters and editors have not been absolved of the responsibility to be, first, Americans citizens and, then, partisans or ideologues as they examine our social, political, and economic reality, whether at the local or national level.

The American people deserve better, and it is our responsibility to deliver on our obligation as journalists. The national news media does them a disservice by pursuing "he says/she says" journalism, and not exploring deeply all issues that affect the quality of life in America and our national interest. It is admittedly difficult for all journalists to research, gather the facts, get those facts straight, and report the news that is most critical to the events, developments, and issues shaping all our lives in local communities and the nation.

On our show we work at it diligently and, yes, even relentlessly, day in and day out. Maintaining that perspective and sense of obligation is why *Lou Dobbs Tonight* features complex stories like the Dubai Ports World deal and reports on stories both dull and complex like free trade, the outsourcing of American jobs to cheap overseas labor markets, the decline of public education, drug addiction, the war on terror, and injustices similar to the outrageous prosecution of two former Border Patrol agents. We cover those stories "repetitiously" and "relentlessly" because they require in-depth reporting and analysis and, yes, because of my populist advocacy. Our reporting reveals the establishment elite and the government at their worst, and our issues reporting is not limited to three minutes every six months, but is often presented day in and day out, for months and even years. That's how long it often takes to unearth the facts, to report on complex issues that evolve over time—and we report a story to its conclusion. We are often blamed or credited, depending upon the ideological and partisan interests blaming or crediting, for influencing the conclusions we draw. I firmly believe that that is the obligation and responsibility of our broadcast, and it is exactly what our audience expects of us.

Other broadcasts have different obligations. I see my obligation as an advocacy journalist who is both an independent and a populist to get to the facts, to analyze issues from the uniquely American perspective, to represent the interests and values of our citizens and nation wherever and whenever possible, and to speak out against partisan ideologues, establishment elites, and special interests who disregard the American way and who see their interests as superior to the American dream. I don't ask my colleagues to in any way abandon their objectivity, only their neutrality as citizens as a condition of their objectivity. I do believe that traditional journalism would be invigorated by greater editorial independence, and I hope my fellow journalists will consider what I'm asking of every American concerned about our nation's future: to surrender their Democratic and Republican partisan registration, abandon their liberal and conservative ideologies, eschew orthodoxy, and become truly independent.

13

Independent Thinking and
the American Spirit

Every good citizen makes his country's honor his own, and
cherishes it not only as precious but as sacred.

—Andrew Jackson

The arrogance of our establishment elites is apparently boundless and, as such, threatens our very existence as a nation. The elites in nearly every quarter of our society—whether academic, media, business, or politics—are members, they believe, of superior orthodoxies, possessed of a one-world view that gives absolute primacy to the interests of business and international commerce, diminishes our national sovereignty, and debases citizenship, whether individual or corporate. They have become aggressive supporters of the postmodern view that Americans are less citizens than consumers, that they are less citizens than units of labor, and that our nation is nothing more than a significant segment of a one-world economy. They not only reject views and opinions that conflict with their own but resist and flail against the empirical reality that discomfits and disturbs their business, economic, and geopolitical philosophy and ideology.

The establishment elites have raised so-called free trade to the level of a personal and societal belief system that is as ardently faith-based as any religion. How else to explain their refusal to recognize thirty-one consecutive years of U.S. trade deficits or a U.S. trade debt that is rising faster than our national debt? How else to explain their attacks on independent thinkers and empiricists who question their economics with facts, critics whom they look upon as heretics?

America's establishment elites have finally been compelled to at least acknowledge some of the facts of our environmental reality and consider the possibility of a threat posed to the planet by global warming. They will not, however, risk disfavor with their orthodoxies by asking the obvious and urgent question: Where is the harm to our economy and society in conserving energy and being responsible consumers? Aren't responsibility and conservation both tenets of conservatism? Liberals, it seems to me, should likewise question the social and economic impact on American citizens of their own orthodox views on the broadest possible involvement of government in American daily life and the diminishment of U.S. sovereignty in favor of global organizations and institutions such as the United Nations and World Trade Organization.

As we move toward the presidential election of 2008, each of us who considers himself or herself to be a responsible, engaged American citizen must ask important questions of all the candidates who seek our votes. Many of the questions are profound and do not have ready answers—questions such as, Why does America require a growth economy based on the necessity of ever-rising population in order to be prosperous? Why is it that establishment elites are far more comfortable with the remote rather than the proximate? This president and this Congress can propose and debate raising gasoline mileage standards over a one- or two-decade period but not act to clean up an estimated 114 dangerously contaminated Superfund sites that threaten the health and lives of millions of Americans.

From the first page of this book, I've declared myself an American, an independent, and a populist who is far more interested in the common good and our national interest than in any other political consideration. Not only must we end the marginalization of working Americans and their families by our government and political system, but we must return them to primacy in public policy. I believe that an active engaged citizenry still has the capacity and opportunity to control our nation's destiny.

Throughout these pages I've tried to present my view of the facts and the issues I believe should be of greatest concern to the American people, and to examine the impact of this country's elite orthodoxies on our public policy, our society, and our economy. Candidates for president seldom fail to remind us of how powerful the United States is, and the responsibility to the world that our superpower status entails. As I hope I've demonstrated, that status does not automatically grant us omniscience or guarantee the inevitability of the American Dream for generations to come. We are a nation that has squandered trillions of dollars and amassed staggering debts. The holders of that debt hold promissory notes on our nation's future and on the prospect of our children's prosperity.

We are, in fact, a dependent nation not only because of our unthinkable indebtedness but also because we have left ourselves vulnerable, by permitting our elites to serve themselves and their interests without regard for all Americans. We have failed an entire generation of young Americans by allowing the decline of society's great equalizer, our public schools. Instead of addressing that failure, our politicians have chosen to divide us into partisan camps, with liberals calling for magnet and charter schools and conservatives calling for vouchers. As an independent populist, I believe we should demand only one choice— and that choice is to restore public education in every neighborhood and community in the nation so that every young American has the opportunity for a quality learning experience.

We must ask why our establishment elites and elected officials have not mobilized our society against drug and alcohol abuse and addiction. Why, for more than three decades, have they fought only timidly the war on drugs? Why is it that the United States, with less than 5 percent of the world's population, consumes two thirds of the world's illegal drugs?

Why have we allowed ourselves to become victims of political correctness rather than beneficiaries of free expression and independent thought? Language has become so abused in the media and in public institutions that too many of us can no longer distinguish between indifference and intolerance, permissiveness and progress.

We Americans must find one another and take up the cause of truth and justice, demand our rights of citizenship and fulfill our responsibilities as citizens, and yield our consent to be governed only to those deserving of our trust. Responsible citizens must demand more public investment in our infrastructure, our national power grid, and our airports. Americans must no longer accept corporate America's rationalization of business practices that cost middle-class jobs and our communities their lifeblood.

We have to ask our leaders why the state of Massachusetts can implement a rational, cost-effective health care system that covers all of its citizens, but the federal government will not. What more must we do to make the knowledge of our world-class medical researchers and physicians available throughout America? Why, as our population rises, are applications to medical school declining? How can we honor better and pay more those who provide health care, whether doctors, nurses, or technicians?

Why is it that the world's only superpower is permitting its business elites to invest in plants and factories in China instead of—as many of us believed would happen with the passage of NAFTA fourteen years ago—in our nearest neighbors, Mexico and Canada?

Why do we dispatch our troops to more than forty nations around the world and, six years after September 11, refuse to secure our own borders and ports?

What is America's destiny, and how will we achieve it? Should America ignore or rationalize its limitations as a superpower or remain committed to its historically recent role of world policeman? Should the United States continue to account for almost a third of the world's arms spending, or should we look to our allies to assume a responsible proportionate economic burden of defense spending?

By the middle of the twenty-first century we will witness significant global population growth. World population will increase by a billion people—to 7.6 billion—in 2020. It is projected that by 2050 the world will be populated by almost 9.5 billion people, roughly 50 percent more than are living today. We will witness an inevitable intensification of global competition for dwindling, natural resources.

American foreign policy, which has been at best haphazard and at worst reckless at the outset of this century, must be conducted with full recognition of new global economic, sociological, and political realities. In my opinion, Americans must insist on a change in the direction of America's foreign policy and in our international trade policy as well. For all these reasons and those I've enumerated throughout this book, we Americans now face the necessity of organizing and managing our individual lives prudently, taking active roles as citizens in our nation's public life, and seeking out national leaders of character and capacity commensurate with the challenges and contests that are before us.

I sincerely and firmly believe that it is time to set aside partisanship, ideology, and elitist orthodoxy to affirm our great national values of individual liberty and equality, and to resist all who would deny any of our citizens those rights. And I believe just as firmly that we must preserve the sovereignty of the nation that has given us those rights and the American Dream.

Just as previous generations have worked and sacrificed to assure us the benefits and blessings of life in America, I hope, for a time at least, that we can come together and embrace our values, rights, and purpose. I believe that America's populist spirit is in resurgence, that we as citizens will serve one another best as independents rather than as partisans, and that we must choose optimism over arrogance, confidence and self-reliance over fear. Let us commit to electing leaders of substance and principle who understand that this country's greatest resource is its citizens and who will nurture our awakening American spirit.

Our foreign policy is riddled with inconsistent and unrealistic assumptions about the changing shape of the world in which we live. The absence of a clear worldview—in social, economic, and political terms—invites, at best, disappointment and, at worst, disaster.

America's free-trade policies, in particular, are positioned to invite disaster. What happens when we no longer pretend that trade is free? At that point our national leaders will have to address foreign policy with clear eyes and the understanding that the contest for natural resources and capital may well make "trade wars" on all-too-literal expression.

Our current trade deficit now amounts to more than three quarters of a trillion dollars a year. We've lost three million manufacturing jobs in the last three years alone, most of which have been exported over-seas. Many of our politicians talk about "free trade," but what they really mean is "give the multinational corporations in this country anything they want."

Congress mandated economic as well as environmental impact statements on domestic policies fifteen years ago. Unfortunately, it did not extend the requirement to foreign policy and trade. In my opinion, Congress should do so immediately.

While I'm neither a one-world liberal nor a militaristic neoconserva-tive, I do believe we have to assess where we are, and where we are heading, as a nation, a society, and a political economy. I believe it's likely we'll continue to consume a disproportionate amount of resources and wealth relative to the rest of the world's population, and I also believe our standard of living and quality of life will be severely challenged, if not confronted outright. Our political leaders should be considering, in public forums and debates, what policies we'll pursue to defend our access to those resources, and what we as a nation can do to inspire and support progress for the rest of the world. We should be asking ourselves whether the consumer culture we've created, with our tremendous demands for oil, minerals, wood, water, and other resources, is the soci-ety we want and whether it defines our way of life, or whether American values will determine the society in which we live.

The American spirit is manifest throughout our society and our his-tory. We are an optimistic people; we are problem solvers and not shirk-ers. We have been a proud, hardworking, and caring people, and we have always considered ourselves to be Americans first. We have always been idealistic, and at the same time prudent and unafraid of sacrifice. We have throughout our history demanded our independence and self-reliance, our individual rights of liberty and equality. We have overcome much, from our Revolutionary War through the Civil War, World War I, a decade of the Depression, World War II, the Korean and Vietnam wars, and the Cold War. And now we have a lot of work to do.

Engaged in long wars in Iraq and Afghanistan and a war against radical Islamist terrorism, we also face rising global economic com-petition for resources and challenges to our way of life from within, including a declining standard of living and failing public education for millions of Americans. We can no longer ignore any of these threats and challenges, and our nation cannot afford to allow our elites to waste more time, money, energy, and precious American lives in thoughtless and careless pursuit of agendas and goals that neither honor our traditional values nor assure that the American way of life will prevail in this new century.

The American spirit imbues us with the strength to meet these challenges with hard work and sacrifice, as there will surely be both. There is no question that we the people must assume our responsibilities as citizens and be full-throated in our expression of that spirit in our homes, communities, and nation. We will soon have the opportunity to choose new leaders who understand and respect our independence and right of self-determination. We the people still possess the power to chart the course of our destiny. With a new commitment to our nation's traditions and values, and to work and sacrifice for one another as citizens, this will undoubtedly be the day of the independent American, assuring that ours will be a bright and certain future as a free people and nation.

Let's get to work.

Notes

Introduction

p. 5 **"We as a people"**: State Department: "Today, the United States accepts more legal immigrants as permanent residents than the rest of the world combined," usinfo .state.gov/xarchives/display.html?p=washfile-english&y=2006&m=October&x=20061 003162245jmnamdeirf0.4331629.

9/11 Commission Hearing: "The United States admits more legal immigrants every year than all the rest of the nations of the world combined." http://www.9-11commission .gov/hearings/hearing6/witness_ting.htm.

1: A Superpower Struggles

p. 14 **With the average cost**: Richard Sammon, "Democrats Get Good Start on 2008 Money Chase," *Kiplinger's*, May 7, 2007.

p. 16 **The Census Bureau estimates**: www.census.gov/main/www/popclock.html.

p. 16 **Our diversity is unrivaled**: "U.S. Population Hits 301 Million," USINFO, January 1, 2007, usinfo.state.gov/xarchives/display.html?p=washfile-english&y=2007& m=January&x=20061229124618bcreklaw0.1818201.

p. 16 **By 2050, we're expected**: "Executive Summary: Our Changing Nation," Population Resource Center, August 2001, www.prcdc.org/summaries/changingnation/ changingnation.html.

p. 17 **The average voter turnout**: "Presidential Election Turnout," Committee for the Study of the American Electorate, 2000.

2: Inflection Points

p. 19 **The preservation of**: First Inaugural Address, April 30, 1789.

p. 26 **The revised G.I. Bill**: GI Bill History, U.S. Department of Veterans Affairs, www.gibill.va.gov/GI_Bill_Info/history.htm.

p. 35 **"I want to talk to you"**: President Jimmy Carter, "The 'Crisis of Confidence' Speech," transcript, July 15, 1979.

p. 36 **There were nearly three thousand**: Jack Ehnes, "Corporate Governance Protects Your Pension," CalSTRS, Winter 2007, www.calstrs.com/eNewsletters/RE/ 2007Winter/Corporate_Governance.htm.

p. 37 **The bailout for these businesses**: Timothy Curry and Lynn Shibut, "The Cost of the Savings and Loan Crisis: Truth and Consequences," FDIC Banking Review, December 2000.

3: Two Parties, No Choice

p. 47 **President Bill Clinton made:** Presidential Visits Abroad, U.S. Department of State, www.state.gov/r/pa/ho/trvl/pres/5188.htm.

p. 49 **The legislation was defeated:** Four key freshmen senators voted against cloture on S1639: Tester, Webb, McCaskill, and Brown. Senate Roll Call on S.1639, www.senate.gov/legislative/LIS/roll_call_lists/roll_call_vote_cfm.cfm?congress=110&session=1&vote=00235; also thehill.com/leading-the-news/senators-webb-tester-mccaskill-are-key-votes-2007-06-20.html.

p. 50 **As Frank Newport of the Gallup:** *Lou Dobbs Tonight*, June 20, 2007.

p. 53 **As of today, 142 million:** "Voting and Registration in the Election of 2004," U.S. Census Bureau, www.state.gov/r/pa/ho/trvl/pres/5188.htm.

p. 53 **Thus, 51 percent:** "Editor's Forecast: Race for the House," Gallup Poll, November 6, 2006.

p. 54 **Those who claim:** Rassmussen Reports, July 1, 2007.

p. 54 **My show reported that:** *Lou Dobbs Tonight*, June 1, 2007.

5: The Imperious Presidency

p. 65 **The President is merely:** *Kansas City Star*, May 7, 1918.

p. 68 **"I am not at all convinced":** "Eagleburger Questions Possible Iraqi Move," CNN.com, August 22, 2002.

p. 68 **"Although the United States":** James A. Baker III, "The Right Way to Change a Regime," *New York Times*, August 25, 2002.

p. 70 **"It would have been a mistake":** Speech by Secretary Richard Cheney, "The Gulf War: A First Assessment," The Soref Symposium, April 29, 1991, web.archive.org/web/20041130090045/ and www.washingtoninstitute.org/pubs/soref/cheney.htm.

p. 73 **Alito drafted the blue print; Here are a few examples:** Charlie Savage, "Bush Challenges Hundreds of Laws," *Boston Globe*, April 30, 2006; also, Robert Pear, "Legal Group Says Bush Undermines Law by Ignoring Select Parts of Bills," *New York Times*, July 24, 2006.

p. 74 **"While this president":** Committee on the Judiciary, Statement of Senator Patrick Leahy, Ranking Member, Judiciary Committee Hearing on Presidential Signing Statements, March 15, 2006, and June 27, 2006.

p. 74 **It found that a third:** "Presidential Signing Statements Accompanying the Fiscal Year 2006 Appropriations Acts," Government Accountability Office, June 18, 2007.

p. 76 **"The purpose of the NPC":** National Petroleum Council, Origin and Operations, www.npc.org.

p. 78 **The current account deficit:** "U.S. Current Account Deficit Increases in 2006," Bureau of Economic Analysis, March 14, 2007.

p. 78 **The trade deficit has been a drag:** There were actually two revisions to this list, and the number right now is seventeen of the twenty-six quarters under President Bush that have been reported. It was much worse in his first term—in thirteen of sixteen quarters trade was a drag on economic growth, www.bea.doc.gov/bea/dn/nipaweb/TableView.asp.

6: Debtor Nation

p. 81 **The cost of federal entitlement programs:** In 2007, nearly 50 million Americans will receive more than $602 billion in Social Security benefits: www.ssa.gov/pressoffice/basicfact.htm; also, www.cbo.gov/ftpdoc.cfm?index=3521&type=0; also, www.cbo.gov/ftpdoc.cfm?index=7731&type=0.

In fiscal year 2007, spending by the federal government will amount to $2.7 trillion, or one fifth of the nation's economic output, the Congressional Budget Office (CBO) projects. The three major federal entitlement programs—Medicare, Medicaid, and Social Security—will account for about 45 percent of those outlays, or about 9 percent of gross domestic product (GDP). If policymakers leave current laws unchanged, federal outlays will claim a sharply increasing share of the nation's output over coming decades, driven primarily by growth in the health-related entitlement programs, www.cbo.gov/ftpdocs/78xx/doc7851/03-08-LongTerm%20Spending.pdf.

p. 81 **Foreclosures on homes:** David Streitfeld, "Foreclosures in State Hit Record High," *Los Angeles Times,* July 25, 2007.

p. 83 **Here are highlights:** ASCE Report Card for America's Infrastructure, 2005 Grades.

p. 86 **American consumers have amassed:** Federal Reserve Board, Statistical Release, Consumer Credit, July 9, 2007.

p. 86 **Nearly two thirds:** Rick Popely, "Long Auto Loans Hurt Car Sales," *Baltimore Sun,* June 2, 2007.

p. 86 **Our credit card debt:** CardWeb.com, Historical Table of U.S. Bank Credit Card Loans, 2000.

p. 86 **Credit cards constitute:** Federal Reserve Board, Statistical Release, Consumer Credit, April 6, 2007.

p. 87 **Today the average household:** "Income Climbs, Poverty Stabilizes, Uninsured Rate Increases," U.S. Census Bureau News, August 29, 2006.

p. 87 **More than $1.8 trillion:** GAO, "Credit Cards: Increased Complexity in Rates and Fees Heightens Need for More Effective Disclosures to Consumers," September 2006; CardTrak "Card Debt" April 2004 issue.

p. 88 **Only a third of us:** Pulse of Democracy: Social Security, Gallup Poll, November 2005.

p. 88 **Some 30 percent:** Mitchell Schnurman, "The New Trend: A Working Retirement," *Star-Telegram,* June 6, 2007.

p. 89 **This fund will only:** "A Summary of the 2007 Annual Reports," Social Security and Medicare Boards of Trustees, April 23, 2007.

p. 90 **"We find that a typical":** Caroline L. Freund, "Current Account Adjustment in Industrialized Countries," International Finance Discussion Papers, Board of Governors of the Federal Reserve System, December 2000.

p. 91 **"Our trade deficits":** Remarks by Ambassador Susan C. Schwab, Deputy United States Trade Representative, Thunderbird University, Glendale, Arizona, March 20, 2006.

p. 91 **"From Chile to":** Remarks by Ambassador Karan Bhatia, Deputy U.S. Trade Representative, Yonsei University, October 24, 2006.

p. 91 **"The advocates of free trade":** "Isolationist Ignorance in Action: Watch Lou Dobbs Ascend to the Pinnacle of Protectionist Prevarication," *The National Review,* April 30, 2007.

p. 93 **The United States imported:** American International Auto Dealers, February 2, 2006.

7: Shadow Government

p. 95 **[T]here are more instances:** June 16, 1788.

p. 97 **The protection of Iraqi:** Tom Squitieri, "Role of Security Companies Likely to Become More Visible," *USA Today*, April 1, 2004.

p. 99 **The first efforts at:** E. S. Savas, "Privatization: Past, Present, Future," Annual Privatization Report 2006, Reason Foundation, City University of New York.

p. 100 **"Since late 1982"; By the end of 2005:** "Army's Guard Program Requires Greater Oversight and Reassessment of Acquisition Approach," Report to Congressional Requesters on Contract Security Guards, U.S. Government Accountability Office, April 2006.

p. 102 **The estimated number involved:** "Rebuilding Iraq: Action Still Needed to Improve the Use of Private Security Providers," U.S. Government Accountability Office, June 13, 2006; see also www.latimes.com/news/nationworld/world/la-naprivate4jul04, 0,5808980.story?coll=la-home-center.

p. 102 **"Nobody had really":** John C. K. Daly, UPI Intelligence Watch, July 26, 2006.

p. 103 **According to the latest:** Ibid.

p. 103 **"The lack of a legal":** "Price Introduces Private Security Contractor Legislation Bill to Enhance Accountability and Oversight of Battlefield Contractors," press release, Office of Congressman David Price, January 10, 2007.

p. 104 **Coordination between the U.S.:** "Rebuilding Iraq," U.S. GAO; see also www.latimes.com/news/nationworld/world/la-na-private4jul04,0,5808980. Story?Coll= la-home-center.

p. 106 **Among these are:** Leonard C. Gilroy and Adam B. Summers, "Detailing Foreign Management of U.S. Infrastructure: Numerous U.S. Ports, Airports, Roads, Water Facilities Already Run by Foreign Businesses," Reason.org, March 15, 2006.

p. 106 **According to those proprivatization:** Ibid.

p. 107 **Take the 91 Express Lanes:** Caltrans, Division of Innovative Finance, AB 680 Private Toll Road Program, Route 91 Express Lanes, www.dot.ca.gov/hq/paffairs/about/toll/status.htm; also, Leslie Miller, "Foreign Companies Buy U.S. Roads, Bridges," Associated Press, July 15, 2006.

p. 107 **In 2006 Transurban Group:** "Agreement Reached for Private Firm to Assume Control of Pocahontas Parkway Toll Facility in the Richmond Region," press release, Virginia Department of Transportation, May 2, 2006.

p. 108 **In 2005 the Chicago Skyway:** Public Private Partnerships Case Study: Chicago Skyway, United States Department of Transportation, Federal Highway Administration, www.fhwa.dot.gov/PPP/chicago_skyway.htm.

p. 108 **"[A] 40-year old":** Mitchell E. Daniels (governor of Indiana), "Reforming Government Through Competition," Reason Foundation Annual Privatization Report 2006.

p. 109 **Terms of the deal:** Rad Sallee, "Contractor Sues to Keep Trans-Texas Details Hidden," *Houston Chronicle*, June 27, 2005.

p. 109 **The Texas legislature:** Kimberly Piña, "Corridor Project Faces Two-Year Halt in Light of Opposition, Questions," *Houston Chronicle*, May 21, 2007.

p. 110 **"We drive foreign cars"**: "Setting the Record Straight on Toll Roads and Public-Private Partnerships in Texas," press release, Reason Foundation, May 11, 2007.

p. 110 **In order to squeeze**: Timothy Egan, "Tapes Show Enron Arranged Plant Shutdown," *New York Times*, February 2005.

p. 111 **Today Veolia handles**: Facts About Veolia Water North America, Veolia, www.veoliawaterna.com/about/media/default.htm.

p. 111 **As of 2007 RWE**: RWE Group's Investor Relations: Divestment of the Water Business, www.rwe.com/generator.aspx/investorrelations/faq_27s/rwe-group/thameswater/language=en/id=253678/page.html.

p. 112 **American Water's management**: Gwen Mickelson, "Felton Water Eminent Domain Case to Stay in County," *Santa Cruz Sentinel*, May 10, 2007; Public Citizen, RWE/Thames Water: A Corporate Profile, March 2003, www.citizen.org/documents/RWEProfile.pdf.

p. 112 **However, a follow-up survey**: FeltonFLOW, www.feltonflow.org/reasonsurvey.html.

p. 113 **"Duties such as customer"**: Sandy Springs, Georgia, press release, November 14, 2005, files.sandysprings-ga.org/releases/11-14-05_careers.htm.

p. 113 **Within twelve months**: Eric Lipton," 'Breathtaking' Waste and Fraud in Hurricane Aid," *New York Times*, June 27, 2006.

p. 114 **She claimed that the backlog**: *Lou Dobbs Tonight*, June 19, 2007.

p. 114 **"Reason is a 501(c)(3) nonprofit"**: 1999 Reason Foundation Annual Report: *Reason* magazine's list of supporters, 2007.

p. 117 **In 1992, there were**: "The United States Nonprofit Sector," 2006 Report, National Council of Nonprofit Associations, www.ncna.org/_uploads/documents/live//us_sector_report_2003.pdf.

p. 117 **To be tax-exempt**: Charities & Non-Profits: Exemption Requirements, Internal Revenue Service, www.irs.gov/charities/charitable/article/0,,id=96099,00.html.

p. 119 **These companies and lobbying groups**: "Corporate America's Trojan Horse in the States: The Untold Story Behind the American Legislative Exchange Council," Alecwatch, 2002, www.alecwatch.org/11223344.pdf.

p. 119 **"Unique to ALEC Task Forces"**: ALEC. org, www.alec.org/model-legislation.

p. 120 **"These bills provide"**: Ibid.

p. 120 **"In 2004 alone"**: Nathan Newman and David Sirota, "The Battle for the States," SirotaBlog, February 2006, www.davidsirota.com/index.php/the-battle-for-the-states/.

p. 120 **It, like other members**: "Corporate America's Trojan Horse in the States," Alecwatch.

8: God and Politics

p. 125 **In fact, church members**: Gregory A. Smith, "Attitudes Toward Immigration: In the Pulpit and the Pew," April 26, 2006, pewresearch.org/pubs/20/attitudes-toward-immigration-in-the-pulpit-and-the-pew.

p. 125 **On his show, Charlie Rose**: *Charlie Rose*, December 11, 2006:

Charlie Rose: Speaking of lobbyists, do you believe that the American Jewish lobby has had an undue influence on American foreign policy?

Lou Dobbs: I should have included that in the book, I think. I think that there is a very good argument that the Jewish lobby has had a disproportionate influence on U.S. government policy. At the same time, it has been a conflicted and confused policy. So I guess I would have to blame the Jewish lobby for what has been a half-century of horrible, horrible U.S. policy in the Middle East. I guess they can take a disproportionate blame as well, right? Because we have permitted this small state to be in almost perpetual conflict from the time that Harry Truman recognized its existence in 1948. To me, that's an inexcusable failure of U.S. foreign policy.

p. 122 **Approximately 60 percent:** "U.S. Stands Alone in Its Embrace of Religion," Pew Research Center for the People and the Press, Pew Global Attitudes Project, December 19, 2002.

p. 127 **The IRS sent out:** Associated Press, "IRS Warns Churches to Stay Neutral in Upcoming Campaign Season," *USA Today*, July 18, 2006.

p. 127 **Forty active investigations:** *Lou Dobbs Tonight*, September 28, 2006.

p. 129 **Johnson's support of:** "History of the 501(c)(3) Political Activity Prohibition," OMBwatch, www.ombwatch.org/article/articleview/2852/1/41?TopicID=2.

p. 129 **Reed and his organization:** Jeffrey H. Birnbaum, "Washington's Power 25: Which Pressure Groups Are Best at Manipulating the Laws We Live By? A Groundbreaking *Fortune* Survey Reveals Who Belongs to Lobbying's Elite and Why They Wield So Much Clout," *Fortune*, December 8, 1997.

p. 130 **"In 2006 the Government Accountability":** "Improvements in Monitoring Grantees and Measuring Performance Could Enhance Accountability," Faith-Based and Community Initiative, Government Accountability Office, June 2006.

p. 130 **James Dobson's evangelical:** Associated Press, "Conservatives Protest Popular Doll-Maker," October 14, 2005.

p. 131 **Mahony is now spearheading:** www.usccb.org/mrs/votersignups.shtml; also www.nytimes.com/2006/04/20/washington/20immig.html?ei=5090&en=598125e3dfe3e1a2&ex=1303185600&partner=rssuserland&emc=rss&pagewanted=print.

p. 128 **"There is no doubt":** Interviewed on *Lou Dobbs Tonight*, September 18, 2006.

p. 132 **Nearly two thirds of us:** Pulse of Democracy on Religion, Gallup Poll News Service, conducted January 15–18, 2007.

p. 132 **"What houses of worship cannot do":** *Lou Dobbs Tonight*, September 18, 2006.

p. 133 **Colson has become:** David Van Biema, Cathy Booth-Thomas, Massimo Calabresi, John F. Dickerson, John Cloud, Rebecca Winters, and Sonja Steptoe, "The 25 Most Influential Evangelicals in the U.S.," *Time*, February 7, 2005.

p. 133 **A Pew survey found:** Trends in Political Values and Core Attitudes: 1987–2007, Pew Research Center, March 22, 2007.

p. 134 **A series of lawsuits:** *Lou Dobbs Tonight*, February 28, 2007.

p. 134 **The median age of:** Survey of Ordinands to the Priesthood, Georgetown University Center for Applied Research in the Apostolate (CARA) for the class of 2007.

p. 134 **Of the 42,307 priests; And while the number of priests:** from *The Official Catholic Directory 2007*, www.usccb.org/comm/statisti.shtml; "The Study of the Impact of Fewer Priests on the Pastoral Ministry," executive summary, U.S. Conference for Catholic Bishops, June 2000.

p. 135 **Haggard's backing and loyalty:** Jeff Sharlet, "Inside America's Most Powerful Megachurch," *Harper's*, May 13, 2005.

9: Crossing the Line

p. 137 **You cannot dedicate:** Address to Naturalized Citizens at Convention Hall, Philadelphia, May 10, 1915.

p. 138 **when only 5 percent of the cargo:** menendez.senate.gov/newsroom/record .cfm?id=262967; also, holt.house.gov/pdf/Holt_floor_remarks_on_the_SAFE_Port_Act _050406.pdf; also *Lou Dobbs Tonight*, May 16, 2006.

p. 141 **There are as many as:** Robert Justich and Betty Ng, "The Underground Labor Force Is Rising," Bear Stearns, January 3, 2005.

p. 145 **"We have a serious":** *Lou Dobbs Tonight*, June 28, 2006.

p. 145 **we admit more than two million:** "Temporary Admissions of Nonimmigrants to the United States: 2005," DHS, Office of Immigration Statistics, July 2006, www .dhs.gov/xlibrary/assets/statistics/publications/2005_NI_rpt.pdf.

p. 146 **My conversation on the air:** *Lou Dobbs Tonight*, June 17, 2007.

p. 150 **Only 5 percent of all the cargo:** *Lou Dobbs Tonight*, April 25, 2006.

p. 150 **Thousands of tons:** "Drug Trafficking in the United States," U.S. Drug Enforcement Agency, May 2004; also, www.gao.gov/new.items/d06200.pdf.

p. 151 **The FDA didn't follow up:** *Lou Dobbs Tonight*, April 23, 2007.

p. 152 **And the FDA only investigates:** Ibid.

p. 152 **The year with the highest:** Data provided by FDA Office of Public Affairs directly to staff of *Lou Dobbs This Week*, May 20, 2007.

p. 152 **The FDA has said:** *Lou Dobbs Tonight*, May 31, 2007.

p. 153 **You should know:** *Lou Dobbs Tonight*, May 29, 2007.

p. 153 **Though the United States permits:** "Temporary Admissions of Nonimmigrants to the United States: 2005," DHS, Office of Immigration Statistics, July 2006.

p. 154 **At the same time:** Lexis-Nexis, April 27, 2007.

p. 155 **This compromise package:** Fareed Zakaria, "Time to Solve Immigration," *Newsweek*, November 13, 2006.

p. 155 **"it seems likely that":** Robert E. Rector, "Amnesty Will Cost U.S. Taxpayers at Least $2.6 Trillion," Heritage Foundation, June 6, 2007 (WebMemo #1490).

p. 156 **"[O]n top of all of this":** *Lou Dobbs Tonight*, May 17, 2007.

p. 156 **Each year a quarter of:** www.numberusa.com/hottopic/overall.html; also, *Lou Dobbs Tonight*, May 8, 2007.

p. 157 **The White House then:** *Lou Dobbs Tonight*, June 26, 2007.

p. 162 **How many African-American:** *Lou Dobbs Tonight*, April 23, 2007.

p. 165 **"The North American Council":** Testimony of Dr. Robert A. Pastor, vice president of international affairs, professor, and director of the Center for North American Studies, American University, before a hearing of the Subcommittee on the Western Hemisphere, U.S. Senate Foreign Relations Committee, June 9, 2005.

10: Eating Our Young

p. 169 **A Pew Research study:** "Once Again, the Future Ain't What It Used to Be," Pew Research Center, May 2, 2006.

p. 170 **The American family's income:** Greg Ip, "Not Your Father's Pay," *Wall Street Journal*, May 25, 2007.

p. 171 **An increasing number of schools:** Norman Draper, "Schools Dropping Valedictorians," *Minneapolis-St. Paul Star Tribune*, May 31, 2007.

p. 172 **The number of households:** U.S. Census Bureau 2006 Current Population Survey (CPS), Annual Social and Economic Supplement (ASEC), March 2007.

p. 172 **More than a third:** CDC, National Vital Statistics Report, Volume 55, Number 1, September 29, 2006.

p. 173 **In those married households:** "How Not to Be Poor," National Center for Policy Analysis, January 15, 2003; also, "Poverty Dynamics in Four OECD Countries," Organization for Economic Cooperation and Development, 2000.

p. 173 **Today, 56 percent:** U.S. Census Bureau 2006 CPS.

p. 174 **We are now spending:** National Education Association, Rankings and Estimates: Ranking of the States 2005 and Estimates of School Statistics 2006, November 14, 2006; also, "National Spending Per Student Rises to $8,701," Rankings & Estimates: Rankings of the States and Estimates of School Statistics, 2005, U.S. Census Data, April 2006.

p. 174 **That is more than:** Spending Per Primary School Per Country, Organization for Economic Co-operation and Development, 2001.

p. 174 **Canada spends only:** "Comparative Indicators of Education in the United States and Other G8 Countries," National Center for Education Statistics, 2004.

p. 174 **Too often the money:** NYC Dept. of Education 2005–2006.

p. 174 **Our eighth-graders:** Trends in International Mathematics and Science Study (TIMSS) 2003, National Center for Education Statistics.

p. 174 **Less than 40 percent:** The Report of the 2000 National Survey of Science and Mathematics Education, Horizon-Research, Inc, National Science Foundation, grant number REC-9814246.

p. 175 **A Business-Higher Education Forum report:** "Securing America's Leadership in Science, Technology, Engineering and Mathematics (STEM)," Business-Higher Education Forum, www.bhef.com/Solutions/stem.asp#background.

p. 175 **"The Federal government has not":** ASCE Report Card for America's Infrastructure, 2005 Grades.

p. 176 **It is estimated that:** "U.S. Voter Turnout Up in 2004," press release, U.S. Census Bureau, May 26, 2005.

p. 176 **Even achieving those goals:** *Lou Dobbs Tonight*, March 24, 2005.

p.176 **For blacks and Hispanics:** The Civil Rights Project at Harvard/Urban Institute Study, February 25, 2004.

p. 176 **A high school degree:** "How Not to Be Poor," NCPA; also, "Poverty Dynamics In Four OECD Countries," OECD.

p. 177 **Those students who drop out:** *Lou Dobbs Tonight*, June 21, 2007.

p. 177 **The L.A. school budget:** *Lou Dobbs Tonight*, June 20, 2007.

p. 177 **"I think that really":** Ibid.

p. 178 **"We need immediate national action":** Ibid.

p. 179 **Charter schools are similar:** Washington Charter School Resource Center, wacharterschools.org/learn/reasons.htm.

11: A Nation in Denial

p. 181 **Let us not forget:** Ronald Reagan, 1986.

p. 182 **"Drug company spending":** "Prescription Drugs: Improvements Needed in FDA's Oversight of Direct-to-Consumer Advertising," General Accounting Office GAO-07-54, December 14, 2006.

p. 182 **The number of TV ads:** John Abramson, *Overdosed America: The Broken Promise of American Medicine* (New York: HarperCollins, 2004), p. 152.

p. 183 **"DTC advertising":** "Prescription Drugs: FDA Oversight of Direct-to-Consumer Advertising Has Limitations," General Accounting Office, October 2002.

p. 183 **A decade ago fewer than:** "Prescription Drug Use in the Past Month by Sex, Age, Race and Hispanic Origin: United States, 1988–1994 and 1999–2002," National Center for Health Statistics, 2006.

p. 184 **Today, 24.2 percent:** Ibid.

p. 184 **CNN reported the story:** Elizabeth Cohen, "ADHD Drug Use for Youth Obesity Raises Ethical Questions," CNN, March 22, 2007.

p. 185 **In 2005, of adults ages:** Drug-Free Workplace Advisor, "How does substance abuse impact the workplace?" U.S. Department of Labor, May 2007.; see also "General Workplace Impact: Substance Use and Abuse in America Today, www.dol.gov/asp/programs/drugs/workingpartners/stats/wi.asp.

p.185 **The number of teenagers now using:** Joseph A. Califano, *High Society: How Substance Abuse Ravages America and What to Do About It* (Public Affairs, 2007).

p. 185 **Methamphetamines have become:** "The Meth Epidemic in America," National Association of Counties, Volume III, July 18, 2006.

p. 186 **More than two thousand kids:** "Fatalities and Alcohol-Related Fatalities Among 15–20 Year Olds—2003 v. 2002," MADD and NHTSA FARS, 2004.

p. 186 **Seventeen hundred college kids:** R. Hingson et al. "Magnitude of Alcohol-Related Mortality and Morbidity Among U.S. College Students Ages 18–24: Changes from 1998 to 2001," *Annual Review of Public Health*, vol. 26, 259–79, p. 200.

p. 186 **"The troublesome thing is":** Lou Dobbs Tonight. March 28, 2007.

p. 187 **and today Afghanistan produces:** "Summary Findings of Opium Trends in Afghanistan, 2005" U.N. World Drug Report, United Nations Office on Drugs and Crime, June 2007.

p. 187 **"President Bush understands":** Office of National Drug Control Policy, press release, February 9, 2007.

p. 189 **"of the 26 million addicts:** Lou Dobbs Tonight, March 28, 2007.

p. 189 **Drug abuse and addiction:** "The Economic Costs of Drug Abuse in the United States, 1992–2002," Office of National Drug Control Policy.

p. 189 **The numbers for alcohol:** "Updating Estimates of the Economic Costs of Alcohol Abuse in the United States: Estimates, Update Methods, and Data." Prepared by Henrick Harwood and The Lewin Group, National Institute on Alcohol Abuse and Alcoholism, 2000.

p. 189 **In addition, more than:** Correctional Populations and Facilities, Prisoners in 2005, U.S. Department of Justice.

12: Media Madness

p. 191 **A popular government:** James Madison to W. T. Barry, August 4, 1822.

p. 193 **"What matters to us":** press release for Steve Capus, NBC News president, April 11, 2007.

p. 200 **During the week she died:** "Anna and the Astronaut Trigger a Week of

Tabloid News," Project for Excellence in Journalism, PEJ News Coverage Index: February 4–9, 2007.

13: Independent Thinking and the American Spirit

p. 208 **This president and this Congress:** "EPA Document Lists Firms Tied to Superfund Sites," The Center for Public Integrity, April 26, 2007.

Index

War on the Middle Class
How the Government, Big Business,
and Special Interest Groups Are Waging War
on the American Dream and How to Fight Back
The middle class is an endangered species. Corporations are shipping its jobs overseas. Politicians are betraying its interests. The news media are feeding it sensation in place of information. The result is not just declining incomes but dysfunctional schools and unaffordable health care, adding up to a widening gap between haves and have-nots. In *War on the Middle Class*, CNN anchor and radio personality Lou Dobbs delivers a clear and powerful report from the front lines on this state of affairs, identifying the forces behind it and what we can do to fight back.

ISBN 978-0-14-311252-5